Wretched Aristotle

Aristotle: Ludovisi Collection.

Wretched Aristotle

Using the Past to Rescue the Future

Jude P. Dougherty

LEXINGTON BOOKS

A division of
ROWMAN & LITTLEFIELD PUBLISHERS, INC.
Lanham • Boulder • New York • Toronto • Plymouth, UK

LEXINGTON BOOKS

A division of Rowman & Littlefield Publishers, Inc.
A wholly owned subsidiary of The Rowman & Littlefield Publishing Group, Inc.
4501 Forbes Boulevard, Suite 200
Lanham, MD 20706

Estover Road
Plymouth PL6 7PY
United Kingdom

British Library Cataloguing in Publication Information Available

Library of Congress Cataloging-in-Publication Data

Dougherty, Jude P., 1930–
Wretched Aristotle : using the past to rescue the future / Jude P. Dougherty.
p. cm.
Includes bibliographical references and index.
ISBN 978-0-7391-4006-2 (cloth : alk. paper)
ISBN 978-0-7391-4008-6 (electronic)
1. Aristotle—Influence. 2. Civilization—History. 3. Civilization, Western—21st century. I. Title.

B485.D68 2009
909'.09821—dc22 2009025152

Printed in the United States of America

™ The paper used in this publication meets the minimum requirements of American National Standard for Information Sciences—Permanence of Paper for Printed Library Materials, ANSI/NISO Z39.48–1992.

For Mary W. Rakow

Contents

PART III CONTEMPORARY MORAL ISSUES

Acknowledgments

The author gratefully acknowledges the following for permission to reproduce in whole or in part the articles previously published by him:

Modern Age (ISI Publications)

"Santayana on the Role of Religion in Society," Vol. 37 (2), Winter 1996, 116–123.
"Indestructible Islam," Vol. 44 (4), Fall 2002, 324–332.
"Socialist Man: A Psychological Profile," Vol. 46 (1–2) Winter/Spring 2004, 12–22.
"Using the Past to Rescue the future," Vol. 49 (1), Winter 2007, 3–11.
"Science and the Shaping of Modernity," Vol. 51 (2), Spring 2009 (in press).
"Wretched Aristotle: Using the Past to Rescue the Future," in *On Wings of Faith and Reason: The Christian Difference in Culture and Science*, ed. Craig Steven Titus, Arlington, Va.: The Institute for the Psychological Sciences Press, 2008.

Introduction

This book is an attempt through a series of interrelated essays to identify the essential features of Western culture. They have been written in the context of an ongoing debate concerning the nature of the public philosophy that undergirds the freedoms we take for granted. The approach is historical, something rarely attempted by contemporary philosophers who prefer to philosophize in an analytical mode or to limit themselves to textual exegesis or to micro-history, procedures that are often removed from the ongoing concerns of political and social life and have little to do with the pursuit of wisdom. A thesis that underlies all of these essays is that modernity cannot be understood apart from its break with classical antiquity.

About eighty-five years ago, philosophers and literary intellectuals as diverse as Edmund Husserl, George Santayana, and Paul Valéry, aware of the declining influence of Christianity, spoke of "the crisis of Western civilization." All three placed their hopes on the revival of the classical sources of Western culture, with Valéry insisting, in addition, on the acknowledgment of a debt to Roman law and to Roman Catholicism. We know that the proposed European Constitution as initially drafted failed to acknowledge both and subsequently was denied unanimous approval. . . . Husserl and Santayana, even in their prescience, could not have imagined the multicultural diversity that confronts today's secularized Europe, a Europe unable to control its borders or to assimilate the flood of immigrants from the Middle East and Africa. As power gravitates to Brussels, the Dutch, the Polish, and others are beginning to have reservations about a European Unity that would deprive them of control over their own destinies. In the face of a centralized bureaucracy that tends to suppress regional differences, national identity is beginning to be reasserted. With increased globalization and its attendant multicultural cosmopolitanism, not only national identity but ethnic identity has increasingly come to be valued. As the United States confronts its own problem of maintaining unity in the face of cultural diversity, there may be lessons that Americans can learn from the European experience given that many of the same problems exist on both sides of the Atlantic.

When Oswald Spengler published his multivolume study, *The Decline of the West*,[1] few outside of professional academic circles understood his thesis or took the epitaph seriously. Today, a century later, no cultural historian can ignore the intellectual shift that took place in the last half of the twentieth century, one that seriously eclipsed the spiritual resources which formerly animated it. As a philosopher of history, Spengler's study of the past and his cyclical view of history led him to the pessimistic conclusion that just as other cultures before it have decayed, Western culture has not only peaked but faces a period of irreversible decline. For more than 200 years the Western intellectual tradition has been subjected to the nihilistic forces launched by the Enlightenment. It is evident that the eighteenth-century repudiation of the classical and Christian sources of Western culture has produced a lasting effect in the social order. Europe seems to be living off a dying past, perhaps nearing the end of a once great culture, not unlike that experienced before the fall of Rome when internal corruption made possible the barbarian invasion. The decline of morals apart, the birthrate of the native European population alone would attest to decline. The ruling elites of Brussels and the European capitals seem confident that the constitutive elements of what was once called "Christendom" can be maintained without reference to their source. Absent Christianity, Europe has little to defend but its material culture as it faces a tide of immigrants that threaten its very character. The newcomers, largely from the Middle East and Africa, who are attracted by the material culture of Europe remain attached to their old ways and in refusing to assimilate extract privileges and exception to the common law that further contributes to their alienation within the larger society. The question arises, how tolerant can Europe be in the face of a largely Muslim influx whose Islamic leaders are convinced that they will one day rule the continent.

The issue of national identity was addressed from an historical perspective in a work published in 2004 by Samuel P. Huntington who pointedly asks from an American perspective: Who are we? Starting from the premise that the United States once possessed a common ethnic core—one may say, an Anglo-Protestant soul—Huntington believes that sometime between 1920 and 1970 it lost that soul, succumbing to a liberal virus that sapped its strength.[2] Seventy-five years earlier, George Santayana employed the same metaphor in speaking of Christianity in the West when he wrote: "Our society has lost its soul. The landscape of Christendom is covered with lava: a great eruption and inundation of brute humanity threatens to overwhelm all of the treasures that artful humanity has created."[3] Huntington is convinced that the United

States remains an overwhelmingly Christian nation, yet he is not oblivious to the moral and cultural decline that he believes has weakened the moral fabric of the nation. He attributes that erosion not to gains made by non-Christian religions but to the increased influence of a small but influential number of intellectuals and publicists, atheists, and materialists, who in the name of multiculturalism attack the identification of the United States with its Christian founding and, indeed with Western civilization itself, rejecting not only their country's religious tradition but its cultural heritage as well. In repudiating the inherited, they wish to create a country that does not belong to any civilization, one devoid of a cultural core. They substitute for the rights of individuals the rights of groups, defined largely in terms of race, ethnicity, gender, and sexual preference. The implications, Huntington believes, are enormous. Absent a common core of conviction, he asks: can a nation maintain a rule of law or maintain the freedoms taken for granted? In the United States, there may yet exist a common political creed, but Huntington is convinced that creed is not enough. Political principles, he argues, are a fickle base on which to secure a lasting community. Shared belief in the rule of law, parliamentary democracy, and liberal free trade all presuppose something more fundamental. These ideas are European, he insists, not Asian, African, or Middle Eastern except by adoption. They make Western civilization unique.

Eric P. Kaufmann, covering much the same ground as Huntington, agrees that America has lost its Protestant soul, but he believes that that loss is a good thing, preferring instead the cosmopolitan multiculturalism that eradicates all religious and ethnic differences. He is convinced, contrary to Huntington's profile of contemporary America, that we have already adopted multiculturalism as the official ideology of the American nation. He finds overwhelming manifestations of the multiculturalist spirit in school and university curricula, in the social sciences, and in humanistic discourse as well as in our political and legal systems.

Kaufmann is pleased that the older America has passed away and that its memory is almost beyond recall. "Those of us who consider ourselves liberal," he writes, "find it very difficult to accept that any group has the right to impose its hegemony over a nation state's realms of political, economic, and cultural activity.[4] Citing Jürgen Habermas in support, he is convinced that dominant ethnicity must give way to multiculturalism, but a multiculturalism "garnished with a constitutional patriotism that is highly inclusive and abstract."[5] But what of the current liberal hegemony? By Kaufmann's own account the once-dominant WASP has been replaced by the illiberal multiculturalist, whose numbers may be small but who controls the organs of opinion through the universities and the media. It has been acknowledged for decades that there is an unbridgeable chasm between the academy and middle America. The eighty-five percent who in some sense value the religious component of their culture are effectively silenced by a like percentage in the academy who give their allegiance to the left and the programs for which it stands. Voting patterns clearly attest to the overwhelming left leaning of the academy, but apart from that one need only consult the publication lists of major university presses in the English-speaking world to see how biased the lists are in favor of the politically correct and the irreligious left. Scholarly treatises abound that rewrite Western history, leaving out Christianity. Kaufmann may welcome the eclipse of Christianity, but he should acknowledge that the once-dominant ethnicity of Protestant America did not hinder the growth of American Catholicism or prevent the emergence of the anti-Christian multiculturalism movement. It remains to be seen whether the self-proclaimed liberal will be so tolerant? Aristotle, in the *Nicomachean Ethics*, reminds us that a successful republic depends on virtue in the people and warns that a bad moral state, once formed, is not easily amended. The undisciplined will, whether it be that of an individual or of a collective, is not capable of remaining fixed on an appropriate end. Is it likely that an American political creed is capable of replacing the unifying role once played by Protestant Christianity?

Who, indeed, stands to profit from the diminished role of Christianity? It should be evident even to the inveterate liberal that a polity cannot exist without virtue in the people. Has not the marginalization of Christianity been accompanied by a significant moral and cultural decline? What would Kaufmann substitute for biblical morality? The atheistic, cosmopolitan multiculturalism in its revolutionary drive cannot help but bring to mind other cultural revolutions, e.g., that of the French whose drive for *liberté, egalité, fraternité,* once achieved, brought on the bloody scourge of the Jacobins; or that of the Bolsheviks, a revolution that was soon followed by Stalin's purges and gulags; or Mao's Marxist triumph that led to the cultural revolution and deaths numbered in the tens of millions. History seems to teach that leftist triumphs bring chaos and destruction in their wake. The political agenda of the multicultural, cosmopolitan left, given that it is so out of touch with the traditions and common sense of the people, can only be implemented through coercion of one form or another. Heretofore the liberal agenda has achieved its objectives, not through consensus but principally by judicial decree and by financial sanctions imposed by the state. In the pursuit of new goals, boldness bred of past success, can only lead to totalitarian rule. A free people will not readily abandon their traditions or embrace the ephemeral goals of the left.

True, there can be no return to times past. Although many profess Christianity, religion speaks with a divided voice. There is no common creed or moral code. "Christianity" is at best a sociological designation, as much an abstraction as "cosmopolitan multiculturalist." Charles Fried, in discussing the role of religion in society, rightly asks what counts as religion, given our heterogeneous population. In speaking of the relationship between church and state, he concedes no value to religion, equating it before the law with unbelief. Whatever deference is paid to religion is a matter of humanitarian grace. This view is ascendant among our intellectual elites.[6]

John Courtney Murray, writing a generation ago and perhaps influenced by the pessimism of Arnold Toynbee, held out little hope that an ideologically polarized America could survive the "new barbarism" of the left that he saw threatening the life of reason embedded in law and custom. The perennial work of the barbarian, he held, "is to undermine rational standards of judgment, to corrupt inherited wisdom by which people have always lived, and to do this not by spreading new beliefs but by creating a climate of doubt and bewilderment in which clarity about the larger aims of life are dimmed and the self-confidence of the people destroyed."[7] Murray in his own day feared the consequences of what he perceived as a moral vacuum and the loss of freedom to which it would inevitably lead. Today he would likely conclude that the prospects for the immediate future are not too bright. The concept "West," he consistently held, has no meaning apart from Christianity. Jurgen Moltmann makes a similar point in a treatise on "The Tradition of Eschatological Hope," where he explores the role that tradition plays in preserving equilibrium within a people by grounding hope and mitigating fear.[8] Traditions, he believes, insofar as they are alive and binding, current and familiar, and taken as a matter of course link fathers and sons across the generations and provide continuity in time. When this unquestioned familiarity becomes problematical, an essential element in tradition is already lost and traditions lose their propitious force.

The essays which comprise this volume address these and other issues in an attempt to show the importance of classical antiquity for an understanding of Western civilization. The lead essay begins with the reception of Christianity into the West. "Wretched Aristotle" is a derogatory term used by Tertullian, a second-century Christian apologist, who excoriated the use of philosophy in the service of evangelization. His words echo through the centuries. Later evangelists will speak of "putrid Aristotle" and castigated the Scholastics, notably Aquinas, for their use of Aristotle in their attempt to elucidate the words of the Gospels. Much of modern philosophy itself is a repudiation of the realism characteristic of Aristotle and the Scholastic tradition. One's attitude toward Aristotle and the Stoics determines positively or negatively one's understanding of the nature of law. Absent a Greek or Christian sense of hierarchy, standards collapse, the vulgar becomes indistinguishable from the noble.

In the first part of this collection, the reader will find articles on Aristotle, on the Stoics, and on the Benedictine contribution, notably that of Cassiodorus, to the preservation of classical texts. A constant theme permeating these essays is that there is a natural order which governs thought and directs human behavior. It is taken for granted that human nature is a constant and that the ancients, no less intelligent or observant than we, have much to teach us across the ages. Steady progress has been made in the natural sciences because of the sophisticated instruments of modern technology, but there are no instruments that bring us closer to an understanding of human nature than those available in antiquity.

These essays move from an appreciation of classical antiquity to its relevance in discussions of contemporary social and political issues. The topics addressed are often moral, but the moral itself is seen as anchored in an ontological perspective. If there is no such thing as "human nature" or "an order in nature" to be empirically uncovered, the ancients who presupposed these principles have nothing to say to us. Their works are of antiquarian interest only and can be put aside. In fact, the shelves of college bookstores are filled with textbooks that begin the history of philosophy with Descartes in the seventeenth century, ignoring all that went before. Disconnected from its ancient sources, much of modern philosophy takes for granted a material universe devoid of purpose. I argued to the contrary that a material universe can only support positive law, not the moral order recognized by the Stoics and Aquinas. Part II of the book is devoted to the nature of religion and its role in society and to the reciprocal influence of science and culture. Part III of the book draws attention to the philosophical determination of moral norms, to conflicting notions of the common good, and to the logical implications of a repudiation of teleology in nature or a divinely ordered universe.

The attentive reader may detect the repetition of some themes that pervade these essays. All were initially written as lectures and were delivered to academic audiences over a period of six years on three different continents. They are unified by the theme that the West cannot be understood or defended apart from an acknowledgment of its Hellenic and biblical sources.

NOTES

1. Oswald Spengler, *The Decline of the West* (New York: A. A. Knopf, 1926–1928).
2. Samuel P. Huntington, *Who Are We?: Challenges to America's National Identity* (New York: Simon & Schuster, 2004).
3. George Santayana, *The Winds of Doctrine* (New York: Charles Scribner's Sons, 1913), 5.

4. Eric P. Kaufmann, *The Rise and Fall of Anglo-America* (Cambridge, Mass: Harvard University Press, 2004), 284.

5. Kaufmann, *Rise and Fall*, 284.

6. Charles Fried, *Saying What the Law Is* (Cambridge, Mass.: Harvard University Press, 2004).

7. John Courtney Murray, *We Hold These Truths* (New York: Sheed & Ward, 1960), 13.

8. Jurgen Moltmann, *Theology of Hope* (New York: Harper and Row, 1967), 291.

Part One

THE RELEVANCE OF ANTIQUITY

Chapter One

Wretched Aristotle

"Wretched Aristotle!" The words are those of Tertullian (c. 160–c. 220), better known perhaps for his rhetorical question, "What does Athens have to do with Jerusalem?" In Tertullian's words, "God has spoken to us: it is no longer necessary for us to philosophize. Revelation is all that is required. He who believes in the word of God knows more than the greatest philosophers have ever known concerning the only matter of vital importance."[1] Tertullian was not the first or the last to reject the use of classical learning in an attempt to understand the truths of the Gospels. Tatian, who preceded him by at least a generation, similarly rejected all efforts to employ Hellenistic learning in biblical exegesis or Christian apologetics. Centuries later, Luther, like his ancient predecessors, was to rile against classical learning, particularly Aristotle, and the use made of Greek and Roman learning by the Scholastics. As he said, "Virtually the entire *Ethics* of Aristotle is the worst enemy of grace."[2] Reason is contrary to faith, Luther maintained, and it is impossible to harmonize the two. Modern versions of this notion are to be found in the anti-metaphysical and fideistic views of Kierkegaard and his twentieth-century disciples such as Karl Barth, Rudolf Bultmann, and Paul Tillich.

By contrast with Tatian and Tertullian, Justin Martyr and Clement of Alexandria used all the intellectual tools available to understand and defend the faith. Similarly, Justin Martyr, a Greek who flourished in the middle decades of the second century, brought to his apologetics a knowledge of Plato, Aristotle, Pythagoras, and the Stoics. He had read Plato's *Apology*, *Crito*, *Phaedrus*, and *Phaedo*, and other works that are still found on the reading lists of introductory courses in philosophy in many liberal arts colleges throughout North America. As a result of his study, Justin concluded that philosophy leads to Christianity as its fulfillment. The "rational" bequeathed by the Greeks is complemented by "revelation."[3] Pagan philosophy is not to be feared for it is consistent with biblical teaching. Plato, he thought, was superior to the Stoics in knowledge of God, though inferior to them in ethics. The same esteem for portions of Greek philosophy came to be shared by Athanagoras, Theophilus of Antioch, Clement of Alexandria, and others.

Clement became so immersed in Greek philosophy that some regard him as more of a philosopher than the theologian he certainly was. Refusing to adopt the style of contemporary apologists, he took as his mission the straightforward teaching of the faith to unbelievers. To that end he found philosophy indispensable. The Greeks had prepared the way for the reception of the truths of the Gospels, and Clement was convinced that Providence in directing historical events willed the existence of philosophers "because like a good shepherd, he wanted to put his best sheep at the head of his flock."[4] Jewish law and Greek philosophy, he maintained, are the two rivers at whose confluence Christianity has sprung forth. Sacred Scripture allows us to make use of profane learning without mistaking philosophical wisdom for the superior wisdom of Christianity. Since no one philosophical school possesses the whole truth, the first task of the Christian philosopher is to eliminate from philosophy all that is false. The only completely useless philosophical sect, Clement thought, is that of Epicurus. With respect to the others, Christianity acts as a selective guide. Assuredly the doctrine of Christ is sufficient unto salvation, but philosophy can be used to lead men to Christ and further used to elucidate the teachings of Christ once they have been accepted.[5]

Origen of Alexandria (185–ca. 254), an Egyptian, is considered one of the great names in the history of Christian thought despite his many theological errors from an orthodox Christian viewpoint. A prolific writer, sometimes called a universal genius, he became a Christian biblical exegete worthy of translation by St. Jerome. Origen possessed an extensive knowledge of Greek philosophy—Aristotelian, Platonic, Stoic, and Epicurean. He adopted the basic elements of Plato's cosmology and psychology while borrowing his terminology and definitions from Aristotle. One of his students said of him, "He required us to study philosophy by reading all existing writings of the ancients, both philosophers and religious poets, taking care not to put aside or reject any . . . apart from the writings of atheists. . . . He selected everything that was true in each philosopher and set it before us, but condemned what was false."[6]

Eusebius of Caesarea similarly exploited the notion that the Greek philosophers and poets were providentially sent by God in preparation for the Gospel. That judgment has been echoed through the ages, most often expressed in the common dictum, "Christ came in the fullness of time when the intellect of the West was prepared to receive the truths of the Gospel." Without doubt the perspective of Justin, Clement, and Eusebius is found and developed in the scholasticism of the thirteenth century.

Nevertheless the dismissal of Greek learning and philosophy by Tatian and Tertullian did not pass away but remains today as the belief of a major sector of Protestantism. Luther, in keeping with his doctrine of Adam's fall and its debilitating effect on human intelligence wrote, "Aristotle is to theology what darkness is to light." And further, "Aquinas [as a result of his indebtedness to Aristotle] . . . never understood a chapter of the Gospels."[7] It is impossible to reform the Church, Luther declared, if scholastic theology and philosophy are not torn out by the roots with Canon Law. In contrast to Clement, Luther claimed that "one should learn philosophy as one learns witchcraft, that is, to destroy it; that is, as one finds out about errors in order to refute them."[8]

Luther's disparagement of philosophical reason was to receive support in the eighteenth century from the British empiricists who effectively undermined confidence in reason's ability to move from the seen to the unseen. Kant confirmed the death of natural theology by his *First Critique*, and it has become commonplace in the dictum of William James that since Kant it is no longer necessary to consider proof for the existence of God. Enlightenment philosophy, in robbing faith of its rational preamble, led to the fresh examinations of the nature of religious belief. Perhaps the most notable leader of that effort was Søren Kirkegaard.

In the long line of theologians stretching from Luther himself to Brunner, Barth, and Bultmann, Søren Kirkegaard holds a unique place. He was the first to state, in more-or-less modern form, the case against the use of philosophy as a preamble to theology. Luther had stated it before him, but the rationalism Luther opposed was the comparatively modest rationalism of the Schoolman and Erasmus. What Kierkegaard had to contend with was the rationalism of Hegel and his disciples. Drawing upon Kant in his attack on Hegel, he goes one step further, robbing religion, specifically Christianity, of any "objective" content. Faith, he declares, is not a matter of belief that can be set forth in propositional form, nor is religion a rational affair.[9]

Making a distinction between the world of universals (scientific generalizations) and the subjective world (inwardness), Kierkegaard asserted that whereas philosophy teaches us to become objective, Christianity teaches us to become subjective. Evidence for God's existence is an "objective question," but we find no conclusive evidence for His existence. Whether we can demonstrate the existence of God or not makes no difference from the standpoint of faith. Far more important is what happens to the individual when he is called upon to believe that which cannot be objectively known. With respect to objective matters, there will always be doubt, but what is important is what happens to the individual in the face of doubt. The believer is not turned away by objective uncertainty but instead passionately affirms. Kierkegaard calls this "subjective truth."

Subjective truth, we may note, is not truth in the usual sense; it is what is usually called "faith." For Kierkegaard, "Faith is precisely the contradiction between the infinite passion of the individual's inwardness and objective uncertainty. If I am capable of grasping God objectively, I am not believing, but precisely because I cannot so grasp God, I must believe. If I wish to preserve myself in faith, I must constantly be intent on holding fast the objective uncertainty, so as to remain out upon the deep, over seventy thousand fathoms of water, still preserving my faith."[10] The implications of Kierkegaard's thought are played out on the contemporary scene. Belief, of course, is a personal act, an act of assent to propositions acknowledged to be true, but the believer must somehow discern what is true. The Fathers of the Church who made the most of classical learning did so because what they had learned from Greek and Roman sources were truths which cohered with Revelation, and furthermore by employing the categories of philosophical learning, they were better able to grasp the import of Revelation.

Boethius (c. 480–c. 525), sometimes called the last of the Roman philosophers and the first of the scholastic theologians, provides a stark contrast to the fideism of Kirkegaard.

"A person is a supposit of a rational nature," so wrote Boethius fifteen hundred years ago, and that definition has resonated throughout the centuries. Analogously predicated of God, angels, and human beings, Boethius's definition of person remains normative today. In the treatise, *The Trinity is One God, Not Three Gods*, a treatise that we have come to know as *De Trinitate*, Boethius opens with this sentence, "I have long pondered this problem with such mind as I have and all the light God has lent me."[11] For Boethius, to embrace the Catholic faith is not to leap into the dark. The Church from its early centuries has consistently taught the reasonableness of belief, has taught that Christ came in the fullness of time when the intellect of the West was prepared to receive the truths of the Gospel. The early Church Fathers, almost without exception, brought to their study of Scripture the language of Athens, the categories of Aristotle, and the teachings of Plato and of the Stoa. Many of the early fathers, among them St. Basil and the two Gregories, studied at Athens. Marius Victorinus (c. A.D. 280–365), sometimes called "the Augustine before Augustine," was similarly schooled and is considered the first Latin Father to compose a systematic metaphysical treatise on the Trinity. He may have been the first to speak of God as "pure act of *to be*." He was convinced that scriptural statements about the equality and the distinction of Father, Son, and Holy Ghost can be reconciled but only if one does not make philosophical mistakes like Basil of Ancyra did. To the philosopher, Justin Martyr, a convert to Christianity in A.D. 130 and a martyr during the reign of Prefect Junius Rusticus (163–167 A.D.), Greek philosophy and Christianity appeared as one and the same divine revelation. For Justin, Christianity absorbed philosophy, not the other way round. "What ever things were rightly said among men," he writes, "are the property of Christians." Philosophers may partly share in the *Logos*, but Christians partake of the whole.

Boethius in his day will echo the outlook of Justin and Victorinus. Philosophy may be productive of wisdom, but a deeper wisdom is offered to the Christian. To make that wisdom one's own, one has to integrate it to what is known of the natural order. Whatever is inherited becomes our own only if in appropriating it we transform it so that it becomes an intellectual *habitus*, part of ourselves. It is not what is inherited that counts but what a person makes of it. Clearly Boethius made the most of what he inherited and set about making sure that inheritance would be available to yet another generation. His ambition to translate all the known works of Plato and Aristotle was cut short with his execution in 524 A.D.

Boethius, we know from subsequent events, stood at a watershed in the history of the West. He was aware that the world in which he had grown to manhood was doomed and that the world coming into being was not his own. He was not alone in that judgment. The *Imperium Romanum* had come to an end with Alaric's conquest of the city of Rome in 410. In the aftermath of the barbarian invasions of the western part of the Roman Empire in the late fifth and early sixth centuries, cultural life had declined, and the future of the empire was unclear. Rome was no longer the symbol of world order. The Greek literary tradition had all but died, and the Hellenism that well served the Fathers of the Church was losing its hold.

Boethius was one of a few in the upper classes who saw the importance of preserving an inherited literary culture, and he set about transmitting the texts of ancient philosophy to posterity. It was his ambition not only to make available to his countrymen the works of Plato and Aristotle but to show the compatibility of the two, often interpreting Aristotle through the eyes of Plato. Cassiodorus (c. 490–585), a younger contemporary and author of the oldest biography of Boethius, also understood the value of Greek learning and, upon founding a Benedictine monastery on his family's property at Squillace, far from a decadent Rome on the Adriatic in southern Italy, set about having his monks copy ancient texts.

Parenthetically, one may note that our present somewhat resembles that ancient past. In our own country and in much of Europe, education at all levels has lost contact with the classics that heretofore provided the core of a liberal education. The value of classical learning was never contested by leading philosophers of the first half of the twentieth century, yet our universities have all but abandoned the Western literary canon. To read Husserl, Heidegger, and Gadamer, for example, is to appreciate their indebtedness to the Greeks.

George Santayana, the Spanish-born American philosopher, eschewing the pragmatism of his mentor William James, thought of his own work as a restatement of Aristotle's metaphysics.

It is to be remembered that the Aristotelian corpus was not fully available in the West until the advent of the thirteenth century. Boethius had access to the *Organon*, that is, the logical works of Aristotle, but not the *de Anima*, the *Physics,* or the *Metaphysics*. Yet we find elements of the natural philosophy of Aristotle throughout his writing. Distinguishing between faith and reason, Boethius describes philosophy as an effort to understand and explain the world of nature around us. The role of theology is to explain the doctrines delivered through Revelation, but theology must draw upon the categories of being. Sorting and classifying, he first distinguishes between faith and theology, and in an effort to locate theology within the sciences, he further distinguishes three levels of scientific abstraction, that of physics, of mathematics, and of theology, a classification that St. Thomas is to elucidate further in Books Four and Five of his *Commentary on the de Trinitate.*

Throughout the *Theological Tractates* and the *Consolation of Philosophy*, Boethius draws heavily on Aristotelian notions of substance, matter, form, and the incorporeal in order to show that in Christ the divine nature and the human nature are real and really distinct. He makes full use of Aristotle's categories in speaking of God as a "substance" but not as a substance in the usual sense—i.e., as a subject of accidental properties. Having previously made the distinction between the corporeal and the incorporeal, he finds that man by virtue of his immaterial soul transcends the merely corporeal and goes on to show how predicates normally said of man can be analogically predicated of God: predicates such as greatness, simplicity, omniscience, goodness, and justice. From his study of the *Organon*, he appropriates the distinction between substance and accident, between matter and form, soul and body, and, by implication, essence and existence. From his study of Plato, he incorporates Plato's theory of forms and his doctrine of participation. We have studies highlighting the platonic heritage of Thomism. Even more pronounced is the Platonic element in the philosophy of Boethius, yet he remains fundamentally an Aristotelian.

This is not the place to sort out the controversies involving the interpretation of Boethius's texts. This is foremost an appreciation of the transcendental character of his work, but not merely that. Boethius holds interest for us because in many ways we are in a similar position. When the Greek literary tradition was losing its hold at the end of the sixth century, Boethius sensed that a loss of the Hellenic tradition was not in the best interest of Christianity. The tools he needed to understand the Catholic faith were those provided by Aristotle and Plato, and he brought them into service as he attempted to understand the Trinity, the Incarnation, and other mysteries related to the faith. Although occupied in theological reflection, he regarded himself as engaged in the same activity as were Plato and Aristotle, the search for truth about nature and human nature, a philosophical search now complemented by Revelation. There is no need to reconcile reason and faith; they are but two movements in one and the same enterprise. It is the scholar's duty to first study the real nature of anything before he formulates a belief about it. Thus, when discussing the mystery of the Trinity in an attempt to understand how three persons can exist in one God, Boethius first discusses from a philosophical perspective the marks of unity and difference. Men differ neither by genus nor by species but by their accidents. The fact that Father, Son, and Holy Spirit are one is because of the absence of difference with respect to essence. Where there is no difference, there is no sort of plurality according to number. God is nothing other than His own essence. When we say "God is just," we are not mentioning an accidental quality but rather a substantial one. Similarly, God's being and goodness are one and the same.

In the *Consolation* we find discussions of the principles of identity (a thing must preserve its unity to preserve its very being), intelligibility (intelligibility follows degrees of being: to the extent that a thing exists, it is intelligible), and finality (God rules the universe by the helm of his goodness).[12] The *Theological Tractates* produce a slew of distinctions and axioms that are carried in the scholastic tradition through the centuries. In the *de Trinitate* and the other explicitly theological writings such as the *Letters to John the Deacon*, *de Fide Catholica* and *Contra EvTychen*, we find a doctrine of the hierarchy of being and a doctrine of participation and their various formulations. We are told that to the extent that a thing exists, it is intelligible. And its corollary: intelligibility follows participation for the existence of the imperfect in any order whatsoever presupposes the perfect. Being and unity are convertible terms; so, too, being and the good. To maintain itself in being, a thing must maintain its unity. This passage after a series of distinctions, leads Boethius to his famous definition of person. "Nature," he begins, "belongs to those things, which since they exist, can in some measure be apprehended by the mind."[13] What then is a nature? Although a nature can be considered abstractly and predicated of many as a universal, a nature can have substantial existence only as a particular. Nature can predicate of all substances, corporeal or incorporeal. A corporeal nature is further identified as "either that which can act or that which can be acted upon, (for) the power to act and suffer belongs to all corporeals, and to the soul of all corporeals; for the soul both acts in the body and suffers by the body."[14] Speaking of corporeal substances, some are living, some are not. Of living substances, some are sensitive, others insensitive; of sensitive substances, some are rational, some irrational. Of rational substances, there is only one that is immutable and impassible by nature, namely, God.[15] All this leading up to a definition of person: "A person is an individual substance of a rational nature."[16]

I have drawn mainly on the *Theological Tractates*, but I do not want to downplay the relevance of the *Consolation* for our own time.[17] Boethius was clearly aware of the distinction between *fides* and *ratio*, so much so that many serious scholars could not believe that the author of the *Consolation* was also the author of the *Tractates*. Due to the work of Alfred Holder and Herman Usener, that controversy has been put into a proper light. Boethius of the *Consolation* was clearly working as a natural philosopher, pursuing to the limit the contribution of philosophy to our understanding of suffering and death. It also demonstrates that Christianity is perhaps closer in its understanding of nature and human nature to pagan philosophy than it is to much contemporary thought.

Whereas Boethius's Christianity is not invoked in the *Consolation,* it is noteworthy that not a single Bible quotation is to be found in the *Tractates*, even though they deal exclusively with theological subjects. I have stressed the Aristotelian element in Boethius, but others have emphasized the Platonic. Clearly Boethius employed the work of both as he grappled with theological and what we call "end of life" issues. After all, as he wrote to Deacon John, who later became Pope John I, I shall translate into Latin every book of Aristotle that comes into my hands and all the dialogues of Plato. Experience had taught him that unless the handing down takes place, there can be no enrichment.

NOTES

1. As quoted by Etienne Gilson, *History of Christian Philosophy in the Middle Ages* (New York: Random House, 1954), 44.

2. As quoted by Jacques Maritain, *Three Reformers* (London: Sheed & Ward, 1950), 30. Maritain draws heavily on F. Ueberweg/M. Heinze, *Grundriss der Geschichte der Philosophie*, Vol. III, 1914. See also *Reformation Writings of Martin Luther,* Vol. I: *The Basis of the Protestant Reformation,* trans. Bertram Lee Wolf (London: Lutterworth Press, 1952), 184–185. Luther uses the term, "wretched fellow."

3. Cf. Gilson, *Christian Philosophy*, 11–14.

4. Cf. Gilson, *Christian Philosophy*, 32.

5. Cf. Gilson, *Christian Philosophy*, 29–34.

6. Gregory Thaumaturgus in *Origenem oratio*, quoted by M. L. Clarke, *Higher Education in the Ancient World* (London: Routledge & Kegan Paul, 1971), 126–127.

7. As quoted by Maritain, *Three Reformers*, 30–31.

8. Maritain, *Three Reformers*, 31.

9. A primary text for Kierkegaard's doctrine of belief is *Either/Or*, 2 vols. Vol.1 trans. David F. Swenson and Lillain Marvin Swenson; Vol. 2 trans. Walter Lowrie (Princeton: Princeton University Press, 1944).

10. Søren Kierkegaard, *Concluding an Unscientific Postscript* [*Afsluttende Uvidenskabelig efterskrift (1846)*], trans. D. F. Swenson (Princeton: Princeton University Press, 1941), 182.

11. Boethius, Anicius Manlius Severinus. *The Theological Tractates: The Trinity is One God, Not Three Gods*, trans. H.F. Stewart and E.K. Rand, and *The Consolation of Philosophy*, trans. "I.T." (1609), revised by H.F. Stewart (London: William Heineman, 1918), 3.

12. Boethius, *Consolation*, 82.

13. *De Trinitate*, 79.

14. *Theological Tractates*, 79.

15. *Theological Tractates*, 83.

16. *Theological Tractates,* 85.

17. The *Consolation* has been a source of inspiration through the ages. It has been translated into English more than 41 times, and by such notable figures as Alfred the Great, Chaucer, and Queen Elizabeth I. It has been called the model of Dante's *Vita Nuova*. The translation I use here dates to 1609. It is that of an otherwise anonymous author, known simply as I. T., updated in 1918 by F.H. Stewart.

Chapter Two

Tom Wolfe's Epictetus

Although classical philosophy does not occupy the place it once held in the curricula of liberal arts colleges, scholars still pursue classical studies, but those studies remain largely within a somewhat isolated community of like-minded professors and students. Still, those studies may occasionally gain public attention in interesting ways. Tom Wolfe's novel, *A Man in Full*, is a case in point.

One of the pivotal figures in *A Man in Full*,[1] while serving a prison sentence discovers the teachings of the Stoic philosopher Epictetus. The fictional character, Conrad Hensley, is perhaps the only innocent in this tale of greed and ambition set in present-day Atlanta. Conrad is not the first in life or fiction to discover the consolation of philosophy while incarcerated. Whether intentionally or not, Wolfe makes the point that there is much to be learned from Stoic philosophy. As a satirist, Wolfe has few contemporary rivals. Although he has chosen fiction as the vehicle to convey his social observations, his insights are worthy of serious consideration. The novel's protagonist, Conrad Hensley, is made to discover something that seems to be lost or losing ground in some of our most venerable institutions of higher learning, where classical studies have too often been driven out of the core curriculum in favor of the trendy. By accident Conrad has been sent a book whose title is simply *The Stoics*, but the title page promises "The complete writings of Epictetus, Marcus Aurelius, C. Musonius, Rufus, and Zeno. Edited with an introduction by A. Briswold Bemis, Associate Professor of Classics, Yale University."

As a result of reading *The Stoics*, Conrad becomes convinced that with courage he can endure and overcome the inhuman conditions into which he has been thrust. Although cast among evil and dangerous men, he finds within himself the will and ability to surmount adversity. Surrounded by bars and treated by guards as if he were an animal in a cage, his reading of Epictetus gives him a sense of his own worth, an awareness that he is not just an animal but possesses in himself a "divine spark." This realization is accompanied by the notion that he is not alone in his struggles. There is a higher being—Zeus—whose help is to be sought. With hope he seeks the aid of Zeus, not realizing that by invoking Zeus he is praying. Miraculously he is liberated from jail and subsequently finds a new life, looking back upon his misfortune as a trial or test of his own inner mettle. Epictetus has given Conrad the awareness that he has dignity as a human person and the comforting thought that he is not alone in his struggles.

Among Western philosophies Stoicism is easily the most influential school of thought. Regarded by many as the loftiest and most sublime of philosophies, it flourished for about five hundred years from the time of its founder, Zeno (340–265 B.C.) to the death of the Roman Emperor, Marcus Aurelius (121–180 A.D.). Paul the Apostle is thought to have employed Stoic themes in his letters and oral teaching. The Stoic outlook can be found in Boethius, Ambrose, Tertullian, and in many of the early Church fathers. During the Middle Ages, elements of Stoic moral theory were known and used in the formulation of Christian, Jewish, and Muslim theories of man and nature and of the state and society. Thomas Aquinas is especially indebted to the Stoic Cicero. In later centuries Francis Bacon, Thomas More, Erasmus, Malanchthon, Montesquieu, Spinoza, Descartes, and Pascal drew upon the Stoics. The Stoics were the well-loved companions of the American founders, notably Thomas Jefferson, James Madison, John Marshall, and Daniel Webster, not to mention John Quincy Adams who felt so ill at ease in France until his beloved books on Cicero arrived.

Those exposed to some classical philosophy will remember that Epictetus flourished in the first quarter of the second century A.D. Although he wrote nothing, his teachings were recorded by his pupil Arrian and survive in two extant works, *Discourses* and *The Encheiridion*. As related by Arrian, Epictetus, in an effort to excite men to virtue, taught that men are not responsible for ideas that present themselves unbidden to their consciousness, but they are wholly responsible for how they use them; hence the need for virtue. According to Epictetus there are "two maxims we must ever bear in mind: one, apart from the will there is nothing good or bad, and two, we must not try to anticipate or direct events, but merely to accept them with intelligence."

Epictetus was convinced that behind all events there is an all-embracing providence whose thought directs the universe. It is the wise man who seeks to uncover the laws of nature and who lives by their light, allowing his reason to guide his conduct and restrain his emotions, thus avoiding the excesses of human nature that lead to disquietude and anxiety. The highest virtue and supreme good consists in obedience to the universal law of reason. Man is free when he freely wills that which reason decrees.

In common with Stoic thought, which emphasized the brotherhood of mankind, Epictetus maintained that all men are sons of God by virtue of their rationality and are kindred in their rationality with the divinity itself. Thus man is capable of learning to administer his earthly commonwealth and his life in accord with the will of God, which is synonymous with the will of nature. Individual well being cannot be secured apart from the common good. The aim of education, Epictetus taught is to view the world as a whole, to grow into the mind of God, thus making the will of nature one's own.

The perennial merit of Stoic philosophy lies in its ability to transcend ethnic, religious, and geographical boundaries. It is a philosophy available to all. Although from the vantage point of a Thomas Aquinas, a Thomas More, or a Jacques Maritain it may not be the definitive ethical guide, it nevertheless addresses the basic human condition, speaking of virtue and vice, the rule of law, and the unity of mankind.

Today the moral discourses of Epictetus as recorded by Arrian are available in more than a dozen editions. Everyman's Classical Library, with a translation and introduction by Elizabeth Carter,[2] served as an English-language source for much of the twentieth century. Thus it is all the more regrettable that classic studies have been abandoned not only at the university level but even more so in secondary education. Exposure to the Latin language in the high school years has always carried with it some knowledge of Cicero and Seneca as ancient texts were employed in language instruction. When a significant proportion of the student population was obliged to study the Latin classics, those students acquired in the process a common vocabulary, a set of distinctions and definitions and with these a moral compass that encouraged virtues such as fidelity, courage, veracity, and piety.

A secondary by-product of the early study of Latin is the confidence it engenders in students of all ethnic and racial backgrounds. It is commonly acknowledged that in the United States no racial or ethnic group is at a disadvantage when it comes to studying Latin. Blacks in urban schools have competed with suburban whites on an equal basis, performing equally well in written and oral delivery. Appetites whetted at the secondary level frequently acquiesced to further training at the collegiate level, albeit apart from and sometimes in spite of career-oriented studies.

Today the common experience of Latin studies is absent in the education not only of a professional class, but in that of those devoted to the so-called "humanities." Communications majors may be not only monolingual but unacquainted with the great Latin writers and orators of antiquity. The linguistic and reference bond among physicist, theologian, and historian has been broken to the disadvantage of all. A return may not be possible as confidence in Western culture has been replaced by admonitions to recognize diversity in which achievement and lineage are blurred in an attempt to create a false sense of equality: not merely before the law, but culturally. Standards disappear, the classical reference to nature, to a sense of hierarchy, and to the recognition of excellence, ignored or contravened, leads inevitably to debasement both at the personal and communal level. Gender studies emphasizing differences between male and female are untenable when compared with Stoic teaching regarding the commonality of human nature, the brotherhood of mankind.

As proposed economic and political prescriptions for curing our disintegrating society are found to be inadequate, there may be an increasing readiness to consider a deeper diagnosis. The study of Stoic texts by itself is not likely to change contemporary attitudes toward nature and human nature, but it may bring to their readers' attention certain unchallenged notions, among them the notion of progress. Cultural historian Christopher Dawson has said that the most destructive notion in the history of Western culture is the idea of progress, that somehow the inherited must be repudiated in the drive to ever superior forms. But if human nature has not changed since antiquity, the ancients may have something to tell us across the ages, deconstructionists and post-structuralists notwithstanding.

Today it is not unusual to find prominent authors in both literature and the natural sciences asserting that physical reality, no less than social reality, is at bottom a social and linguistic construct. Well-known physicists are on record averring that physical reality is nothing but a scientist's act of registration. One feminist has suggested that the astronomer/mathematician should record, along with her instruments' readings, the rhythms, music, and dance she simultaneously experiences in her own body. It is not uncommon to find statements that proclaim "historical and social reality" to be nothing but acts of interpretation. Marxists have long declared that scientific knowledge, far from being objective, reflects the political zeitgeist. Disciples of Derrida tell us that we can no longer assume with ease that nature exists "out there" to be mapped and discovered without evaluating our own roles in the process of investigation. Post-modern critics of science proclaim that physics has irrevocably banished the notion of objective reality.

As an antidote to the disintegrating force of multiculturalism, Stoicism points to the unity of the human race, its spiritual solidarity, and the need ever to keep the common good in mind. In antiquity it was universally recognized that the integrity of the State itself required on the part of the populace a common allegiance to a set of beliefs and principles, usually provided by religion. Impiety and atheism were taken seriously. In the *Laws*, Plato even prescribed the death penalty for the second offense of atheism, the first being forgiven as a youthful transgression. Temples and statues of gods were the visible symbols of national unity. The state religions of modern Europe are but a legacy of the recognition that a common intellectual outlook is required for political unity. Even the so-called religious wars following the Reformation were motivated more by politics than by religion. Dawson, quoted above, in speaking of the ideological diversity of the modern Western world, regards that diversity as a handicap. "There are Christians and rationalists," he writes, "liberals and conservatives, socialists and materialists, nationalists and internationalists. This ideological division and conflict is a source of weakness insofar as it provides a series of opportunities for totalitarian powers to apply the techniques of disintegration just as they do in the case of the conflicts of political interest between different Western States."[3] Although Dawson was writing during the cold war and thinking globally, the insights of this metahistorian are even more relevant today than they were when first written.

From its founding the United States has enjoyed the unity provided by an inherited view of law and society, drawn principally from English common law and biblical morality. English common law itself is traceable through medieval Canon Law to Roman law, notably represented by the Stoic statesmen Cicero and Seneca. The present-day accommodation of minorities and the perennial conflict between secular humanist and Christian have undermined this common legal and moral foundation. No longer is it possible to appeal to moral principles shared by all or at least by the vast majority. Appeals invoking the outlook of the "silent majority" or the "moral majority" meet with derision by the secular media. The fact that traditional religious beliefs and moral norms are subscribed to by an overwhelming majority counts for little when squared off against a vociferous opposition. The question that Wolfe forces us to confront is this: Whence the source of unity which is required for the rule of law. Do all have to agree? Is a consensus even possible among ideologically opposed factions?

Religious communities have sought a third way for some decades with a call for ecumenism, a call to forget fundamental differences and concentrate on programs of action mutually agreed upon. But some ideological differences are so deep and point so directly to action that consensus or even accommodation seems remote. What rights or even respect should majorities command? If the majority outlook is not to prevail in policy or legislation, what should? The opposing view? We are all too familiar with the studied, thoughtful claims of an authority which are "balanced" in the media by the ignorant, off-the-cuff remarks of a dissident, as if both points of view had equal merit. With such a practice, it is obvious that truth is not the objective. Unfortunately, when the true and noble are not supported, they fall by the wayside.

Every view, no matter how absurd or socially destructive, is accorded equal validity. Unhappily, when there is no sense of excellence, vulgarity has equal standing with the noble and uplifting.

The Stoics are there to remind us that truth can be achieved, and they remind us too of certain perennial truths about human nature and the nature of law. On the subject of truth, Epictetus says, "If a man objects to truths that are all too evident, it is not easy to find an argument with which to change his mind. . . . When a man caught in an argument hardens to stone, how can you reason with him any longer?"[4]

At the level of the state, subjectivism translates into what has come to be known as "procedural democracy," wherein competing claims to the good are treated as equal, the government remaining neutral among them. The common good is accorded no special standing; it is merely one claim among many. While majority interests may not be synonymous with the common good, still less so are the eccentric claims that seek to replace it. The question which remains to be answered is: What contributes to or leads to an appreciation of, or leads one to keep the common good in mind? Some would say personal moral virtue, a sense of community, call it "solidarity," and a willingness to respect the wishes of others—in short, good will. Aristotle would call it "civic amity." To discover what disposes one to such an attitude requires an inquiry at another level. Here we may face a major shortcoming of Stoic doctrine. The "brotherhood of mankind" as taught by Epictetus did not imply doing anything for the physical benefit of others. Stoic "solidarity" is not warm and outgoing. Its doctrine of endurance does not entail what we would call "charity." Its redeeming and enduring feature is its equating of law with right reason. The effect of identifying law with reason is to internalize law, making it something like the voice of conscience, the moral law within. Zeus is the ultimate source of law, the law-giving pilot of the universe. But his will is reflected in the customs of a people, to which, assuming normalcy, the Stoics were willing to give the force of law. The assumption is that custom is served well and has withstood rational scrutiny or it would not have acquired such status.

In its time Stoicism was not apolitical. Historians look upon it as a conscious attempt to revitalize the political organization of the known world, and it met with considerable success. The design for the Augustan principate was shaped by Stoic theory. The Stoic spirit spread with the empire, and one of its most notable effects may be the rationale it provided for the conferral of Roman citizenship and equality before the law throughout the whole empire.

Given its lengthy history, it is difficult to talk about Stoicism with needed precision. One would have to distinguish among the Early, Middle, and Late Stoa. Yet one is tempted to draw certain parallels between that period in antiquity in which the Early Stoa came to be and our own time. Stoicism was called into being when the political revolution affected by Alexander the Great stripped the individual of the insulated shelter of the city-state and forced him to come to terms with and find a place in an enormously expanded political setting. Perhaps Stoicism caught on because it clearly pointed to the importance of the individual, even in the midst of empire, insisting that in nature there are no distinctions among men: noble or commoner, Hellenic or barbarian. All function physically in the same way; differences are merely a matter of convention and cultural circumstance.

While Stoicism will forever remain a rich source of wisdom, speculative and practical, there can be no thought of turning back or blindly endorsing an outlook suited to institutions and patterns of life in another age. The noblest aspects of its teaching were transformed by Christianity, which in turn became the guiding moral force throughout the West until challenged by the Enlightenment. The so-called "age of reason" was to rob morality of its metaphysical grounding, so evident to the Stoic and to the Christian. In denying the existence of a supreme law giver, the rationalism of the Enlightenment denied the intrinsic intelligibility of nature and a natural moral order. The consequences of the Enlightenment rejection of a natural-law morality are only in the twentieth century being felt in their logical conclusion.

To diagnose the ills of contemporary society, one needs to step back and view it through the lens of history. It is often said that only a dying culture ignores its dead. The first-century Roman historian Titus Livy (59 B.C.–A.D. 17) recommended to a failing Rome a consideration of "the kind of lives our ancestors lived, of who were the men and what the means, both in politics and war, by which Rome's power was first acquired and subsequently expanded."[5] Although Livy was a contemporary of Augustus, he produced a memorable passage applicable in our own time. "I would have [the reader] trace the processes of our moral decline, to watch first the sinking of the foundations of morality as the old teaching was allowed to lapse, then the final collapse of the whole edifice, and the dark dawning of our modern day when we can neither endure our vices nor face the remedies needed to cure them."[6]

Werner Jaeger, in his monumental study *Paideia*, warns us that we should not slip into the posture of regarding classical antiquity as merely a piece of history "for education has from the very beginning been closely connected with the study of the ancient world. The ages which succeeded it always regarded classical antiquity as an inexhaustible treasure of knowledge and culture—first as a collection of valuable external facts and arts, and later as a world of ideas to be imitated."

Wolfe's *A Man in Full* may not have the social or political impact of Jonathan Swift's, "A Modest Proposal" (1729), but it may engender renewed interest in a few classical texts that remain ever salient, ever new.

NOTES

1. Tom Wolfe, *A Man in Full* (New York: Farrar, Straus, Giroux, 1998).

2. Epictetus, *Moral Discourses*, trans. and intro. Elizabeth Carter (London: Everyman's Classical Library, 1910). The latest edition of Book I of the *Discourses* is translated with an introduction and commentary by Robert F. Dobbin (Oxford, England: The Clarendon Press, 1998).

3. Christopher Dawson, *The Gods of Revolution* (New York: New York University Press, 1972), 165.

4. Epictetus, *Discourses*, trans. Robert F. Dobbin (Oxford, England: Clarendon Press, 1998), Book I, chap. 5.

5. Titus Livy, *History* (Cambridge, Mass.: Loeb Classical Library, 1924), Vol. I, Preface

6. Livy, *History*, Vol. I, Preface.

Chapter Three

Aristotle in North America

Modernity cannot be understood apart from its break with Plato and Aristotle. Rejecting antiquity, Descartes and Hobbes facilitated the break, although some cite Machiavelli as the founder of modernity, while others cite the British empiricists. Obviously perspective varies from those whose interests are primarily political to those whose interests are metaphysical.

The fortunes of Aristotle are bound up with the fortunes of metaphysics. Once the core of any philosophical curriculum, metaphysics has become, where it is still pursued, one specialized discipline among many. In the golden age of American philosophy, the age of Pierce, James, Royce, Whitehead, and Santayana, the centrality of metaphysics was uncontested, and later, even by the pragmatic naturalists who followed the lead of John Dewey. The eclipse of metaphysics is due in part to the ascendant influence of British analytic philosophy insofar as it reduces philosophy to logical or linguistic analysis. Some will speak of analytic metaphysics, but that may upon scrutiny turn out to be an oxymoron.

Pragmatic-naturalists, such as John Herman Randall, Jr. and Abraham Edel, adapted Aristotle to suit their purpose but remained philosophical realists. They did not subscribe to the analytic philosophy emanating from Oxford and Cambridge. Traditional metaphysical issues, including discussions of substance, causality, and purpose in nature were still pursued, albeit from a materialistic point of view. The materialism of Dewey and his school was driven by an aversion to the so called, "supernatural" and the consequences it implied for the social and political order. Driven by a skepticism with respect to the efficacy of intellect to reason from the seen to the unseen, John Herman Randall, Jr. could produce a book on Aristotle, omitting any reference to separated substance, an immaterial intellect, a prime mover or a self-thinking intellect. In a best-selling textbook, Ernest Nagel, although employing the language of Aristotle, reduced scientific explanation to description and prediction.

In the early days of the American republic, philosophy was the province of the New England divines, those same ministers who laid the foundations of what were to become some of America's most prestigious universities. By the end of the eighteenth century it was recognized that British empiricism and Enlightenment philosophy originating in France and Germany were posing a threat to the Christian faith. *The Journal of Speculative Philosophy*, the first journal of philosophy in the English language, was established at St. Louis in 1867, among other reasons, to combat the secular philosophies arriving from Europe. The chosen mode of counterattack was that of German idealism, particularly the idealism of Hegel. In its first issue, editor William Torrey Harris explained the purpose of the journal. He gave three reasons. In his judgment speculative philosophy provides, first, a philosophy of religion much needed at a time when traditional religious teaching and ecclesiastical authority were losing their influence. Secondly, it provides a social philosophy compatible with a communal outlook as opposed to a socially devastating individualism. Thirdly, while taking cognizance of the startling advances in the natural sciences, it provides an alternative to empiricism as a philosophy of knowledge. Speculative philosophy for Harris is the tradition that begins with Plato, a tradition that finds its full expression in the system of Hegel.

The foremost representative of the speculative outlook endorsed by Harris was undoubtedly Josiah Royce whose Gifford lectures (1900–1901), published as *The World and the Individual*, sought not only to counter the skepticism of the day but to provide a rational foundation for the Christian faith. Royce had little respect for blind faith. The problem created by Kant's destruction of metaphysics he regarded as fundamental. In 1881, Royce wrote, "We all live, philosophically speaking, in a Kantian atmosphere." Eschewing the outright voluntarism of Schopenhauer, Royce sought a metaphysics that would permit him to rationally embrace his Christian heritage. Whereas William James was convinced that every demonstrative approach to God must fail, Royce was convinced that speculative reason gives one access to God. The code words of the day, "evolution," "progress," "illusion," "higher criticism," "communism," "socialism," he thought, evoked a mental outlook that reduces Christianity to metaphor and Christian organizations to welfare dispensaries. What was at issue for Royce was not simply a philosophical problem. The philosophers also tutored the architects of the new biblical criticism, the *Redaktionsgeschichte* movement. David Friedrich Strauss, in his *Das Leben Jesu*, under the influence of the Enlightenment, examined the Gospels and the life of Jesus from the standpoint of the higher criticism and concluded that Christ was not God but a supremely good man whose moral imperatives deserved to be followed. This, Royce could not accept: there is no philosophically compelling reason, he maintained, to embrace a purely naturalistic interpretation of the Sacred Scriptures. The movement inspired by Royce was not without success.

By the last quarter of the nineteenth century, nearly every chair of philosophy, in the newly emerging universities, was held by an idealist. But the intellectual climate was soon to change. Hegel was not able to hold the day in the face of notable achievements in the sciences that demanded recognition of the empirical source of new ways of thinking about nature. Laws of nature are discovered; inquiry is not simply the uncovering of the implicit or the organization of data in the light of the given. To Royce's supposed definitive critique of materialism, opposition was not long in coming. Critiques were mounted in volumes published as corporate philosophical enquiry under titles, such as *The New Realism* (1912) and *Critical Realism* (1920) and were soon to control the day. By 1916 the idealism of the St. Louis Hegelians, as it had come to be called, had given way, and would soon be replaced by the pragmatic-naturalism of John Dewey and his school, an outlook that found expression in another corporate volume, *Naturalism and the Human Spirit* (1944). This signaled the direction the new realism was to take. Under the influence of Kirpatrick and Dewey it became the philosophy undergirding public education in the United States.

At approximately the same time that the young Josiah Royce entered the intellectual arena, Leo XIII, aware of the secular challenge to the Christian faith and convinced that philosophy must be fought by philosophy, recommended, not Hegel, but Aquinas. His encyclical, *Aternae Patris*, by endorsing a fledgling Thomistic movement, gave direction to Catholic philosophy and theology that was to last throughout most of the twentieth century. To study Aquinas is by implication to study Aristotle, and, one might add, Maimonides, Averroes, and Avicenna as well. From the late nineteenth through most of the twentieth century, the philosophy taught in the seminaries and in the Catholic colleges of the period came to be called Aristotelian-Thomistic. The Catholic Church was even dubbed by dissidents, "The Aristotelian Church." In the early years, professors in those seminaries, colleges, and universities drew heavily on Germanic scholarship. English scholars like W. D. Ross and A. E. Taylor were to come later. The specialized studies we now take for granted were largely unknown. There was little comparable to the work we currently associate with Richard Sorabji, Jonathan Barnes, Jonathan Lear, Lloyd Gerson, and G. E. R. Lloyd.

University education modeled on the Humbolt University of Berlin did not arrive in the United States until the founding of Johns Hopkins University in 1876. The first graduate-level faculty of philosophy to be established in the

United States under Catholic auspices was that of The Catholic University of America's School of Philosophy (1895). Although its orientation from the very beginning was that of the realism of Aristotle and Aquinas, the first doctoral dissertation to mention Aristotle explicitly in its title was not accepted until 1929. It bore the title, "Aristotelianism in Thomas Aquinas." The second did not come until 1940 with the publication of a dissertation entitled, "Efficient Causality in Aristotle and St. Thomas." Specialized studies of Aristotle soon followed.

Under the influence of Etienne Gilson, the founder of the Pontifical Institute of Medieval Studies at the University of Toronto, studies, such as Joseph Owens's, *The Doctrine of Being in Aristotle's Metaphysics*, and Gilson's own work inspired like enquiry throughout the Catholic world. Thomistic centers with attendant interest in Aristotle emerged throughout the Midwest, notably at Marquette University, The University of Notre Dame, St. Louis University, and to a lesser extent at the University of Chicago and Indiana University. Their contribution to Aristotelian scholarship was soon paralleled by the highly specialized textual work that came to be the norm in the last decade of the twentieth century. Aristotle's *Prior* and *Posterior Analytics*, his *Physics*, *de Anima*, *Metaphysics,* and *Ethics* were used in courses labeled logic, the philosophy of nature, the philosophy of human nature, metaphysics, and ethics. Catholic scholars were often accused of not knowing the difference between Thomas and Aristotle, attributing to the latter doctrines that could only be found in Thomas. The mode of teaching was usually historical or systematic or a combination of the two, not the textual exegesis in favor today. The aim of teaching was an integrated whole, both speculative and practical. In the classroom, the origin of an idea was not as important as the idea itself and its implications. It was only later when the mode of teaching shifted from the manual or systematic mode to the study of original texts themselves did specialized commentary become indispensable.

It is difficult to separate British and American scholarship, especially as it pertains to Aristotle since most English-speaking scholars spend time in North America, often ending their careers in North American universities. The key philosophical issues are largely the same on both sides of the Atlantic. Where Aristotle prevails, metaphysical demonstration of an immaterial order is accepted; so too the immateriality of the human soul and a natural law outlook as the grounding of virtue. The possibility of scientific explanation is taken for granted. Where empiricism prevails, science is reduced to description and prediction, mind supplants intellect and is accounted for exclusively in terms of brain activity. Natural law, in the absence of a concept of human nature and the recognition of its *telos*, is supplanted with the values we choose to embrace. At times mainstream academic philosophy seems to be a chaotic scramble to avoid supposed outmoded ontological concepts such as substance, essence, or nature with purely descriptive accounts. The idea of an immaterial soul or the concept of a self-existent being, the cause of the existence of things, or the concept of an immaterial intellect responsible for the order in nature are rarely entertained apart from antiquarian interest in a given author. Where empiricism prevails, interest in Aristotle is primarily textual exegesis, pursued in the interest of clarity and internal consistency.

This does not mean that Aristotle is not used. Alasdair MacIntyre in his celebrated book, *Whose Justice, Which Rationality?* (1988), shows clearly the ethical implications of an Aristotelian outlook as contrasted with that of David Hume. John M. Rist in *Real Ethics* (2002) has called for a return to the scientific realism of Plato and Aristotle. Leon Kass in working out a biomedical ethics finds it necessary to return to Aristotle's concept of human nature (*Life, Liberty and the Defense of Dignity*, 2002). Contemporary discussions of the Galileo affair often center on whether Bellarmine had the right to demand demonstration in the Aristotelian sense. Nearly all discussions of natural law find it necessary to resort to the metaphysics of Aristotle, but these are carried out in those quarters that have never abandoned the study of Aristotle.

William James, writing at the beginning of the twentieth century could speak of his Harvard colleagues' "deep appreciation of one another" and of the department's cooperative efforts to convey basic philosophical truths to its students. The Harvard faculty of philosophy, at that time, included Josiah Royce and George Santayana. Josiah Royce was writing books with such titles as *The Religious Aspect of Philosophy*, *The World and the Individual,* and *The Problem of Christianity*; and George Santayana, *The Life of Reason*, *The Realms of Being*, *The Sense of Beauty*. James's own *Varieties of Religious Experience* was what we today would call a best seller. Until the second half of the twentieth century, at least in the United States, philosophy was studied in a more-or-less traditional way. One was expected to know in a cursory way the major figures and movements in the history of Western philosophy. In certain programs, one was also expected to have more than an elementary knowledge of mathematics, physics, chemistry, and biology. Then modernity caught up with the curriculum. Today it is not merely that philosophy has become so specialized that members of the same faculty sometimes find it difficult to communicate with each other. That is one problem to be sure. Specialization, it must be acknowledged, reflects a deeper fragmentation of a once integrated discipline in which the parts were clearly understood in relation to the whole. That fragmentation has resulted in many a careful and valuable study of original texts as can be seen in Aristotelian scholarship alone, but it has also resulted in a kind of trivialization which permits whole careers to be spent on isolated problems in the work of a single philosopher of little consequence, or worse still, on the youthful efforts of a philosopher whose mature works repudiated his early efforts.

When G. E. Moore was asked, "What is the function of philosophy," he could answer, "To give a general description of the whole of the Universe, mentioning all the most important kind of things we know to be in it." C.S. Peirce in his day wanted to be regarded as a laborer in the common enterprise of intellectual inquiry. Peirce is not to be faulted: the division of labor is not the fundamental problem. Given the task of Dame Philosophy, some labor is bound to be subservient. To shift metaphors, the master need not complete every canvas. All profit from the careful analysis and exposition of obscure tests or the production of critical editions of ancient and medieval sources. Yet if one made an empirical survey of the leading North American journals and major university presses, it would be difficult to determine from the articles and books examined the literal meaning of the term, "philosophy." Much discourse seems unrelated to the pursuit of wisdom. It is not surprising that the bulk of philosophical work will be unintelligible even to the educated layman, but some work targets an audience no greater than that provided by a handful of university faculties. How many professional philosophers know the difference between a "fallibilistic meliorism" and a "weak version of universal pragmatics?" It may be that we are in our day experiencing the full effects of a turn that took place three centuries ago. Etienne Gilson has remarked that if one starts with the mind, one ends there. "History," says Gilson, is there to remind us that no one ever again regains the whole of reality after locking himself in one of its parts." Tutored by Descartes and others, modern philosophy in repudiating classical philosophy put the epistemological problem first. Josiah Royce, in paying tribute to Leo XIII for the Thomistic revival, expressed the fear that a resurgent Thomism might give way to the Kantian legions and their demand that the epistemological issue be settled first. The issues which confronted the late nineteenth century intellectual world remain.

Contemporary studies of Aristotle abound, but few may be considered monumental. Most are published as articles in professional journals and are narrowly focused and unrelated to the Aristotelian corpus as a whole. Conferences and symposia devoted to the study of Aristotle often produce significant volumes. No research library can be without the published results, for example, of an international conference held at Deurne, Netherlands, in 1999, published under the editorship of Frans de Hass and Jaap Mansfield, as *Aristotle's* On Generation and Corruption I. The same is true of significant monographs devoted to specific works of Aristotle, such as Jonathan Barnes's *Aristotle* (1989), Daniel Robinson's *Aristotle's Psychology* (1989), Charlotte Witt's *Substance and Essence in Aristotle* (1989), Fred D. Miller's

Nature, Justice and Rights in Aristotle's Politics (1995), Lloyd Gerson's *Aristotle and Other Platonists* (2005), and the list could go on. And then there are studies such as Rom Harré's *Varities of Realism* (1986) and William A. Wallace's *The Modeling of Nature* (1996) that must be regarded as Aristotelian treatises.

These studies attest to the perennial value of the works of Aristotle, who, in spite of relative neglect, is still seen as an indispensable guide in the difficult terrain of metaphysics and epistemology, and, one should add, ethics and politics as well. A little-adverted-to fact is that while technology has broadened the scope of the natural sciences, there have been no similar advances to facilitate the work of philosophy. Instruments from the microscope to the telescope have been augmented in each generation. Particle accelerators with ever-increasing energy have produced startling increases in our knowledge of matter and energy in almost one generation. But in philosophy we are no better equipped than the ancients, who, no less intelligent or observant than we, have much to tell us about nature and human nature from a metaphysical point of view. Aristotle's account of human knowing remains a starting point not easily surpassed. The *Nicomachean Ethics* is of perennial value to the political theorist and continues to serve as a guide to personal fulfillment. The nature and purpose of the polis as described by Aristotle remain a starting point for political theory even in the age of globalization.

Etienne Gilson's *William James Lectures* (1950) rested on the premise that the history of philosophy is much more a part of philosophy than the history of science is a part of physics. Those lectures, presented and published as *The Unity of Philosophical Experience,* argued that no man can carry very far his own philosophical reflections unless he first studies the history of philosophy. "In point of fact," said Gilson, "the First Book of Aristotle's *Metaphysics* is the first known History of Greek Philosophy." Such an assessment, of course, is not a common view. Gilson's approach is clearly at variance with most contemporary philosophy. Under the influence of Gilbert Ryle and the British analysts, the history of philosophy has all but been abandoned. If Josiah Royce or George Santayana were to return to consult contemporary journals of philosophy in the English language, they would be surprised to find that many an article makes no reference to reality and to what one's predecessors may have said about the realm of being but instead consists of a highly sophisticated argument for or against a given abstract thesis whose grounding or presuppositions are likely to go unacknowledged. Within the current intellectual milieu, Aristotle may be examined for the logical structure of an argument without reference or appreciation of the insight to be gained from his acute observation. Aristotle's confidence in the intellect, in the intelligibility of nature, and in the power of reason to reach unseen causes has been replaced—to borrow a phrase from Giovanni Gentile—by "the agnosticism of the schools."

In the aftermath of the Kantian revolution, as Royce would call it, the postmodern world of Nietzsche, Heidegger, and the deconstructionists may be ripe for a return to the commonsense realism of Aristotle. The moral bankruptcy of contemporary philosophy and its cultural implications should be evident to all who take time to reflect on the Pyrrhonism, sophistry, and humbug that pass for philosophical inquiry. Aristotle was not faced with skepticism as a strongly held position in his day, but all the elements needed to provide an antidote to the empiricism and agnosticism of our day are to be found in his legacy. The determined opposition to this once-dominant figure in Western philosophy seems unintelligible unless one attributes it to a kind of willfulness or a disposition to moral relativism.

Chapter Four

Ora et Labora: Benedict's Legacy

Alasdair MacIntyre, to the scandal of many of his contemporaries, ended his book After Virtue (1981) with the judgment that given the decline of Western civilization, "We are waiting not for Godot, but for another—doubtless very different—St. Benedict."[1] No one questions the fundamental contribution of the Benedictines to the preservation of classical learning and the monastic contribution to the civilization characteristic of the West. The distinguished Renaissance scholar Paul Oskar Kristeller, writing from his distinctive vantage point, put it this way: "If we were to take away the Benedictine and Cistercian monasteries, not only the theological but nearly the entire intellectual movement of the Carolingian age and the centuries following it would seem to disappear."[2]

Benedict is more than a symbol. His *Regula Monachorum* became an exemplar of community life throughout the West. Enjoining a monastic combination of intellectual and communal labor, his rule was created in the spirit of Cicero's *De Officis* and Augustine's *De Opere Monach.* It is no doubt the Roman ideal of *virtus*—the natural virtues taught by the Stoics and ennobled by Benedict in the light of the Church Fathers—which caught MacIntyre's eye as he wrote his magisterial work on virtue.

Following Benedict, Josef Pieper, in his multiple works on virtue and on leisure and work, portrays the connection between those virtues required by self-perfection and the very existence of community life, indeed of civilized life itself.[3] In the spirit of Pieper, the following examines the contribution of Benedict and Western monasticism to the culture we are rapidly disassembling.

As citizens of the West, we are heirs to an intellectual and moral outlook which has shaped our culture and its many institutions. Heirs to a legacy symbolized by the cities of Jerusalem, Athens, and Rome, we are empowered by virtue of that inheritance to judge and to evaluate. To know "who one is" is to know one's intellectual progenitors, a decided advantage when all is called into question. Equipped with such knowledge, one is better positioned to distinguish friend from foe, for with the aid of history one can see the implications of ideas spread out and thus be less inclined to embrace contradictories. There is nothing more limiting than the present, devoid of both history and dream. One can be parochial in time as well as in place.

Lynn White, Jr., once said of the Benedictines that they were the first intellectuals in the history of the West to get dirt under their fingernails.[4] It is in the monasteries founded by St. Benedict that we have a witness to the emergence of an intellectual outlook different from both classical and Eastern Christian approaches. Let us then examine the Benedictine perspective and its implications for science and technology, in contrast to the too-speculative Greek approach and the naturalistic and positivistic philosophies of the twentieth century. Reflection on these themes, I think, brings us into the middle of one of the most interesting debates of the past decade.

In his book, *La Formation de la Pensée Grècque*, Pierre-Maxime Schuhl argues that the slave-based society of Athens in the fifth to fourth centuries B.C. created an outlook that was detrimental to the application of science to technique.[5] The social consciousness of the period, with its contempt for manual labor, prevented the mature utilization of the very science to which the Greek genius had earlier given birth. This thesis is reinforced by the work of Benjamin Farrington, who describes the rise and decline of Greek science, accounting for the arrest of the scientific spirit in the third century B.C. by the growing indifference to applied science.[6] Farrington, like Schuhl before him but whose work was unknown to him, connects this indifference to the growth of the institution of slavery. He places a great deal of blame on Plato.

Farrington's assessment takes this form. Science, whatever its ultimate developments, has its origin in techniques, in the arts and crafts, in the various activities by which man keeps life going on, keeps body and soul together. Its source is experience, its aims practical, its only test is that it works. Science arises in contact with things; it is dependent on the evidence of the senses. It requires logic and the elaboration of theory, but its strictest logic and choicest theory must be proved in practice.

Fully to understand the science of any society is to be acquainted not only with the degree of its material advancement but with its political structure. There is no such thing as science in *vacuo*. There is only the science of a particular society at a particular place and time. The history of science can only be understood as a function of the total life of society. Farrington argues that the division of labor in Greek and Roman society has an important influence on the development of science. The presence of a leisured class ensured opportunity for reflection and elaboration of theory. It also gave opportunity for theorizing without relation to facts. The Greek community was marked by a sharp separation of servile workers and free men of leisure, which meant a division between acquaintance with matters of fact and contemplative appreciation. Furthermore, with the development of classes, the need for a new kind of science arose which might be defined as "the system of behavior by which man acquires mastery over man." When the task of mastering man became the preoccupation of the ruling class and the task of mastering nature became the forced labor of another class, science took a new and dangerous turn.[7] Karl Niebyl argues that it was not so much slavery but success in international trade as a result of military conquest that gave the Greeks a privileged economic position.[8] But, like Farrington, Niebyl maintains that the dominant social group became separated from the active productive process, eventually becoming more preoccupied with the problem of maintaining its status quo than with creativity.

Farrington claims that "with the science of Alexandria and of Rome we are in very truth on the threshold of the modern world."[9] When modern science began in the sixteenth century, it took up where the Greeks left off. An interesting puzzle is the question of why modern science did not follow on the heels of Greek science. Before the end of the third century B.C., the major work of Greek science had been accomplished. During the next 400 years there were many extensions of knowledge. There was much reorganization in the body of knowledge, with fresh acquisition of skill in exposition, but there was no great forward drive, no general application of science to life. Science had ceased to be, or had failed to become, a force in the life of society. "Science had become a relaxation, an adornment, a subject of contemplation."[10] It remained for another period, another intellectual climate, to reunite the speculative and the manual.

From the decline of Roman civilization to the rise of the European universities in the twelfth century, a period of approximately 700 years, the Benedictine monasteries were to play an indispensable role, not only as bearers of the classical learning but as cultivators in their own right of science and technology. The educational institutions of the Roman Empire were swept away by the barbarian invasions, or they declined and died with the declining city culture of the Latin world. It was only through the monasteries that the Latin classics were preserved. As Dawson summarized their achievement, "The monastic schools and libraries and scriptoria became the chief organs of the higher intellectual culture in Western Europe."[11]

To speak of monasticism in a general way is not to overlook the various forms of Western monasticism or the differences between Benedictine abbeys, their ups and downs, and their constant reformations, which seem to be a characteristic of all human institutions, secular and religious. Certain outlooks, however, are pervasive because they are bound up with a Christian view of man, of nature, of man's relation to nature, of man's ultimate destiny and the Benedictine sanctification of labor.

If the Greek community was marked by a sharp separation of servile worker and free man of leisure, the same was not true of the community founded by St. Benedict. In the view of Benedict, the wisdom of the Creator has ordained that man, both body and soul, should cultivate both his physical and spiritual powers. In his Rule, Benedict prescribed that at certain hours of the day each monk should be given time for study: "the brethren must be occupied at stated hours in manual labor, and again at other hours in divine reading."[12] The monk must first of all devote himself to the study of Sacred Scripture, particularly the Psalms, for from that source there quietly flows an inexhaustible wealth of sublime wisdom. The Fathers were to be studied; so, too, were theology, philosophy, grammar, and logic. The monk may devote himself to other sciences and to the fine arts, such as painting and sculpture, provided they have the aim of praising God or promoting the welfare of neighbor. Certain arts were necessary for the observance of the Hours and for the maintenance of the liturgy, arts such as calligraphy, painting, music, and, above all, chronology and the knowledge of the calendar. The monks also had to instruct their converts, not only in Christian doctrine but in the Latin tongue, the sacred language of Scripture and liturgy.

It is true that monasticism was born in the African desert as a protest against the whole tradition of the classical culture of the Greek and Roman world. It stood for the renunciation of everything the ancient world had prized—not only pleasure and wealth and honor but also family life and citizenship and society. Its founders and models were ascetics who passed their lives in ceaseless prayer and fasting. But there was much in Oriental monasticism that was repugnant to the disciplines and practical ethos of the Roman tradition. St. Augustine's work on monasticism, *De Opere Monachorum*, is outspoken in its condemnation of the hypocrisy of the long-haired false ascetics and wandering monks who lived in idleness and exploited popular superstition.

Benedict's conception of the monastic life, by contrast, is essentially social and cooperative.[13] As the discipline of the common life, his *Rule* differs from older rules in its strongly practical character. The Benedictine abbey was to be a self-contained economic organism, like the villa of a Roman land owner, save that the monks were themselves the workers and the old classical contrast between servile work and free leisure no longer held sway. According to the *Rule*, St. Benedict intended the abbot to be the manager of the estate of the monastery. The *Rule* lays great stress on the equal treatment of all members of the community, noble or peasant, free or slave. Under the Germanic influence, monks had to be free men. In actual fact they were almost exclusively members of noble families.[14] Benedict's monasteries, by their sanctification of work and poverty, revolutionized the order of social values. The slave-owning society of the empire, the aristocratic warrior ethos, gave way to an institution which stressed the value of manual labor. The effects were not long in coming. The disciplined and tireless labor of the monks brought back into cultivation the lands which had been deserted and depopulated during the age of the invasions. As John H. Newman beautifully described the period, "by degrees the woody swamp became a hermitage, a religious house, a farm, an abbey, a village, a seminary, a school of learning and a city."[15]

The superhuman asceticism of Celtic monasticism, closer to the Egyptian, was not to characterize the Benedictine. The original rule of St. Benedict was outstanding in its balance of prayer, work, study and sleep. It provided for about eight hours of sleep. The common services took about three and a half hours, depending upon the time of the year, while study and readings consumed roughly another four hours. The work time also fluctuated with the season and took six to eight hours. Cluny was, in time, to overemphasize liturgical prayer at the expense of contemplation. Its best-known abbot, Peter the Venerable, was to develop a theology in defense of an exclusively liturgical life without the necessity of labor, which doctrine held that the monk had to be maintained by the Christian people as a public intercessor. In those respects, Cluny may be considered an aberration. It is clear that Benedict himself regarded manual labor as essential.

The copying of manuscripts became a form of labor that was accepted in very early monasticism. Although Benedict did not encourage the reproduction of manuscripts, the practice had begun even before his death. Cassiodorus, who in advanced age founded the Monastery of Squillace, deliberately introduced the copying of manuscripts as a means of preserving the old tradition of learning. His devotion to classical literature and to the vanishing purity of the Latin tongue has preserved for posterity the poetry of Virgil and Horace and the prose of Cicero, Livy, and Quintilian.[16]

Gibbon described the early monasteries as refuges, chiefly inhabited by faint-hearted men of aesthetic and intellectual inclinations, by idlers and wasters looking for an easy life, and by others who were unwilling to face the world. No doubt the monastic life did attract some of the types described by Gibbon, but his report is far from the truth. Responsible scholars paint another picture. It is the picture of active and courageous monks, working among the Franks, facing the hostile Lombards in Italy, and establishing foundations in Ireland, Scotland, England, Iceland, Germany, and the Scandinavian countries. They were sane and hard-headed men who lived with the peasants and shared their labors in plowing and planting, in reclaiming land, and in clearing away forests. Their labors were not without fruit. In the Carolingian period the Benedictine rule became the universal standard of the religious life in the West. The great monasteries became the cultural centers of the Empire. Independent schools emerged in the abbeys, each seeking to outrival the others by increasing its library, by attracting professors of renown, and by drawing students to its intellectual tournaments. These schools promoted the study of the sciences and were to create a legion of remarkable theologians, lawyers, philosophers, and scientists. We need but cite the schools of Cluny, Citeaux in Burgundy, Bec in Normandy, Aurillac and St. Martin at Tours and St. Omer. A roll call of the leading scholars of the age, from Gregory through Bede, Lafranc, and Anselm, would name the abbots of many of those monasteries.

While much of the learning fostered in those monasteries was theological and scriptural, still there was no lack of the kind of learning we would today call humanistic.[17] Nor was there an absence of technological innovation. The science of the period was principally, though not exclusively, concerned with agriculture, responding to the needs and capacities of an agrarian society.

Alfred North Whitehead, whose attempt to understand science in the modern world led to his study of its medieval and Renaissance background, was fascinated by the role played by the Benedictines. "The alliance of science with technology, by which learning is kept in contact with irreducible and stubborn facts, owes much to the practical bent of the early Benedictines."[18] This practical bent of the Benedictines, Whitehead could have added, is witnessed by their interest in medicine, in their concern for the improvement of farm instruments, in the harnessing of natural power, and in the promotion of crafts. By the eleventh century, some abbeys were to have as many as four or five water wheels, each powering a different shop.

In the earliest Benedictine monasteries, studies of medicine are found which were to initiate a long series of works which continued without break until the sixteenth century. Beginning with Bede in the seventh century, a series of treatises was written on astronomy by scholars for purely practical purposes, such as determining the date of Easter, fixing latitude, and showing how to determine true North and telling time with an astrolabe. Another series of practical treatises deals with the preparation of pigments and other chemical substances. It should be noted that technical treatises were among the first to be translated out of the Arabic and Greek into Latin, indicating that the way had been prepared for their reception. In the thirteenth century, the encyclopedias of Alexander Neckham, Albertus Magnus, and Roger Bacon contain a great deal of accurate information about the compass, the calendar, chemistry, and agriculture, reflecting a long tradition of monastic learning. Mention should also be made of the Benedictine contribution to the development of mines, saltworks, foundries, and glassworks in Bohemia, Germany, and Hungary. While it is difficult to pinpoint the origin of certain technological advances, there is evidence that the monasteries contributed to advances in spinning and weaving, in pulling and dyeing, in feltmaking, in the manufacturing of soap, and in the making of barrels and tubs. The cultivation of rye, oats, and hops in the North is thought to be the result of monastic initiative.[19]

By the middle of the twelfth century, the cathedral schools came to replace the monasteries as centers of learning and cultural influence. The introduction of Aristotle into the West in the twelfth and thirteenth centuries was to have immediate and profound influence. In one sense it was a Greek revival, but between the Hellenistic period and the advent of the medieval universities, the European intellect had undergone a transformation. Let us now examine more carefully that transformation.

First, a few comparisons. If we were to compare the Christian attitude toward the pursuit of knowledge, as exemplified in the Benedictine, with the previous Greek attitude, we would find not opposition but, instead, the Christian building upon the Greek. The Christian's belief that nature is intelligible and that processes are directed to ends is something he shares with his Greek predecessors. That nature is the handiwork of the divine, he sees more clearly. God reveals himself not only in Sacred Scripture but also in the book of nature, which is to be studied both for itself and for the insight which it gives us into God himself.

If the Greeks were overly theoretical, the reasons are sociological rather than philosophical. There is nothing in the Greek view of science, nothing in either Aristotle or Plato, which should separate science from technology. That science and technology became divorced in the Hellenic period is the result of historical accident, not of necessity. It is, however, by a kind of necessity that the two are bound together in the Benedictine. For the reasons given by Benedict, the contemplative monk must engage in manual labor. For intrinsic reason the sanctification of work and labor was to become the achievement of the monks.

The Benedictine outlook might also be contrasted with that of the Protestantism which was to arrive on the European scene in the sixteenth century. Essentially a religion of action, Protestantism was hostile to both monasticism and asceticism. Abandoning the contemplative ideal, it substituted in its place the standard of practical moral duty. Albrecht Ritschl regarded this as the most characteristic achievement of the Protestant movement.

Some would contrast the monastic with the later Scholastic view of science and technology. St. Bernard of Clairvaux is sometimes taken as representative of the monastic theologian, and it is well known that at an early age he acquired a strong distaste for the exercise of logic without a practical function. In many contexts, Bernard suggests that all forms of detached knowledge, all scientia, should be used primarily in the service of the individual. The ultimate purpose of knowledge is to combat uncertainty and to prepare the way for salvation. Yet Bernard, a sworn enemy of scholasticism, was to draw heavily upon Abelard as he completed his theology in later life.[20] Whatever his failings, Bernard never denied the worth of theoretical knowledge, even though in his most polemical years he did subordinate all knowledge as well as all action to personal moral growth. In that he remained true to his Benedictine vocation.

A distinction must be made between the neo-Platonism of the late Roman period and the Aristotelianism which was to arrive in the twelfth century. The scholasticism of the later Middle Ages was to return to a fundamentally Aristotelian view of the relationship between science and technology. Plato considered mathematics to be not only a high form of knowledge but also the key to the understanding of all reality. For both Plato and his disciples, the physical structure of bodies and their motion are derived from the geometrical structure of the eternal idea, and this, in turn, was derived from its arithmetical structure. But the same is not true for Aristotle or the Scholastic philosophy built upon his works. Aristotle never denied the validity of pure mathematics nor the validity of mathematics for the study of nature. He was abreast of the mathematics of his day, but he rejected the Platonic and Pythagorean equation of philosophy with mathematics, displaying considerable impatience with those philosophers who expended their energies in searching for the number out of which the world is composed. In Aristotle's judgment, such philosophers had given up the search for the cause of perceptible things and, consequently, had nothing to say about the causes from which change takes its start. Aristotle considered the use of mathematics in astronomy, optics, harmonics, and mechanics as a profitable first step in understanding natural phenomena. There remained the more important task of examining the physical natures themselves and of discovering the causes operative in natural phenomena.[21]

Interpretations of Renaissance science which regard it as the union of Renaissance art with the mathematical idealism of Platonic metaphysics need to be qualified. Led by Voltaire, the rationalist historians of the eighteenth century discounted any possibility of a connection between the triumph of scientific reason, which they located in the period of Galileo, Harvey, Descartes and Newton, and medieval Aristotelianism which preceded that period. The studies of Alistair Crombie, Annaliese Maier, William A. Wallace, and others have shown how dependent the Renaissance was on the Scholastic period.[22] As Crombie remarks, "With the recovery of the full tradition of Greek and Arabic science in the twelfth and thirteenth centuries, and particularly of the works of

Aristotle and Euclid, there was born, from the marriage of the empiricism of technics with the rationalism of philosophy and mathematics, a new conscious empirical science seeking to discover the rational structure of nature."[23]

Other comparisons can be made, for the kind of outlook taken for granted within the renaissance contrasts sharply with that found in much twentieth-century philosophy of science. John Dewey's (1859–1952) pragmatic-naturalism may be taken as an example. In works such as *The Quest for Certainty and Experience and Nature* he was given to scolding the Greeks for a too speculative approach to nature. Dewey had several things against the Greeks. He rejected what he took to be a view of science which identified science with contemplative activity, that is, with a disinterested inquiry into nature, a seeking of knowledge for its own sake. Dewey not only rejected the contemplative view of science but also the notion that there are natures, or structures, independent of the mind and of human interest. He also dismissed the notion of teleology, that nature is ordered or is purposive in its processes. Dewey affirmed instead that inquiry creates the substances it deals with. Knowing is essentially interaction between the knower and the known; neither exists apart or in isolation. Knowing arises with a problematic situation. As such it is an answer to a problem, sufficient for the job at hand but possessing no time-transcending value. Explanations in science are answers to "why" questions, whose meanings are relative to the questioner and his interests. In Dewey's final analysis, science is reduced to description and prediction. He identifies science primarily with *techné*, not with *epistémé*. Not only do we learn by doing, but knowledge is at its best when it is a combination of theory and practice.

One of Dewey's major programs was the introduction of scientific technique to the study of social phenomena. Dewey's objective was not a disinterested report of social processes; rather, knowledge is to be sought for its instrumental value in the pursuit of desired goals. No passive spectator of social structures, Dewey set out to change them with the aid of scientific technique. The schools themselves were subordinated as instruments to be employed in the advancement of the social revolution.

Dewey was aware that he was not only challenging a Greek view of nature and of natural science but also a Christian conception of the nature of things. Nature, he affirmed, is self-intelligible; man is a part of nature, having his origin, growth, and decay within nature. Consequently, a full explanation of man and nature has no need to draw upon an extra or what he called "super-natural" context to account either for the supposed order of things or for the inquiring mind itself, a mind heretofore erroneously regarded as different in kind from the world it encounters.

By contrast, the Benedictine mind, heir at once to classical and Christian learning, is convinced that nature, because it is the handiwork of God, is intelligible, that nature can be known in itself and in its causes. A knowledge of nature is desirable both for its own sake and for the utility it yields. The balanced or well-motivated person will pursue not only the virtues of speculative intellect but of practical intellect as well. In him, the moral and the intellectual will be integrated, with neither subordinated but with each serving the other. The genius of Benedict is manifested in his common-sense appropriation of the best offered by revelation and Greek and Roman traditions. One cannot be a Platonist, a naturalist, or a positivist and be a Benedictine. But one can be a monk and simultaneously be a physicist, philosopher, and gardener.

NOTES

1. Alasdair MacIntyre, *After Virtue* (Notre Dame: University of Notre Dame Press, 1981), 245. MacIntyre's remark is reminiscent of one made by T. S. Eliot, who expressed the utopian thought that a strengthening of monastic life is desirable today, for within the removed preserve of the cloister "uncontaminated by the deluge of barbarism outside" a certain number of people may receive "something more than education for a place in the Civil Service, or for technical efficiency, or social or political success," as quoted by Josef Pieper, *Scholasticism: Personalities and Problems of Medieval Philosophy* (London: Farber and Farber, 1960), 156.

2. Paul Oskar Kristeller, "The Contribution of Religious Orders to Renaissance Thought and Learning," in *Medieval Aspects of Renaissance Learning*, ed. and trans. Edward P. Mahoney (New York: Columbia University Press, 1992), 96.

3. See especially Musse and Kult, trans. Alexander Dru, intro. T.S. Eliot (New York: New American Library, 1963).

4. Lynn White, Jr., "Dynamo and Virgin Reconsidered," *American Scholar* 27 (1958), 187.

5. Pierre-Maxime Schuhl, *La Formation de la Pensée Grècque* (Paris: Felix Alcon, 1934).

6. Benjamin Farrington, *Greek Science* (Baltimore: Penguin, 1961); *The Faith of Epicurus* (London: Weidenfeld and Nicolson, 1967); *Science in Antiquity* (London: Oxford University Press, 1967).

7. Farrington, *Greek Science*, 19.

8. "Scientific Concepts and Social Structure in Ancient Greece," in *Philosophical Foundations of Science*, ed. R.J. Seeger and R.S. Cohen (Dordrecht: D. Riedel, 1976), 376.

9. Farrington, *Greek Science*, 301.

10. Farrington, *Greek Science*, 302.

11. Christopher Dawson, *Religion and the Rise of Western Culture* (New York: Sheed & Ward, 1962), 48. Dawson's view is not shared by all. In a work first published in 1929 and one that has been reprinted in many editions, Sir William Cecil Dampier perpetuates the "Dark Ages" myth. Although contemporary scholarship has moved beyond that simplistic designation for a very rich period, it remains a popular

impression. While Dampier gives no attention to the Benedictines as bearers of classical learning, in the single paragraph where he mentions them in his 544-page treatise, he writes, "In the sixth century the Benedictines began to study compendiums on the works of Hippocrates and Galen, and they gradually spread knowledge of these writings throughout the West. The monks were also practical farmers, who kept alive some knowledge of the art of agriculture." (*A History of Science and Its Relation to Philosophy and Religion* [Cambridge, Mass.: Cambridge University Press, 1966].)

12. St. Benedict, *Rule*, Chap. 48.

13. For a review of the literature concerning Benedict's indebtedness to the *Rule of the Master* and earlier rules, see Owen Chadwick, *The Making of the Benedictine Ideal* (Washington, D.C.: St. Anselm's Abbey, 1981).

14. See Dawson, *Religion*, 51ff.

15. John H. Newman, *Historical Studies II* (London: Longmans, Green, and Co., 1872), 410. Newman's essays on "The Mission of St. Benedict" and "The Benedictine Schools" are certainly among the most eloquent assessments of the Benedictine contribution to Western learning ever written.

16. For an evaluation of the contribution of Cassiodorus, see William H. Stahl, *Roman Science* (Madison: University of Wisconsin Press, 1962), 202–211.

17. Interest went beyond classical and orthodox Christian sources. Peter the Venerable, as Abbot of Cluny, commissioned the first Latin translation of the Koran. Cf. Pieper, *Musse und Kult*, 83.

18. *Science and the Modern World* (New York: The New American Library, 1948), 16.

19. Lynn White's article, "Technology and Invention in the Middle Ages," *Speculum* 15 (1940), still provides an informative overview of then available studies of medieval achievements, as does A. C. Crombie's *Medieval and Early Modern Science* (Garden City, NY: Doubleday, 1959), but both need to be supplemented by more recent studies. See especially *Science in the Middle Ages*, ed. David C. Lindberg (Chicago: University of Chicago Press, 1978). Since the late 1950s there has been an astonishing growth in the number of historians of medieval science. Lindberg's work presents sixteen authors who from a plurality of disciplines set forth and defend generalizations about the aims and developments of medieval science.

20. For a discussion of the relation of St. Bernard to Abelard, cf. Josef Pieper, *Musse und Kult*, 82ff.

21. For an elaboration of this point see James A. Weisheipl, "The Nature, Scope, and Classification of the Sciences," in *Science in the Middle Ages* (Chicago: University of Chicago Press, 1978), 461–482.

22. Wallace's studies have shown that Galileo's method was more closely patterned on that of the late Aristotelians of the Padua school. The most significant aspect of Galileo's work "was not its insistence on experiment, but rather on the fact that 'the book of nature' is written only in the language of mathematics." William A. Wallace, *From a Realist Point of View* (Washington, D.C.: The University Press of America, 1981), 74.

23. Alistair Crombie, *Medieval and Early Modern Science* (Garden City, N.Y.: Doubleday, 1959), 6.

Chapter Five

Ancients and Moderns on the Subject of Property

Attitudes with respect to the acquisition, use, and protection of property are but a manifestation of a deeper philosophy of human nature. This is seen dramatically in our subsequent discussion of the common good and the utilitarian outlook of contemporary liberalism. The academic debate occasioned by the U.S. Supreme Court's consideration of and subsequent ruling in *Eldred* v. *Ashcroft* brought to light conflicting notions on the nature and rights of property. The Court was asked to rule on the constitutionality of the Copyright Extension Act of 1998, which extended the limits of copyright beyond, it was contended, the constitutional specification of a limited time.[1]

The Court's resolution is now a matter of record,[2] and it is not the intent of this chapter to review the Court's ruling but to address the question, "Does the larger society or community which may benefit from the productivity of an author or inventor have a just claim to the fruits of his labor?" Discussions of the rights and duties of property owners date to antiquity. Property is so bound to considerations of human nature that the ancients still speak to us across the ages. Aristotle, for example, recognized the social character of man's condition. In the *Nicomachean Ethics* he acknowledges that man cannot thrive except as a member of a community, but he cautions that we cannot treat the goods of our fellows as if they were somehow our own. Both Plato and Aristotle affirm that self-fulfillment or self-realization may only be attained within a communal environment where citizens are well disposed to one another, yet neither Plato nor Aristotle affirms that we will be "more fulfilled" by living in a "better" society.

Abstract discussions, ancient or contemporary, are not without consequence. In our day, the academy has a peculiar way of insinuating itself into judicial decisions, or—to put it another way—the judiciary seems particularly vulnerable to the Zeitgeist of the academy. Witness the Supreme Court's rulings on church/state issues, tort law, educational policy, and race relations. The Zeitgeist of the academy is no less influential when it comes to issues affecting property, from zoning ordinances to death duties. Ancient reflections on the nature and function of property may be contrasted with post-Enlightenment treatises, notably those by Karl Marx, John Stuart Mill, and John Rawls. The comparison between antiquity and modernity is instructive.

In a famous text on property, Cicero begins with the observation that there is no such thing as private ownership established by nature. "Property becomes private either through long occupancy (as in the case of those who long ago settled in unoccupied territory) or through conquest (as in the case of those who took it in war), or by due process of law, bargain, or purchase, or by allotment."[3] He continues, "Therefore, inasmuch as in each case some of those things which by nature had been common property became the property of individuals, each one should retain possession of that which has fallen to his lot; and if anyone appropriates to himself anything beyond that, he will be violating the laws of human society."[4] Property, however acquired, is increased largely by wisdom, industry, and thrift and rightly belongs to its holder. Yet, says Cicero, citing Plato, we are not born to ourselves alone. Our country and our friends make claims upon us. Fellowship requires that we help one another. "In this direction we ought to follow Nature as our guide, to contribute to the general good by an interchange of acts of kindness, by giving and receiving, and thus by our skill, our industry, and our talents to cement human society more closely together, man to man."[5]

Assistance to others must be rationally grounded, he continues. "For many people often do favors impulsively for everybody without discrimination, prompted by a morbid sort of benevolence or by a sudden impulse of the heart, shifting as the wind. Such acts of generosity are not to be so highly esteemed as those which are performed with judgment, deliberation, and mature consideration."[6]

"The man in an administrative office," Cicero affirms, "must make it his first care that everyone shall have what belongs to him and that private citizens suffer no invasion of their property rights by act of the state."[7] "For . . . it is the peculiar function of the state and the city to guarantee to every man the free and undisturbed control of his own particular property."[8] Cicero speaks of destroyed harmony when property is taken away from one party and given to another or when officials intervene to cancel debt.

Although he speaks of the obligations of property holders, Cicero is clear that need does not create entitlement. Even so, he says, "let it [property] be made available for the use of as many as possible (if and only if they are worthy) and be at the service of generosity and beneficence rather than sensuality and excess."[9] "Acquire, use, enjoy, and dispose, but rationally" is his time-transcending motto. Cicero's concept of "deserving poor" will be adopted by St. Jerome and St. Augustine and other Fathers of the Church when they speak of obligation in charity. Charity to be efficacious cannot be mindless. Both Plato and Aristotle recognized that civic dissension often arose from inequality of wealth, but Aristotle made it a point to criticize proposals to equalize fortunes, particularly proposals justified in the name of preventing revolution.

Ancient theories of property cannot effortlessly serve as a guide to the formation of law affecting property rights today, especially intellectual property. In our age of undreamt technological innovation, innovation constantly in flux, even contemporary statutory law is hard pressed to resolve disputes over property rights. Yet antiquity provides a basis for discussion of modern social theory that often flies in the face of common sense.

The idea that private property is at the root of political and economic evil is the well-known cornerstone of theories advanced by Marx and Engels. In *The Communist Manifesto*, Marx and Engels asserted that the theory of the Communists may be summed up in a single sentence: Abolition of private property.[10] "Property," they maintain, "is not the realization of personality but its negation."[11] The declared aim of Marx is the nationalization of economic assets for the common good. In a Communist society, he tells us, everyone is to contribute according to his abilities and receive according to his needs. From this principle, the regulation of production is a *conditio sine qua non*.

John Stuart Mill, perhaps equally as influential as Marx, infused his brand of liberalism with the same socialist goal, stressing the overriding importance of the equitable distribution of productive wealth. Many of our contemporary intellectuals find in Mill the moral authority for legislation which curtails the right of ownership for the common good.[12]

Among the twentieth-century authors who treat property exclusively in moral terms, the most influential is undoubtedly John Rawls. In *A Theory of Justice* Rawls delineates what he takes to be the principles of a well-ordered society based on "fairness."[13] Rawls proposes to reform or abolish laws and institutions, no matter how efficient and well arranged, if they are "unjust." For Rawls, the essence of injustice is inequality. His ideal is perfect egalitarianism, a principle of equality that he applies not only to material goods but also to intelligence and inborn skills. The advantages afforded genetically ought not to bring the fortunate possessor any special benefits. Why? Because they are unearned.[14] From Rawls's moral perspective, the allocation of talents and abilities must be regarded as "arbitrary." Talents should be viewed as "a common asset," and their possessors should profit from them "only on terms that improve the situation of those who have lost out." If need be, efficiency must be sacrificed in order to attain perfect equality. Marx himself might have been shocked, for Rawls goes far beyond even the most radical of communist theorists in wishing to socialize natural talents by denying to the talented the benefits their talents bring them. Rawls goes further. He rejects "equality of opportunity" as inherently unfair since it means that the less gifted or less industrious will be left behind.

It is to be noted that entitlements to what one has earned or otherwise legally acquired have a completely different status in *A Theory of Justice* than do freedom of speech, freedom of religion, freedom of association, due process of law, and the right to vote and hold office. Property rights are excluded from protection. For Rawls, economically significant property rights are valued not as conducive to liberty but as indispensable features of an economic system which must be maintained for the benefit of all. Reliance on contract, salary agreements, the payment of interest and dividends is economically essential, but its only moral justification is the good of the whole, not an individual's entitlement to what he has earned or otherwise acquired. What the individual is entitled to is determined by the overall system. Individual property rights are the consequence, not the foundation, of a just economic system. Rawls stands in sharp contrast to John Locke, whose theory of property greatly influenced the framers of the U.S. Constitution. Locke speaks of the natural right to life, liberty, and property and argues that the most basic of these is property, for without property there exists neither life nor liberty.[15] Rawls, of course, is not the first in the history of political theory to take the view that property is communal. He acknowledges the influence of Rousseau and Hobbes, but his societal view of property is reminiscent of that of Pierre Joseph Proudhon. In his famous treatise, *What is Property*?, Proudhon answered his own question with the memorable declaration, "Property is theft."[16] Proudhon reasoned, as Rawls was to reason similarly more than a century later, "All capital, whether material or mental, being the result of collective labor, is in consequence, collective property."[17]

But is it realistic to speak of the distribution of talents and the fruit of sometimes extraordinary effort as a common asset? How far should distribution go? In *The Law of Peoples*, Rawls proposes the extension of his principles of justice to the Society of Peoples under the Law of Peoples. "The Law of Peoples," he writes, "is an extension of the liberal conception of justice for a domestic regime to a Society of Peoples."[18] It is not the intent of this brief presentation to offer a critique of Rawls but to suggest that a seemingly benevolent theory of justice, viewed in terms of its consequence, can lead us to utopian ideals far removed from reality. In advancing his theory of justice, Rawls ignores psychological, political, and economic realities as well as recorded history and the findings of anthropologists. Any theorist looking for a rationale to support antitrust legislation and other regulatory efforts to prevent extreme disparities thought to be the effect of so-called "unbridled private enterprise" will find justification in Rawls.[19]

Numerous arguments to the contrary are to be found in economic historians who show clearly that societies which provide firm guarantees of property rights are the very ones that experience economic development. For most economic historians the determinant of economic growth lies in the legal institutions which ensure to enterprising individuals the fruits of their labors. Property guarantees are thus of critical importance. European history suggests that the rise of the West to the position of global economic preeminence lies in the institution of private property.[20] But the West is not alone. Those countries that historically have provided the firmest guarantee of economic independence, especially property rights, are virtually without exception the richest.

Romantic appeals to "the common good," such as those of Mill and Rawls, may be fruitful under some conditions, but absent shared belief in a community, they are likely to be disingenuous. When one appeals to a common good separate from and superior to the private goods of individuals, the function of government (be it that of a legislative, executive, or judiciary body) becomes one of conflict management. Given the way legislation is framed in modern democracies, opposing parties are likely to press for state-awarded privileges, bargaining and negotiating for advantage. Under such conditions the state is not likely to represent a common will but rather becomes the object of adversarial wills. Thus positioned, the state serves not by defining goals which members of society ought collectively to pursue but by removing obstacles to goods privately defined. The "common good" becomes the result of negotiations between private political actors. Such a situation can only lead to social and economic chaos. A compliant or weak judiciary is apt to rule in the light of a supposed common good against an individual claimant, perhaps settling the dispute but undermining other fundamental rights.

Ancient notions grounded in a common concept of human nature remain the foundation of the common law tradition assumed in the English-speaking world, a tradition unchallenged until the advent of modernity. Those ancient texts, Mill notwithstanding, certainly influenced the framers in drafting the U.S. Constitution. Mill's liberalism is often advanced as a political philosophy proper to the foundation of liberty, but those parties who have usurped the name "liberal" in fact advocate control—control over property, trade, wages, hours of work, meat, drink, and amusements, and above all, education.

Moral confusion is not limited to academic circles, always the scene of profound conflict, but is found in the religious sector where churchmen have the power to affect the behavior of many. Western religion for the most part may have succumbed to the liberal Zeitgeist, yet there is a body of relevant social teaching in the Western intellectual tradition that has maintained its roots in classical antiquity and in the Gospels. In the light of that tradition, it can be argued that communication technologies, like other artifacts, rightfully belong to those who create them. They are not a natural resource, communally owned, as fresh water streams or forest preserves may be, but the product of design and industry on the part of an individual or group. That does not mean they lack implications for a community. In that respect they are like mineral wealth or oil and gas fields. But even the worth of natural resources depends on human skill for extraction and marketing, and their value depends on those skills. If the community benefits, it is the result of someone's initiative who deserves his due. The issue before us may be: What claim does a community have on the individual? Under socialist and communist regimes, the maxim: "from each according to his ability, to each according to his needs," has proved to be economically debilitating, if not disastrous. Socialism by its very nature destroys initiative insofar as it expropriates the fruit of individual effort, and leads to suppressive bureaucratic control. No one who subscribes to the principles enunciated in the Gospels can at the same time be a socialist without fear of self-contradiction. Indeed, papal documents have condemned socialism from its very birth. The socialist impulse, thinly disguised as "liberalism," is given to invoking moral principles borrowed from outlooks it does not share. Its remote antecedents are found in the Enlightenment philosophies, Anglo-French and German, of the eighteenth and early nineteenth centuries.[21] But if with Locke, one denies that there are natural structures which govern inquiry, that is, denies with Locke that there is such a thing as human nature, and with Hume denies that causality exists apart from a mind relating before and after, the inevitable consequence is the denial of an empirically determinable natural moral order to which we are accountable. Given the empiricism of Locke and Hume, appeals to solidarity can not be grounded in an anthropology which recognizes a common human nature or the brotherhood of mankind, the ground of natural obligation.

The U.S. Constitution took for granted that the right to private property is a condition of liberty. Property rights, it was recognized, adhere not only to the individual but are also affirmed of the individual in his collective arrangements. If a man is entitled to the fruit of his labor, a corporation is entitled to the fruit of its investment. Yet one may ask, are there no limits? Can there not be unfair competition? Certainly wealth entails responsibility, as Rabbinic literature, Church Fathers, and Papal social encyclicals in common recognize, insofar as they proclaim that what we have we do not own but hold as God's trustee. It can be argued that all theories of property implicitly or explicitly entail a conception of the common good.

Apart from the judgment of the Court in *Eldred* v. *Ashcroft*, one is brought to the conclusion that Article 1, Section 8 of the U.S. Constitution had it right when it declared its purpose to be "to promote the progress of science and the useful arts, by securing for limited times to authors and inventors the exclusive rights to their respective writings and discoveries." The Constitution provides a prudential balance between the protection of property rights and social claims. To expand at will the "limited time" clause is to invite a Pandora's Box of litigation, with opposing parties jostling for legislative, regulative, or juridical preference. The ensuing conflict is likely to result in the arbitrary denial of one or the other—property rights or reasonable communal benefit.

NOTES

1. Article 1, Section 8 of the Constitution reads, "to promote the progress of science and the useful arts, by securing for limited times to authors and inventors the exclusive rights to their respective writings and discoveries."
2. Cf. Eldred v. Ashcroft, 537 U.S. 186, reh'g denied, —U.S.—, 123 S. Ct. 1505 (March 10, 2003).
3. Marcus Tullius Cicero, *On Duties*, trans. Walter Miller (Cambridge, Mass.: Harvard University Press, 1997), I, 21.
4. Cicero, *On Duties*, I, 21.
5. Cicero, *On Duties*, I, 22.
6. Cicero, *On Duties*, I, 49.
7. Cicero, *On Duties*, I, 49.
8. Cicero, *On Duties*, II, 78.
9. Cicero, *On Duties*, I, 92.
10. Karl Marx and Friedrich Engels, *The Communist Manifesto* (New York: International Publishers, 1935), 42–43.
11. As quoted by Richard Pipes in *Property and Freedom* (New York: Alfred A. Knopf, 1999), 52. The disastrous effect of the Bolshevik attempt to implement the economic theory of Marx and Engels is described by Pipes in chap. 5, "Property in the Twentieth Century," 209ff. In his survey of property rights in the twentieth century, Richard Pipes concludes, "the winds have not been favorable to the rights of ownership and all that accompanies them. . . . Even in democratic societies the concept of property has undergone substantial revision, transforming it from absolute dominion into something akin to conditional possession. . . . As a result, the rights of individuals to their assets have been and continue to be systematically violated" (p. 279).
12. John Stuart Mill, *Principles of Political Economy* (Oxford, England: Oxford University Press, 1994), cf. chaps. I, II.
13. John Rawls, *A Theory of Justice* (Cambridge, Mass.: Harvard University Press, 1971).

14. Rawls, *Theory of Justice*, 101–102.

15. John Locke, *The Second Treatise of Government*, ed. Thomas P. Peardon (New York: Macmillan, 1952). The *Second Treatise* was initially published in 1690.

16. Pierre Joseph Proudhon, *Qu'est-ce que la Propriété*? trans. Benjamin B. R. Tucker as *What Is Property?* (New York: H. Fertig, 1966).

17. Proudhon, *la Propriété*, 147.

18. John Rawls, *The Law of Peoples: With the Idea of Public Reason Revisited* (Cambridge, Mass.: Harvard University Press, 1999), 9.

19. A contemporary attempt to defend what is essentially a utilitarian theory of property is found in Stephen Munzer's *A Theory of Property* (Cambridge, Mass.: Cambridge University Press, 1990). Unlike Rawls's abstract moral justification of the welfare state, Munzer takes account of the limitations imposed by the practical, "weaving together," in his own words, "[of] the theoretical and the practical." Concluding an extended criticism of Rawls he writes, "A theory of property should not be an intellectual plaything but an instrument for reforming institutions of property" (p. 469).

20. Cf. Douglas North and R. P. Thomas, *The Rise of the Western World* (Cambridge, Mass.: Cambridge University Press, 1973). Also Douglas North, *Structure and Change in Economic History* (New York: Norton, 1981); Tom Bethell, *The Noblest Triumph* (New York: St. Martin's Press, 1998).

21. For an account of the emergence of modern socialism in the latter part of the eighteenth century and the beginning of the nineteenth, see John H. Hallowell, *Main Currents in Modern Political Thought* (New York: Henry Holt and Co., 1950), 368–397. The term "socialism" he finds was first used about 1830 to describe the teachings of Robert Owen in Great Britain and Charles Fourier and Henri de Saint Simon in France.

Part Two

THE ROLE OF RELIGION IN SOCIETY

Chapter Six

The Ontology of the Artifact

The close relationship between metaphysics and artistic production has been noted since antiquity. Umberto Eco in his *Art and Beauty in the Middle Ages* provides from an historical point of view a succinct statement of the dependency.[1] "Medieval aesthetics began with a heritage received more or less uncritically from the Classical age—a heritage infused, all the same, by a spirit altogether new. Gradually there developed a metaphysics and epistemology of the beautiful and eventually an idea of beauty as an organic value. This was the period of its greatest maturity."[2] When, in the aftermath of the Enlightenment, Aristotelian metaphysics began to lose its following, the rationale of art and poetry became less and less systematic. The foundation was laid for the Mannerist doctrine of genius and imagination. When the artifact conceived as essentially a matter of order, a rendering of the *splendor formae* in the language of Aquinas, was lost, gave way, so too was lost the notion that artistic production has something to do with beauty. This loss is reflected in the very architecture of museums that came to be or were altered in the last half of the twentieth century.

The late nineteenth and early twentieth century witnessed the creation of the great museums of art that today span the United States from New England to the west coast. Private collections amassed by industrial leaders were offered for public appreciation in structures deemed appropriate for their viewing. Kress, Carnegie, Mellon, Frick and Clark are names associated with some of the greatest collections of European masters. The favored architecture of the newly endowed museums tended to be neoclassical Greek, with a few museums opting for the Italian Renaissance style. Museum-goers were no doubt unconsciously led to identify the art museum with expansive stairs leading to massive portals fronted by Doric or other Greek-inspired columns that blended into the building as a whole. A stranger arriving in the city would instinctively identify such a structure as an art museum. The interior matched the promise of the building's façade, expansive corridors, elegant staircases, alabaster fountains, Renaissance courtyards, a delight to the eye promoting a feeling of grandeur. Upon entering the usually paneled, picture galleries, one could view European masters from the early Italian Renaissance to the French Impressionists. Sculpture gardens and specialized collections of primitive American painting or oriental art might be found off one of the many corridors. Collections were usually arranged chronologically unless the donor had mandated that his collection be displayed intact. Viewers were exposed to Botticelli, Raphael, Memling, Van Eyck, Rembrandt, El Greco, Van Gogh, Ingres, David, Corot, Manet, Renoir, and countless others from the thirteenth to the twentieth century.

Then something happened. As collections expanded, new spaces for viewing had to be added, but the art world of the late twentieth century was not that of the late nineteenth. Almost without exception the architecture of the new space deviated substantially from and often clashed with that of the original gallery. Rarely did the expansion reflect the beauty and grace of the original structure. The curve gave way to the straight line, adornment to the slab, and glass replaced marble and stone. One may say that the newly acquired paintings deserved no better. Bizarre architecture seemed suited to bizarre content. Ideological and fanciful organization replaced the chronological. New "isms" took hold: Fauvism substituted arbitrary colors for those of nature on the assumption that there is no reason esthetically for the sky to be blue or the grass to be green. Cubism flattened images and abolished depth. Kandinsky went even further, abolishing all traces of subject matter. Surrealism and Futurism became favorites of the new intelligentsia. Museums often took upon themselves a pedagogical role and became classrooms in defense of the irrational. Curators apparently did not notice that patrons moved quickly through the new galleries, failing to linger as they might before the European masters. The movement to the irrational was no doubt encouraged, if not inspired by, the taste of Joseph Hirshhorn and Peggy and Solomon Guggenheim. Their fortunes enabled them to build independent museums to house their own collections, but their influence extended far beyond. The sea change in the art world tended to reflect the ideological shift of the patrons. The Wall Street fortunes that supported the new were those of financiers and stock manipulators, a different breed from the industrialists of the previous century. The influence of the academy could be detected in the narrative that often accompanied the exposition of the new. Viewers who could spontaneously appreciate a Raphael, a Rembrandt, or a Renoir had to be coached into an appreciation of a Duchamp, a Pollock, or a de Kooning. In the absence of beauty the viewer had to be told what the artist was trying to do, that the dripping of pigments in swirling rhythms or the allowing of paint to run untended down the surface of a canvas, did indeed have some meaning. The explanation? Perhaps the artist wished to "stress the risk and unpredictability of life itself."

Clearly, the academic philosophies of the Enlightenment, Anglo-French and German, had penetrated the art world. A Christian past had given way to an atheistic, materialistic modernism. To use the words of George Santayana, the shell of Christendom was broken. With its loss went a respect for classical antiquity and a respect for natural forms theretofore regarded as the handiwork of God. No longer was there a perceived purpose in nature or a moral order to be observed. The artist was emancipated from all restraint, free to express himself as he saw fit. Spontaneity and indecision were the order of the day. Incomprehensible daubs replaced lovely landscapes, still lifes, and portraits. In their drive to create a new world of forms unrelated to the physical world in which we live, some commercially successful artists seem to take a diabolical pleasure in baffling the public.

Every moviegoer of the past half-century will recognize the motto of a major motion picture studio, "Ars gratia artis." The meaning and implications of that dictum may be debated, but it points to the fact that theories of art matter. Taking his lead from Albertus Magnus, St. Thomas, in discussing the nature of aesthetic experience, identifies three characteristics of the beautiful: integrity, harmony, and clarity or splendor of form (*splendor intellectus*). Just as truth satisfies the intellect and good satisfies the will, beauty satisfies both cognitive and appetitive faculties, that is, it satisfies both intellect and will. Aquinas further describes beauty as resplendence of the substantial form in an object whose parts are well proportioned. From a Thomistic point of view "resplendence" is an objective quality, an ontological quality, one that exists independently of the viewer. The nobility of the form instantiated reflects the nobility of the form as conceived and may tell us something at a deeper level about the integrity of the artist himself. What may seem inspired is often the product of days of thought. Anyone who has had the opportunity to discuss the work of a painter or sculptor with the artist himself will recognize how much of the artist is transferred to the art work itself. The intellectual and spiritual formation of the artist guides his hand even where intractable matter has not yielded to the form as conceived in the mind of the artist.

It is clear that much of the contemporary art world has rejected the notion that beauty is or should be the aim of artistic production. Blatant ideology and commercial success have robbed much contemporary art of integrity as well as splendor. Ideology can subvert artistic production when it is made to serve ends that are not its own, e.g., the proletarian art of the Roosevelt and Stalinist periods. This is not to say that art necessarily loses its integrity when it assumes a pedagogical function. The didactic art of the early decades of the twentieth century insofar as it was designed to serve a socialist agenda may leave us unmoved because of its dehumanizing message. Art deco of the same period, like commercial art everywhere, may fail for other reasons. Art in the service of the temple is a different matter. The architecture, statuary, stained glass, and painting of a medieval cathedral succeeded in creating an ambience that led the viewer to a transcendent and ennobling order. Paintings and sculpture may be weak forms of communication compared with the printed word, but when presented and understood within the context of the theology that informed their creation, they can be overwhelming in their effect. In the service of the temple, the artist's vision is received by a like mind. His meditation understood. The viewer is drawn not just to the sensory qualities of the object but to the immanent qualities of the whole. Nobility of purpose does not, of course, redeem a badly executed work.

Of twentieth-century artists whose work illustrates the relationship of art to faith, one may be drawn to the stained glass of Chagall, to the paintings of Roualt, or to the massive sculptures of Ivan Meštrovi_. Less well known but equally powerful artists are the sculptors, Alex Giampietro and Hamilton Reed Armstrong. The piety of Meštrovi_ is exemplified by his magnificent St. Jerome, currently found in front of the Croatian Embassy on Massachusetts Avenue in Washington, D.C. Like Jerome, Meštrovi_ has his roots in the Dalmatian coast and his faith in the very scriptures that Jerome rendered into Latin.

Giampietro's faith is reflected in a superbly executed "Christ Crucified" and the sculptor's intellectual bent in a museum quality bust of Jacques Maritain whose philosophy of art he espoused. Without diminishing the respect due to Meštrovi_ and Giampietro, I think it fair to say that Reed Hamilton Armstrong is the foremost as well as most prolific of contemporary religious sculptors. His work is infused by a profoundly Catholic mind even when he addresses non-religious subjects. Our Lady could not have a more devoted servant, as his many depictions of her attest. Multiple folio volumes would be required to chronicle Armstrong's output. There are life-sized depictions of Michael the Archangel, Moses, the Prodigal Son, John the Baptist, Thomas Aquinas, and Ibn Gabirol. There are portrait busts of Pius X, John Paul II, Edith Stein, Mother Teresa of Calcutta, King Juan Carlos of Spain, and a magnificent bronze rendering of Holbein's Thomas Moore. From the cast aluminum doors of the parish church in Fuengirola on the Costa del Sol, Spain, to the tabernacle doors of the Oakcrest School in McLean, Virginia, Armstrong's work is suffused with a sense of a sacred calling. His spirituality is manifested in what may be his greatest works, his retable depiction of the "Risen Christ" and his "The Trinity" and "*Christus Lux Mundi.*" Armstrong's work is to be found on both sides of the Atlantic in private collections, churches, and public spaces. Ibn Gabirol stands in a public Square in Málaga and Moses and Aquinas in a courtyard at the Ave Maria School of Law. A tribute to grandparents graces the Garden of Joachim and Anna in Torremolinos, Spain. A recent bronze of the medieval Islamic scholar, Ibn Albeitar, brought tears to the eyes of its donor when first exhibited. Numerous commissions await fulfillment.

Religious subjects themselves do not make a work of art religious. From a Christian perspective, we live in a created universe where everything that exists is religious because it imitates God in its operations as well as its being. In a finite and analogical way, the artist participates in the divine creative act. In a Christian universe the artist is called to praise God by cooperating with His creative power, by increasing, to the extent that he can do so, the sum total of being and beauty in the world. To make things and to make them beautiful are one and the same thing. This calling is exemplified at the highest level when the work is destined for the temple. Thus understood, creative art is not limited to imitation but encompasses the creation of new forms. Yet what is created cannot help but reflect the personal imprint of the artist, the vision and harmony, or lack thereof, found within the depths of his soul.

It seems evident that in the contemporary art world, be it architecture, painting or sculpture, little is taken from nature, or referred even implicitly to an order in nature. Absent the recognition of an ordered universe, freedom seems to be exercised in the name of freedom itself.

Although Armstrong's Ibn Gabirol graces a public square in Málaga, it is neither Armstrong nor Ibn Gabirol that is likely to be identified with that city. Within the art world, Málaga is best known as the birthplace of Picasso. Like Armstrong, Picasso was baptized in the Catholic faith, and, like Armstrong, his early training made him an able draftsman. Picasso's "Altar Boy" is a pleasing illustration of both his faith and skill, but at the age of nineteen, Picasso left home for the bohemian life of Paris. The experience was formative in more ways than one. The personal and artistic freedom he found there led both to his loss of faith and to a rejection of the artistic tradition of the academy. Modern anarchism had claimed another adherent, leading his artist father, Don José Ruiz y Blasco, to decry "a shameful waste of talent." Picasso's art was to become agonized and shrill. His canvasses transformed everyday subjects into bizarre images in which he took almost perverse liberties with human anatomy. Enlisted in the cause of International Communism, many of his works became grotesque symbols of brutality and darkness. From a commercial point of view, Picasso has to be considered the most successful artist of the twentieth century. Museum directors, art dealers, and wealthy connoisseurs vied for his work. His paintings sold for the largest sums ever paid to a living artist. That success may also attest to a radical change in the intellectual, one could say, spiritual, climate of the century. One need not compare a Meštrovi_ to a Picasso to illustrate that change. It is exemplified in the life work of Picasso himself. One can delight in his early work while eschewing the latter. The correlation between loss of faith and loss of perspective is a subject not often addressed by art historians.

I conclude with an insightful passage written more than a hundred years ago by Leo N. Tolstoy: "Christian art . . . should be catholic in the original meaning of the word, i.e., universal, and therefore it should unite all men. And only two kinds of feeling do unite all men: first, feelings flowing from the perception of our sonship to God and the brotherhood of man; and, next, the simple feelings of common life, accessible to everyone without exception—such as the feeling of merriment, of pity, of cheerfulness, of tranquility, etc. Only these two kinds of feelings can supply material for art good in its subject matter."[3]

NOTES

1. Umberto Eco, *Art and Beauty in the Middle Ages* (originally, *Sviluppo dell'estetica medievale* in *Momenti e problemi di storia dell'estetica*), vol. 1, 1959, trans. Hugh Bredin (New Haven, Conn.: Yale University Press, 1986).
2. Eco, *Art and Beauty*, 2–3.
3. Leo N. Tolstoy, *What Is Art?* trans. Almyer Maude (Library of Liberal Arts, 1899).

Chapter Seven

The Failure of Positivism and the Enduring Legacy of Comte

When Desiré Mercier (1851–1926) began his study of theology at the University of Louvain in preparation for ordination to the priesthood, the reigning philosophy of the day was that of Auguste Comte. Mercier was to become Director of the Institut Superieure de Philosophy of Louvain and eventually Cardinal Archbishop of Malines. Even in his student years, Mercier was aware that the philosophy of Comte directly challenged his religious vocation. Comte was convinced that men must forego theological and metaphysical speculation to concentrate on observation of facts if they are to arrive at intellectual maturity. Although Comte belonged to the first half of the nineteenth century, his philosophy was aggressively promulgated in the latter half by his disciples Taine and Durkheim. This is not the place to recount Mercier's professional struggle with the epistemological issues that led Come to metaphysical agnosticism and Mercier to the philosophical realism of Aristotle and Aquinas.

The aim of this chapter is to suggest that Comte's positivism, grounded as it was in the British empiricism of the day, not only ruled out metaphysics but ruled out theoretical physics as well, both for the same reason, Comte's denial of the efficacy of causal reasoning. According to Comte's positive philosophy, physics errs as does metaphysics when it postulates abstract entities as explanatory causes. Comte, of course, wrote years before theoretical physics came into its own with atomic and subatomic explanations for natural phenomena. To Etienne Gilson's remark that metaphysics has a way of burying its undertakers, we may add that the success of nineteenth- and twentieth-century physics has laid to rest positivism as a philosophy of science.

It needs to be said, however, that while events of the past century have undermined the empiricists' foundation of positivism, the outlook is apt to survive any and all critiques for reasons that have little to do with the philosophy of science. Comte, generally accorded the title "Father of Positivism," is also regarded as one of the progenitors of sociology. Influenced by Locke and Hume and for a time materially supported by Mill, Comte recognized the social implications of the empiricism emanating from the British Isles, implications which led directly to a secular humanism which he codified in his "religion of humanity." Although Comte's interests led him away from the philosophy of science per se and into the field of sociology, the term he coined came to be used in the wider sense of a philosophy of knowledge which limited knowledge to sensory experience.

It is positivism in the wider sense and not Comte's social philosophy which is the subject of this enquiry, although the two are intertwined. The thesis of this essay is that Comte's social philosophy rests on a philosophy of science long outmoded, but his influence, direct or indirect, remains formidable in the social sciences. In many respects Comte was a product of his age, unifying an outlook which had already gained acceptance among the intelligentsia. Ancient truths about nature, human nature, and cognitive ability had already been successfully challenged by eighteenth-century philosophers on both sides of the channel, ostensibly with the support of the newly ascendant mathematical sciences of nature.

Reflections on the nature and capacity of human knowledge did not await the advent of eighteenth-century mathematical physics. Plato's discussion of science and Greek claims to knowledge will forever remain a starting point for the philosophy of science. It was Plato who bequeathed to Western philosophy the insight that all science is of the universal. Aristotle concurred, but he found the universal not in some unseen realm of archetypes but in the nature common to members of the species. Aristotle taught that by a process of abstraction we come to know the essence, nature, or quiddity of a thing, prescinding from its accidental features, which it may or may not have while remaining the thing that it is. Such is the object of science, the nature of an entity, the structure of a process, their properties and potentialities. Yet to have scientific knowledge is not simply to know what is, not simply to have uncovered a law of nature. For Aristotle, to have scientific knowledge is to know the entity, process, or property in the light of its cause or causes. Presupposed by Aristotle are two principles: the principle of substance and the principle of causality, both principles rejected by the British empiricists.

Positivism, in whatever specific form it takes, in effect denies at once the intelligibility of nature and the power of intellect to grasp "the more" that is given in the sense report. A contemporary Aristotelian, by contrast, will affirm that there is more in the sense report than the senses themselves are formally able to appreciate. Locke, in denying the reality of substance, reduces what we call substance to a constellation of events or sense reports.

According to Locke, we use terms which imply substances, but this usage is merely a shorthand way of pointing to something without repeating at length all the properties we associate with that something or constellation.

Hume's account of causality similarly limits knowledge to a simple sense report. We experience succession, Hume tells us, not causality. "Cause" is the name we give to the antecedent, contiguous in place, continuous in time, and habitually associated with the consequent which we designate "effect." If there are no natures or substances independent of the mind's creating them, if there is no causality, the enterprise called metaphysics collapses. For after all, metaphysics is based on the assumption that the realm of being is greater or wider in designation than the being reported by the senses. If the material order reported by the senses is all there is, then the most general science of reality is natural philosophy or the philosophy of nature. If there is an immaterial order of being as well as the material world of sense, then the most general science is the philosophy of being, also known as metaphysics or ontology. One can conclude to or reach the immaterial order only by a process of reasoning. Such reasoning has led mankind through the ages to affirm the existence of God, to posit an immaterial component of human knowing and a spiritual or immaterial soul.

It is not the purpose of this essay to argue for the existence of a transcendent realm but to suggest that same sort of reasoning that leads one to affirm the existence of God also leads one to affirm the existence of the submicroscopic. As Comte himself recognized, causal reasoning is common to both natural theology and theoretical physics. The efficacy of causal reasoning is dramatically seen in those sciences where the postulated entities of one generation become the encountered of another. It can be shown that limiting knowledge to the sense report has implications not only for the natural sciences but for law, the social sciences, and theology as well. On a strict positivist account, science is in effect reduced to description and prediction, the social sciences are denied their object, "human nature," and of course natural theology is denied its object since there is no way to reason to the existence of God.

The questions which Mercier early on addressed are these: Do the natural sciences actually limit themselves to or conform to the positivist equation of knowledge with the empirically given? Is there not more to physics, chemistry, biology, and astronomy than mere description and prediction? We attempt to show that there is. But first a remark on the success of positivism as a theory of knowledge. Perhaps viewed historically it would be better to call it a program.

Auguste Comte was not a socially disinterested philosopher of knowledge. Positivism is a form of materialism, and many philosophers of the eighteenth and nineteenth centuries were perfectly willing to shed the notions of "God," an "ordered nature," and an "immaterial realm" for social and political reasons. If man is not accountable to a nature created and ordered by a benevolent God, many strictures are removed, institutions even rendered obsolete. It is not that in times past philosophy taught all that ecclesial authorities proclaimed about the source and end of human life, but as long as philosophy claimed an ability to reason to a first efficient cause and an ultimate final cause, it served as a prolegomena, if not a prop, for theology and religion. Comte himself wished to replace an inherited Christianity with his own "religion of humanity." H. G. Wells is reputed to have said what Comte wanted was Catholicism without Christianity.

In the rush to embrace an iconoclastic epistemology, many of Comte's disciples failed to pay much attention to actual practice in the sciences. Hume notwithstanding, reasoning on a causal basis from the observed to the unobserved was and is common practice in the natural sciences. The existence of bacteria was inferred long before the microscope displayed their reality. In physics and chemistry molecular structures were inferred long before electron microscopes and particle accelerators graphically confirmed their reality. It is not misleading to say that in physics, causal explanation is taken for granted. The encountered is routinely explained by that which is not encountered. No one who looks at the course of nineteenth- and twentieth-century theoretical physics can affirm that science is simply description and prediction. Molecular biology is replete with examples of once-inferred structures' falling within the range of the observable with the passage of time. Clearly there is more to causality than Hume would allow. To search for an explanation is to look for a cause. While Comte did not fully embrace the skepticism of Hume, he did hold that scientific theories are merely the coordination of observed facts. The sciences, he tells us, subsume phenomena as observed facts which are descriptive, not explanatory. It is the status of theories and conceptual schema which is the central issue between realism and positivism in the philosophy of science. Much of what we know in contemporary theoretical physics is known by inference. Molecules, atoms, electrons, protons, neutrons, mesons, and their activity are inferred. In talking about them we form conceptual schema which the positivist, heir to centuries-old nominalism, treats as convenient ways of handling complex data. On the positivist's account, the conceptual scheme of "atom" is a mere convenience. The data are real enough; they are given in measurements of one sort or another, but to posit an inexperienced source is to make an unwarranted intellectual leap. To interpret that data as flowing from a structure independent of the mind is to go beyond what is given in experience. Contrary to this scenario offered by the contemporary heirs of Auguste Comte, Henri Poincaré, and Ernest Mach such as Hilary Putnam and Larry Laudan, it can be argued that Aristotle's philosophy of knowledge provides us with the basis for a realistic interpretation of our scientific knowledge of nature.

At the root of the positivist's account of science is the acceptance of Hume's notion of causality. Science, on Hume's principles, is reduced to description and prediction. But contemporary philosophy of science has a difficult time holding on to a Humean conception of causality. No physicist is content with merely describing sequence. The inquisitive mind looks for explanations. Structures are inferred. The difference in kind among natural structures is said to account for difference in phenomena. In attempts at explanation, structures are usually given visual representation; data are usually expressed in equations and linked to an imagined structure. While much of what we know about atomic phenomena can be expressed mathematically, such knowledge lacks explanatory power unless it is linked to a mechanism thought to be responsible for that which is measured.[1] The inferred mechanism is presented diagrammatically, schematically, or pictorially by means of a model. Modeling requires images. Commonly recognized are two types of models, iconic and sentential. A picture, or a diagram, is an iconic model; an equation, like other statements, is a sentential representation of something judged to be the case. Not everything we know can be expressed sententiously. That we also think by means of pictures and diagrams is something Aristotle recognized when he described thinking as consisting of both imagination and judgment.

For the purpose of illustration permit me to relate an episode in the history of science which I take to be a rich source of relevant material. In late December 1938, Lise Meitner and her nephew Otto Frisch, one a theoretical chemist, the other a physicist, walked in the woods near Göteborg, Sweden. The problem before them was one created by the German physicists Otto Hahn and Fritz Strassmann, namely, the seeming formation of barium from uranium. That the nucleus of the uranium atom could be split was at that time unthinkable. Attempting to understand the reports of Hahn and Strassman, Meitner and her nephew allowed their imagination full play. In the conversation which took place between them, Meitner and Frisch recalled that Bøhr had once suggested that the nucleus of an atom resembled a liquid drop. If a drop could divide itself into smaller drops by elongating until a constricted neck formed in the middle and then could tear itself apart into two drops, perhaps something like this could happen to the uranium nucleus. Strong forces would resist, just as surface tension resists such a break-up in a drop of water. But nuclei are electrically charged, and this might diminish the effect of the surface tension. Lise Meitner began to do some calculations on the back of a letter and on some scraps of paper. Frisch followed her calculations. Yes, the charge of a uranium nucleus might be a "wobbly uncertain drop, ready to divide itself at the slightest provocation, such as the impact of a neutron." When the two drops parted they would fly apart with tremendous energy, an energy calculated by Meitner to be approximately 200 million electron volts.

Lise Meitner remembered at this point how to compute the masses of nuclei from the so called "packing fraction." If the uranium nucleus divided, the two particles formed would be lighter than the original nucleus by about one-fifth of the mass of the proton. With some quick arithmetic, she multiplied the lost one-fifth of mass by the speed of light squared. It came out almost exactly at 200 million electron-volts. The lost one-fifth would supply exactly the 200 million election-volts of energy with which the drop would tear apart. The importance of their insight was not lost on them. "So here was the source of all that energy," said Frisch. It is reported that the two looked at each other with incredulity and then again with triumph.

In a paper reporting their discovery for the British journal *Nature*, they described the division of the nucleus as "fission." The source of the term itself is interesting. As they were writing the paper, Frisch had asked a young biologist what he and his confreres called the splitting of a cell. "Fission," he replied, and Frisch had the word he needed. Ruth Moore, from whom this account is taken, writes, "the process was simply, accurately and perceptively named for all time."[2] Next came the task of testing their theory by experimentation.

The first point I wish to make is that Meitner and Frisch were clearly searching for an explanation of something that begged to be understood. They were looking for the mechanism responsible for the phenomena reported by their German colleagues. Although the data they were attempting to explain seemed implausible, they nevertheless accepted that data on the authority of Hahn and Strassman. Meitner and Frisch, as well as the scientific world on both sides of the Atlantic, believed the Hahn-Strassman report to be accurate. Need I note that the acceptance of the work of others is normal procedure in the sciences? Most theoretical physics is based on the authoritative reports of colleagues.

In their attempt to understand, there is no doubt that Meitner and Frisch were looking for a cause. Their search led them to an imagined source. Note also the role of analogy or metaphor. The source of the energy released was imagined to be something like a drop of water, elongating and dividing. The nucleus was conceived in visual terms as a fluid. Clearly the mind was proceeding by analogy, from something better known to something less known. The familiar was serving as a model for the unfamiliar. The mechanism responsible for the phenomena was understood by means of an iconic model. The mind was not satisfied by a mere mathematical description of the phenomena reported. Not surprisingly the value of the Meitner/Frisch explanation was recognized universally. But was the explanation correct? If it were, it could not simply be checked by repeating the experiment which gave rise to it in the first place, although laboratories in Europe and North America eagerly repeated the experiment. For Aristotle, explanations are different from mere reports. For a contemporary mind schooled as an Aristotelian, an explanation in order to satisfy has to link a causal mechanism to the phenomena observed, phenomena which are initially reported as raw data, very often in equation form. Meitner, Frisch, Bøhr, Fermi, and the many others who quickly saw the implications of the explanation began to integrate their new knowledge with other things they accepted. The plausible explanation became the accepted one as all that was known about the nature of uranium and its various isotopes cohered. Every attempt at interpretation was tested with every possible real or imagined experiment. The Meitner/Frisch explanation was dependent upon previous success in the construction of a model for the uranium atom. That model was initially constructed in an attempt to explain the cause of certain phenomena associated with the sensorially distinguishable and describable element uranium. Now the model was employed to explain something never intended, namely the break up of the atom into barium and krypton.

There are several points that may be emphasized: 1) the implicit philosophical realism evident in the thought of Meitner and Frisch. 2) The fact that their model actually provided a plausible mechanism for the phenomena observed. By means of the model, properties were associated with their structural cause. The Meitner/Frisch mode of procedure followed what I take to be a realist account of scientific method. In attempting to understand the properties or activities encountered, the mind renders them intelligible by means of an imagined source. To provide a reasonable source is the function of the model. It is not simply a question of before and after since the source is never directly experienced. There is a linking of behavior to that which is thought to behave by means of a plausible mechanism that can only be thought by means of a model. I stress, it is not simply a question of sequence, contiguity in place, continuity in time, and a habit of associating those events designated cause and effect; rather the mind is led to affirmation because the inferred cause is thought to be responsible for the phenomena in question. The cause must be presented to the mind by means of an image, not just any image but one rendering a plausible mechanism. The mind immediately rules out a multiplicity of images in favor of likely candidates. As mere logical possibility gives ground to material or real possibility, images are quickly discarded. The closer one comes to a true explanation, the fewer the images that can be entertained. Finally only one imaged source is regarded as plausible, and it is given the status of genuine cause. The imagined structure can be said to be, in Aristotelian language, "instantiated." I am using "structure" here not as a synonym for substantial form in the Aristotelian sense but as a quality consequent upon extension, certainly reflective of form, but not identical with form itself or with essence.

The knowledge we have of the structures of the submicroscopic is by inference, yet the mental mechanisms by which we attain and hold that knowledge is not much different from the everyday or common-sense knowledge we have of the world of sense experience.

There is one process of coming to know, but as Aristotle understood it, the awareness of commonality and the mental expression of that commonality seem to be distinguishable acts. Controlled knowing of the sort that takes place in the sciences is analogous to what may be taken as true of ordinary or common-sense awareness. I have in mind the deliberate focusing on commonality which takes place in controlled or scientific induction and the deliberate creation of images in order to understand that commonality and difference. It can be argued that, following Aristotle, controlled induction and model formation are but systematic attempts to do what the mind does naturally at a prior stage in coming to know. Through the process of induction the soul is "led to" or "brought to" the universal as present in the particular. When one of a number of logically indiscriminate particulars becomes the focus of interest, the earliest universal is present in the soul. In the flux of the particulars the soul is gradually able to perceive the first constant and unchanging universal. The plurality of individuals is required to focus the mind's vision gradually on that universal which is present in all individuals but is finally perceived as such by the mind in one particular instance. This is the intuition (*nous*) that apprehends the commonality of the nature under consideration and is the originative source of scientific knowledge.

Contemporary debates bring to mind ancient disputes, particularly those relating to Aristotle's *De Anima,* III, 5. The terminology is sometimes new, but the age-old problem of universals haunts present discussion. This problem is sometimes framed in its contemporary setting as the problem of the relation of language to reality. W. Quine, for example, has argued that the referent of a term is not determinately fixed, and consequently reference is inscrutable in the sense that we can have no sure knowledge of what our speech is referring to.[3] Hilary Putnam holds that even an ideal theory, that is, one which is compatible with all possible observations and satisfies all theoretical and operational requirements, can employ different models. Since multiple models can satisfy all epistemic conditions, there is no non-arbitrary way of selecting one of them as the unique model representative of the posited structure. If there are alternative possible models of a theory, how can we know which one approximates reality? Putnam maintains that reference cannot be fixed by the mind's affirming a reality represented by the intentional model since that would require the unintelligible notion of our minds having access to reality that is unmediated by the theory whose reference is in question. Putnam also rejects the view that reference is determined by a causal relation between a structure independent of the mind and the language user since such a view would presuppose realism.[4]

In another text, Putnam seems to be saying that the only reality to which we have access is "reality as it appears to us."[5] Putnam is, of course, not alone in maintaining such a position. Idealists such as Nicholas Rescher maintain almost the same thing. The realist will counter that Putnam's position is flawed by the fallacy of equivocation. In one sense, to say that some item is mind-independent is to say that the item exists independently of the existence of any human mind. In another sense, to say that some item is mind-dependent is to say that it cannot be apprehended by the human mind in a way that is unmediated by some schema. The fact that some item is not mind-independent in the latter sense does not entail that it is not mind-independent in the former sense, and it is the former sense that is at issue in the realist conception of truth.

Niels Bøhr recognized that theoretical concepts that are devoid of any perceptual content are problematic. He called them "idealizations," but I think that in the mathematical sense there is no such thing as a straight line or a triangle in sensorially experienced reality. If theoretical concepts are to have any genuine explanatory force, they cannot lose all connection with ordinary sense perception. Once science goes beyond the critical level where its concepts lose all connection with ordinary perceptual experience, it can no longer be regarded as providing a description of an actual mechanism. It should be noted that, in line with Bøhr's description of scientific practice, Aristotelian realism does not require that true statements be regarded as conveying mental pictures that faithfully and completely depict the inherent properties of the object in itself. Science is always open ended. There is always more to be known; there are always better representations to be attained. But the mind, in achieving a better grasp of "what is," is not moving from the false to the true but from the less precise to the more precise. The progressive character of scientific enquiry is connected with its communal nature. Progress is usually the result of many minds working on the same problem with someone coming up with an idea no one articulated before.

In this context, P. F. Strawson's contemporary defense of an Aristotelian realism is worth noting. In Strawson's language the possibility of descriptive identification and reidentification of particulars imply not only a spatio-temporal world of external objects but intersubjective communication.[6] Material objects are ontologically basic from the point of view of particular identification. They are particulars that can be identified and reidentified without reference to particulars of a different sort. Basic particulars must be publicly observable objects of a sort that different observers can literally see, or hear, or touch. Other sorts of particulars are not basic in this respect.

To conclude, as Etienne Gilson has noted, "Being is neither intuited by a sensibility nor understood by an intellect; it is known by a man. An organic chain of mental operations links the sense perception of what is known as being to the abstraction and to the judgment through which man knows it as being."[7] We affirmed earlier the axiom, "There is no intellection without accompanying sensation." But to recognize that principle is not to instantiate every image that accompanies thought. Some images are involuntary, spontaneously arising in the presence of their object, others are well-crafted, well-designed, themselves the product of much thought, created to represent as closely as conceivable the real. In the sciences we call them "models." A model is an idealized or postulated representation of an unobservable entity or process. Elements employed in their representation are analogous to entities at least partially understood from elsewhere. Associated with the model is a theory indicating how the envisaged mechanism is expected to behave and so permitting specific predictions to be made. The crafting of a model is not arbitrary. In their initial vagueness and generality the models are thrust upon us and held by us in a sensuous way by the imagination. But the intellect is not satisfied with vagueness. It wants precision even in the images it employs when judging and reasoning. If the images do not come, if they are not immediately evoked, it may be that the source of the phenomena indirectly grasped by statistical reports has not been truly identified; we do not yet know what to make of our finding. Sometimes the language we use may be misleading as, for example, when we talk about the "spin of a K meson." This does not militate against the realist position. It simply means that not all that is encountered is understood. We may for the time being have masses of data that require interpretation. Sometimes the mathematics may lag behind the data, sometime the postulated mechanism behind the statistically expressed correlation. The whole thrust of the scientific enterprise is to render intelligible that which does not explain itself. The continuity between prescientific and scientific knowledge is assumed in a realist's account of knowing. In our own day, the globally distributed character of independent reports, the similar proffering of tentative explanations, the employment of common images to represent, indicate that the mind is not fabricating but discovering.

One often reads that scientific reports of nature supersede each other with remarkable frequency, that the reports to which we now subscribe have falsified previous reports taken to be true, and that we have reason to suspect that our present way of looking at things will give way to others. This is sometimes taken as evidence of the arbitrariness and unreliability of the conceptual schemes we currently employ. But the history of science discloses no such thing. In every period there have been false starts, but where explanations have been recognized as substantiated, they remain, sometimes as vague accounts that have been rendered more precise by the refinement of data or the rigor of explanation. Enhancement is not falsification. The advancement of our knowledge of nature does not refute the realist's description of the cognitive process but reinforces it. Explanatory notions such as "bacterium," "cell," "molecule," "atom," "circulatory system," "nerve fiber," were first theoretical entities before they became objects of direct or indirect perception.

To return to Comte, although the foundation of his theory of knowledge is seriously challenged by the march of events, his legacy in the social sciences remains. His law of stages is taken for granted by social theorists, many of whom have never directly encountered Comte.[8] His legacy remains in the work of Lucien Levy Bruhl, Emile Durkheim, and Hippolyte Taine, and their twentieth-century disciples. Few challenge the materialistic assumptions of contemporary anthropology, sociology, and psychology or look for the source of the relativism which pervades much contemporary educational theory.

The challenge that Mercier faced as a student remains but with this difference. Today he could draw upon volumes of contemporary work in the philosophy of science which have taken a realist turn as many philosophers have recovered a realist perspective often directly inspired by Aristotle in their attempt to remain true to actual practice in the natural sciences. British empiricism may entail the materialism taken for granted by many social theorists, but it is rarely seen as an adequate philosophy of science.

NOTES

1. For a fuller discussion of models in the natural sciences see Rom Harré, *Principles of Scientific Explanation* (Chicago: University of Chicago Press, 1970) and William A. Wallace, *The Modeling of Nature: Philosophy of Science and Philosophy of Nature in Synthesis* (Washington, D.C.: The Catholic University of America Press, 1996).

2. Ruth Moore, *Neils Bøhr: The Man, His Science and the World They Changed* (Cambridge, Mass.: MIT Press, 1985).

3. W. Quine, *World and Object* (Cambridge: MIT Press, 1960); W. Quine, *The Roots of Reference* (LaSalle, Ill.: Open Court, 1974).

4. Hilary Putnam, "Models and Reality," in *Realism and Reason: Philosophical Papers*, Vol. 3 (Cambridge, Mass.: Cambridge University Press, 1983).

5. Putnam, *Models*, 207.

6. P. F. Strawson, *Individuals: An Essay in Descriptive Meta-physics* (London: Methuen, 1959), 38ff.

7. Etienne Gilson, *Being and Some Philosophers*, 2nd ed. (Toronto: Pontifical Institute of Medieval Studies, 1952), 206.

8. Comte's law of three stages may be stated simply. Everywhere in all matters, social phenomena begin in a theological stage, pass through a metaphysical stage, and terminate in a positivistic or scientific stage. Cours de philosophie positive was published in six volumes between 1830 and 1842. The influence of Comte is difficult to underestimate. Taine, Mill, and Durkheim were important early disciples. Later, so also were Levy-Bruhl in France and John Dewey in the United States, although "disciple" may be too strong a word in the case of Dewey. Suffice it to say that Dewey accepted uncritically the "law of three stages."

Chapter Eight

Judicial Decision within the Rule of Law

Statutes are created by decisions of legislative bodies, but the power of the courts to interpret statutes is in effect the power to remake them. In an oft-quoted passage, though one that I have not been able to trace to its source, the Episcopal Bishop Hoadly is reputed to have said, "Whoever has absolute authority to interpret any written or spoken laws, it is he who is truly the Law-giver to all intents and purposes and not the person who first wrote or spake them."[1] One does not need to review many decisions of the federal judiciary in the United States to recognize the truth of that statement.

The recognition of the element of interpretation involved in applying the law introduces a number of questions. What is a proper basis for interpretation? Are there principles that determine judicial decision making? How far can the judge legitimately make the law? What recourse does or should the people have when confronted with a bad judge made law. Do extralegal principles, or considerations, play any part in decision making? Is there a basis for law independent of legislative intent?

These are important questions at any time, but they take on a kind of urgency when social structures are in a state of flux, when time-honored customs and mores are questioned, and when institutions previously effective in the defense of inherited norms surprisingly have been rendered impotent. As more than one cultural historian has shown, there is evidence to affirm that the West is passing from a Christian past to an outright secular future, with no assurance that the latter will be an improvement over the former. With public values in transition, it is to be expected that the judge's conception of law, its sources and its scope will be crucial, for it is through his decisions that the shape of social practice will in a large measure be determined. Whether one agrees with Plato that the function of law is to make men good, the laws enacted, or reshaped through judicial decision, do in fact form men's consciences. Some theories of law require the judge to exercise considerable restraint; others would give him untrammeled freedom in the employment of his judgment. The danger present in the latter is manifest. It does not require much imagination to envisage the law under the influence of certain social theories becoming hostile to the family, to private education, to religion or to desirable aesthetic goods, especially when the latter are to be purchased at the expense of individual freedom.

Given the importance of the judiciary in both the English speaking common law traditions and Continental code traditions and the influential role that legal philosophy plays in shaping decisions, I propose to examine two and suggest a third legal theory on precisely the topic of judicial decision making.[2]

As I read it, there are three major schools of legal theory that command attention and that may be regarded as influential in the English-speaking world. Note that I am focusing primarily on Britain and North America, in part to delimit my subject matter; principally, however, because of the peculiar role which the judge plays in the common-law tradition, where judicial decision not only disposes of the case at hand but established principles of law to be taken into account in future decisions. The three theories which I propose to examine exist in a pure form only in textbooks of jurisprudence. Although they may be blurred in the legal philosophy of any individual, still they are distinct and distinguishable, and when embraced give their holder a specific outlook upon the law.

One goes by the name of "legal positivism"; the other is known as "American realism" or sometimes as "sociological idealism," and the third is the classical natural law outlook. None is new, and the tenets of all three schools are well known. The first is associated with the name of Austin in the nineteenth century and in a more sophisticated version with the name of H. L. A. Hart in recent decades.[3] The second is the philosophy of Oliver W. Holmes, Roscoe Pound, and Benjamin Cardoza,[4] which in the lifetime of most of us has moved from a theory abstractly considered to the work-a-day philosophy of the courts in the United States. The third is identified with Aristotle and Aquinas in antiquity and the Middle Ages and with Hooker and Burlamaqui in the period preceding the American Revolution. In a sense both legal positivism and American realism are positivistic in the sense that they both eschew a metaphysical grounding of legal principle. Yet, surprisingly, both tend, at least in some proponents, to identify with a natural law tradition.

According to Austin, law is that which the legislatures and courts enunciate and enforce. The legislature is particularly important in his view. Sovereign in a way in which the court is not, it is free not only from limitations imposed *ab extra*, but also from its own prior legislation. At least three theses are fundamental to the legal positivism represented by Austin. First, the law of any community is to be understood as the special rules it has embraced for the purpose of proscribing certain types of behavior. These rules can be identified by tests having to do with their pedigree. Valid legal rules can be distinguished from the spurious and from mere custom by looking to their source. If their adoption is deliberate and compliance is enforced through sanctions dependent upon the use of public power, then the rule is to be regarded as civil law. Secondly, the law of any community is to be identified exclusively with the rules so tested. If one's case is not covered by such a rule, that case cannot be settled by applying the law. Thirdly, to affirm that one has a legal obligation is to say that his case falls under a valid legal rule. In the absence of a valid legal rule, there is no legal obligation. What is required by morality is not required by law unless specifically legislated. Laws may reproduce or satisfy certain demands of morality, but there is no necessary correspondence between the two orders. Hart finds equally unacceptable the view that there is an unlegislated law, and the view that legislated law which conflicts with morality is not genuine law. Like many in the positivist tradition, he was scandalized by the Nuremberg trials following the close of World War II. In brief, the legal positivist places the emphasis on will and sanction. Law is precisely what the lawmaker declares it to be and nothing more. Law does not exist antecedently to the legislative fiat; law is not discovered, it is decreed. In the absence of decree, there is no law. Similarly, in the absence of enforcement, rules do not have the force of law.

A strikingly different attitude prevails among those who subscribe to the principles of legal activism, typical of the American realist school. With this group, there is a decided shift in interpretation. Law is not to be regarded as that which has been decreed by a legislative body; rather, it is that which has been ruled to be so by a judge. It is understood that in interpreting a statute, the judge has taken into consideration not only legislative intent, but the best interest of the community as well, insofar as these are known to him through the aid of the relevant social sciences. To the legal realist, law is not simply a statute or code; properly understood, it is the means utilized by society for the achievement of certain definable social ends. Put another way, law is an instrument of social engineering in which the conflicting pulls of political philosophy, economic interest and ethical values constantly struggle for recognition against a background of history, tradition, and legal technique. While all of these factors may be reflected in the legislative act itself, they are preeminently present in the judicial decision. In the last analysis, the decision of the courts and not legislative intent is determining.

It is always difficult to characterize a movement, particularly one which eschews systematization and presents itself merely as an outlook, yet certain features of the legal activist view can be distinguished. For one thing, it tends to be rule-skeptical. This can be seen in its pragmatic interpretation of decision making, where it deliberately downgrades the role played by principle. Holmes's theory of judicial decision is roughly Dewey's instrumentalist view of human reason. According to this view, the judge in ruling does not draw conclusions in the light of general principles. Rather, he starts with a problematic and often confused situation. The process of clarification involves the sorting out of multiple questions. With a clear delineation of the problem, a possible solution suggests itself. Law is thus an experimental process in which many factors determine the conclusion reached. Legal principles, legislative intent, and the probable consequences of a ruling are only some of the generic considerations taken into account. So understood, the arguments used by a judge or advocate are not to be taken at face value. They are to be recognized rather as the art of trained craftsmen to make a decision plausible after it has been reached. Law exists primarily in facts and deeds, not in statutes or legal principles.

On this pragmatic view, of the many factors which the judge must take into account when ruling, one of the most important is the practical consequences of his decision. To determine these consequences, he must rely not simply on his own experience, but must turn to those sciences that explore human behavior in society, e.g., economics, sociology, psychology, and criminology. To study law as it works and functions is to investigate the social factors that make the law, on the one hand, and the social results, on the other.

An important feature of this outlook is the scope permitted by the judge. Pragmatic jurisprudence obviously provides a much larger field of free play for the judge in deciding cases than certain forms of positivism would allow. In his application of precedent, as in the interpretation of statutes, the judge must take note of major shifts in public opinion and social policy. He must steer his way between subservience to government and remoteness from constantly changing social pressures and economic needs. In the works of W. Friedman, "Law is a flexible instrument of the social order; it is dependent upon the political values of the society it purports to regulate."[5]

The two positions just described provide answers to the question of whether there are principles apart from those explicitly stated by the law that the judge must take into account in rendering his decision. The positivist tends to deny that there are; the pragmatist insists that there are, and that these are largely the envisaged consequences of the decision as determined by the relevant social sciences. Both positions obviously fail to respect the role of philosophically derived principle.

Obviously, we need not embrace either view. A third position is available which mediates between the two extremes and incorporates the best insights of both. This is the natural law position of Aristotle, the Stoics, and Aquinas and in our own day defended by Jacques Maritain, Yves Simon, and John Courtney Murray. This outlook presupposes a metaphysics, perhaps for completeness, a theistic metaphysics that is not apt to be shared by those in the positivistic or naturalistic camps. There are, nevertheless, features of the natural law outlook which may recommend it even to the metaphysically timid. It is my proposal that we reexamine classical natural law theory as a meta-ethics rather than as a body of norms. Jacques Leclercq has suggested the even stronger thesis that "natural law has never been systematically studied," but he wrote nearly a century ago.[6]

To shift the focus a bit, I now set forth the elements which I consider essential to the natural law approach. Often, natural law is construed as a set of normative propositions which, because of their universality and supposed necessity, in some fashion transcend periods and cultures. Presented as a body of conclusions, natural law appears as fixed or static, and is apt to be rejected out of hand in an age accustomed to look upon the acquisition of knowledge as an ongoing process. But when considered as a meta-ethic, it can be argued that natural law theory has a contribution to make on several fronts. In providing a theory about the determination of norms, it speaks to topics such as ethical reasoning, the movement from descriptive to normative assertions, the use of science in ethics, the extralegal grounds for judicial decision, judicial activism, and the societal basis of law. Furthermore, when so construed, it receives significant support from several quarters not usually identified with natural law tradition which have in ethics stressed the empirical determination of the nature of man and those goals suitable for him.

Natural law, when considered as a meta-ethic, is more advice with respect to procedure than a set of conclusions. The advice amounts to this: proceed with confidence that intelligence can determine in a general way what is good for man. This assertion presupposes that nature is intelligible, and that the human intellect can ferret out the secrets of nature. Put another way, natural law encourages the observer to look for regularities in nature, human and otherwise. Regularity indicates structure, and a knowledge of structure, in turn, yields functional explanation which has a major role to play in the determination of norms.

The confidence that nature is intelligible was a distinctive feature of the Greek mind, which gave birth to the concept of natural law. Intelligibility, for the Greek, owed itself to design, and was explained variously by an ultimate final cause drawing all things to itself, or in terms of a demi-urge, a divine-like artificer. The Christian Middle Ages, of course, were convinced that nature is the handiwork of God and that things are as they are as a result of a divine plan. In both the Greek and Christian traditions, there are the common affirmations that things have natures which indicate tendencies and that both are the product of intelligence. Aristotle, for example, maintained that from a consideration of what a thing is in its tendential aspects, one can determine what is suitable for it: in other words, that which is its good. From consideration of what man is, one can determine what ends he ought to pursue. For Aristotle, the supreme end of man is happiness, which consists primarily in intellectual activity, all other pursuits being subordinate or instrumental to that one. Aquinas adds principally that ultimate fulfillment consists in an eternal beatitude in which man's intellectual and appetitive faculties will find complete satisfaction. For Aquinas, ultimate beatitude is possible even if temporal beatitude of the Aristotalian sort escapes one by reason of chance or by reason of the poverty of the human organism.

In these reflections, we can observe the beginning of a natural law methodology. No conclusions are ready-made. This is evident in both Aristotle and Aquinas, although there is a difference in starting points and emphasis. Aristotle's ethical quest begins with a man already in society with given mores. Those mores which have already formed him play a determining factor in the conception of the good he finally works out. Aquinas, while not denying the validity of Aristotle's insight, begins with confidence that nature is the handiwork of the divine and with the conviction that the divine intellect is the root of an order which the human intellect is able to perceive. What this order is remains to be discovered. Hence, Aquinas's emphasis on reason. In his famous "Treatise on Law," he tacitly identifies law with reason; elsewhere, he develops a methodology which reason is to follow.[7]

It is significant that Aquinas does not attempt to deduce the content of natural law. It is also significant that Aquinas draws no clear-cut distinction between natural and civil law. His famous definition of law, "Law is an ordinance of reason, promulgated by he who has responsibility for the care of the community," while formulated to be predicative of all law, is primarily a definition of civil law. Where so-called natural law leaves off and civil law begins, there is no hard and fast line. True, there is this difference: civil law is articulated in some fashion by civil authority, whereas natural law is not. Yet the difference is not determinative. Natural law can be articulated by a church or an academic community, and is reflected in the ordinances of a community. By whom it is articulated is not a significant distinction. Nor is it significant that the state does not articulate all that is affirmed by the community of scholars. Deserving of emphasis is the fact that law, natural or civil, is the product of reason figuring out what is good for the race, that is, men taken as individuals and as members of the community designed to serve their common interests. This suggests that the principal difference between natural law and civil law is the difference between the constant and the variable.

Aquinas, like anyone in the natural law tradition, recognizes that there are certain constants in man, and that these can be discerned. These constants are the grounds for those normative enunciations which will remain the same from generation to generation, or for that matter, whenever and wherever man is found. The variables are cultural, economic, and topographical. The proportion between the constant and the variable is not worked out. Aquinas is not generous in mentioning constants. The assertion that the natural law is immutable can easily misrepresent Aquinas's position. As he presents his views in the "Treatise on Law," most of the content of the natural law is variable, which suggests that one should be careful in emphasizing content, if, in fact, law is something that is constantly evolving. This can be stressed, for there is evidence to believe that a fresh reading of Aquinas will show that too much is made of the distinction between natural and civil law. Aquinas, in this treatise, is affirming principally that law is rooted in something other than the will of the legislator. When he distinguishes between the immutable and temporal aspects of law, he is recognizing that in certain basic features, man is everywhere alike. This is why the ancients can speak to us across the ages.

It should be clear that not everything that is legislated or determined to be law by a law-making assembly or court is in fact to be treated as law. Aquinas will not give the force of law to those enactments which clearly fly in the face of reason and in the face of experience. One may assume, however, that when legislative bodies are interested in determining the equitable, and conditions are propitious, they will in a large measure, perhaps as far as humanly possible, succeed. This is not to ignore that much legislation is a tissue of compromise, often reflecting conflicting and contradictory insights and principles. Free intelligence and good will will produce good law, not inevitably, but for the most part, and this law, I maintain, is continuous with the dictates of nature, or natural law if you will. On this, indirect support is provided from an unsuspected quarter, namely by H. L. A. Hart. Though he maintains the distinction between the positive laws of a community and its mores, he finds that they frequently overlap or coincide. I am arguing that the difference is principally in the mode of articulation.

It is worth stressing that reason for Aquinas is not to be identified with deduction. The natural law is not to be deduced from intuitive or antecedently known principles. Anthropology will play the same role in his ethics as it does for Aristotle. Here Aquinas's moral philosophy is to be contrasted with the purely formal ethics of Kant, where anthropology has little or no role to play. It is through induction, not deduction, that the moralist is aware of certain constants in man. It is through induction that the philosopher can generalize about man in a changing environment. How much permanence and how much change are, again, questions to be settled by reference to the data of the sciences.

If the changing aspect of law is emphasized, the dilemma created by a too rigorous universal creating hardship cases is mitigated. Aristotle deals with the hardship case in the area of civil law by proposing a sort of equity which would make adjustments where the case was in fact an exception to the universal. Aquinas insists that the law must conform to reason. If it does not, it does not bind in conscience. In the practical order of civil matters, he would not be adverse to Aristotle's solution. Clearly, Aristotle, by his discussion of the equitable, and Aquinas, with his emphasis on reason, could defend themselves against a charge of "moral absolutism."

The foregoing conception of natural law rests upon two ontological pillars: 1) the conviction that there are natural structures, and 2) the conviction that the processes of nature are purposive; in the language of Aquinas, upon the principles of essence and finality. But do these exhaust the commitments which are required to support a natural law outlook? Is it possible to subscribe to a natural law basis for morality without first establishing the existence of God? The answer to this question seems to be in the affirmative. There are many who would find themselves agnostic with respect to the question of God's existence, and yet would like to recognize "that arbitrary will is not legally final," that civil law and conscience are to be measured against an independent scale. A moral scale.

To have a natural law ethics without the supporting principles of essence and finality seems impossible. These principles may be called something else, perhaps "structure" and "function," and admit of a plurality of interpretations, but their recognition, if even in a tenuous form, seems necessary to natural law theory. But what of their ultimate foundation? Can one be committed to natural law and remain theologically an agnostic? History again provides a clue. Natural law has not always been associated with a belief in a divine governor or lawgiver, and even where it has been, it can be argued that its characteristic tenets have not been logically dependent upon that belief. Aquinas insisted that natural man, without revelation, can know what is good.

Some of these notions are reflected in a commonly made distinction between the notion of "legal principle" and that of "legal rule." "Principle" refers to a standard that is to be observed because it is a requirement of justice or fairness or some other dimension of morality. Legal principles are rendered in maxims such as "No man may profit from his own wrong doing," "No man may found a claim on his own iniquity," "No man may acquire property by his own crime." Rules, on the other hand, are enactments of legislative bodies. So distinguished, principles provide reasons with a given line of argument. They incline a decision one way, though not conclusively, and they survive intact when they do not prevail. They do not necessitate a decision because there may be other principles inclining a decision in another way. Rules, however, dictate results; if a contrary result is reached, in effect, the rule has been abandoned or changed. Principles may be controversial, but that is to be expected. They are not demonstrable in the sense that we can usually show the validity of a rule by locating it in an act of parliament or congress or in some judicial precedent. Principles are defended by appealing to conceptions of human nature, to an amalgam of practice, and other principles implied in legislative acts. These are the principles of reason, morality and social utility which, on this view, are the fountainhead of law.

It must be acknowledged, of course, that a judicial decision is a prudential decision often reflecting the mind and personality of the judge as much as the principles invoked in the arguments used to defend his decisions. In any given decision, it may be difficult to distinguish not only between ratio and dictum, but even more so between principle and rule. Yet the several elements are necessarily present.

In defense of the natural law position, it can be argued against the positivist that unless some principles are acknowledged to be binding upon judges, requiring them as a set to reach particular decisions, then no rules or very few rules can be said to be binding on them either. The fact that rules directly, or indirectly through subsequent distinctions, are overruled points to a basis for the decision other than the rule itself. If courts have the discretion to change established rules, there must be standards which determine when a judge may or may not overrule or alter an established rule. It is necessary, though not sufficient, that the judge find that the change would advance some policy or serve some desirable social goal. Not any principle will justify a change. A justified change cannot depend upon the judge's own preference. Any judge who proposes to change existing doctrine must take account of some important standards that argue against departure from established doctrines. One of these would certainly be the doctrine of legislative supremacy, a set of principles and policies that require the courts to pay a qualified deference to the acts of the legislature or parliament. Another would be the doctrine of precedent, which requires consistency in interpretation in the name of equity and efficiency.

It is to be noted that the doctrines of legislative supremacy and precedent incline toward the status quo, each within its own sphere, but they do not command it. When it is argued that a particular rule is binding, it is implied that the rule is affirmatively supported by principles which the court is not free to disregard, and which are collectively weightier than other principles which argue for change. This certainly takes account of one of the principal aims of the legal activist, but it also indicates the need for restraint. A balanced view does not ignore the fact that changed social circumstances and developments in human knowledge do occur and do affect the application of precedent. Much law is the product of its own period and environment and thus does not remain static.

Nevertheless, there are limits to how far the judge can legitimately make the law. Even where a judge has to lay down a rule for the first time, it is seldom that he cannot find guidance of some kind in the mass of previous decision and enactment. By invoking precedent, the judge recognizes the authority of a prior decision because to him it appears to be a correct statement of law. When precedent is admittedly founded on error, his obligation to follow it ceases. The whole effort of the judge is to find the law, not to manufacture it. The judge is always working within materials which exist in the present or the past. His concern is not properly with the future effect of the rule, but with the application of what he believes to be the existing rule to the concrete case before him. He cannot, however much he may wish to do so, sweep away what he believes to be the prevailing law and substitute something else in its place. On this third view, the court sits to administer the law, not to make new law.

Compare now the function of the court to that of the legislature in making the law. The legislature is not confined to law in the present or in the past but may do as it wills with respect to the future. Though it is true that the legislature frequently works on existing and even ancient material, it can make new law in a sense which is precluded to the judge. It legislates where the judge interprets. By no possible extension of his office can a judge legitimately introduce new rules for the compensation of injured employees, for the rate of taxation, for the appropriation of public monies or for the disbursement of natural resources. Yet the legislature does function in such a manner. Thus it is seen that only in a secondary sense does the court properly make law. Every act of interpretation shapes something new, but the creative power of the courts is limited by existing legal materials. Whereas it can be said that the courts find material and shape it, the legislature can be said to manufacture entirely new material.

There are a number of factors to be advanced in support of this view. For one thing law must harmonize with the body of general principles accepted by the populace as a whole. The legislature is likely to be more responsive to the code of prevailing convictions, call it popular consciousness or public opinion. Legislators are representatives of the people who invest them with authority. It would be naive to maintain that representation means a mechanical carrying out of a mandate. The mandate of any representative body or any single individual within it can be only in the most general terms. Yet the principle of representative government does ensure that a plurality of community interests is represented in the legislative process. Legislation is hammered out as competing interests vie for ascendancy. These are the interests of taxpayers, of manufacturers, of laborers, of builders, of craftsmen, of educators, or parents, of corporations, and of recipients of legislative benefice. The legislation shaped as a result of the conflict of community interests is usually a tissue of compromises. Rarely does any one group succeed in dominating the legislature for any length of time. Though logrolling and pork-barreling are common practices, there are checks and balances. Representatives are elected to terms of office and may be recalled, and their enactments, at least in the United States, are subject to judicial review.

The competition of special interest groups in a legislature seems less a danger to sound legislation than an activist court pursuing certain ideological goals in opposition to the good sense of the people. The courts seem peculiarly vulnerable to ideological pressure, especially when those ideologies enjoy the support of the media and the academy.[8] In the United States, the prevailing views in the universities seem able to influence the courts in a way in which they are not able to influence the legislatures. This is not to minimize the role played by other instruments of opinion such as the communications media. But the media themselves tend to reflect the reigning values of the academy. It was William F. Buckley who first said, "I would rather be governed by the first one thousand names in the Boston telephone directory than by the faculty of Harvard College;" the quip does have its point. Though this is not the place to examine the problem in detail, there are reasons why one can often have more confidence in the enlightened judgment of the common man than in that of the academician. In the law which pertains to the regulation of commerce and industry, the technician's testimony is invaluable. But in the determination of social goals, similar testimony, free of ideological advocacy, is hard to find. This stems in part from the fact that the social sciences as social sciences are in no position to recommend social goals. But it is also due in part to the very nature of the academic enterprise where knowledge is frequently advanced only through a dialectical process of give and take. Academic discourse typically proceeds by means of advocacy. A thesis is taken and pushed to its limits. Balance of judgment is frequently lacking. An entire career may be carved out of the brilliant and continuing defense of a position that will eventually be rejected. The ivory-tower metaphor used to describe the academy is not without some justification. Be they one-sided or not, academic debates eventually have their effects on the social order. The public may lag behind opinion makers in its moral attitude, but the effects of the nihilism characteristic of the academy can be found in today's diminished moral standards and their social consequences throughout the West. John M. Rist speaks of "the ethical hangover from a more homogeneous Christian past" that remains influential outside academic circles. Biblical morality still holds but "diminishingly restrains academics, media people, and lawyers from making unabated statements (say, in defense of direct lying or misinforming)."[9] Rist advocates a return to a real ethics, which for him begins with Plato, Aristotle, and the Stoics, what we have been calling a natural law approach, as an antidote to the outright lying and humbug that characterizes much of contemporary moral discourse.

NOTES

1. Quoted by Leon Fuller, *Anatomy of the Law* (London: Penguin, 1971).
2. Graham Hughes identifies three major influences on American juridical philosophy in the twentieth century, the two schools under examination here and that of Hans Kelsen. In spite of the eminence of Kelsen in European thought and of the fact that "every American writer of legal philosophy in the past two decades has felt obliged to take account of his general position," Hughes admits that there has been no school of American Kelsenians. "Rules, Policy and Decision Making," *Law, Reason and Justice* (New York: New York University Press, 1969), 102.
3. See J. Austin, *The Province of Jurisprudence Determined*, 2nd ed. (London: J. Murray, 1861); Reprinted (New York: Burt Franklin, 1971), and Hart, cited earlier.
4. Benjamin Cardoza, *The Nature of the Judicial Process* (New Haven: Yale University Press, 1921); Roscoe Pound, *An Introduction of the Philosophy of Law* (New Haven: Yale University Press, 1961).
5. W. Friedman, *Law in a Changing Society* (London: Pelican, 1964), p. 13; in Friedman's judgment, American legal realism is the product of pragmatist and behaviorist approaches to social institutions. For his analysis of American realism, see *Legal Theory* (London: Stevens & Son, 1944), 292–304.
6. For extended contemporary discussions of natural law see John Finnis, *Natural Law and Natural Rights* (Oxford, England: Clarendon Press, 1988); John Finnis, *Aquinas: Moral and Political Theory* (New York: Oxford University Press, 1998); Russell Hittinger, *A Critique of New Natural Law Theory* (Notre Dame, Ind.: University of Notre Dame Press, 1987); Russell Hittinger, *The First Grace: Rediscovering Natural Law in a Post-Christian World* (Wilmington, Del.: ISI Books, 2003); Ralph McInerny, *Ethica Thomistica* (Washington, D.C.: The Catholic University of America Press, 1982).
7. Cf. Thomas Aquinas, *Summa theologiae* (New York: Benzinger Brothers, 1947), I–II, pp. 90–97, from which this account is taken.
8. Carlin, Howard and Messenger hold that one of the fundamental assumptions of American idealism is the theory that there exists an essential harmony between the interests of the citizen and that of the state. The judge is thus regarded as a benevolent administrator seeking a solution to a social problem rather than an impartial adjudicator resolving a legal dispute. Concern for the person and rehabilitation of the disadvantaged, they argue, entails a conception of the poor as having problems rather than grievances and of needing treatment not justice. These authors frankly

fear a legal philosophy which makes the task of the court not a decision with respect to conflicting rights, but the restoration and promotion of social equilibrium. "Civil Justice and the Poor: Issues for Sociological Research," in *Law and the Behavioral Sciences*, ed. Lawrence M. Friedman and Stewart Macauly (Indianapolis: Bobbs Merrill, 1969), 192.

9. John M. Rist, *Real Ethics* (Cambridge, Mass.: Cambridge University Press, 2002), 2.

Chapter Nine

Modern Interpretations of Religion: The Legacy of Hume and Kant

The failure of the proposed European Constitution to acknowledge the Christian roots of European culture is the outcome of a conflict begun long ago, the inevitable result of the Enlightenment, Anglo-French and German, of the late eighteenth and early nineteenth centuries. No one intellectual can be held accountable for Europe's neglect of its past, but the combined discourses of British, French, and German intellectuals changed the way Europe's cultural elites were to view religion and its role in society. The drama is fascinating, and there are many players, but the leading roles have to be assigned to David Hume, Immanuel Kant, and G. W. F. Hegel.

David Hume is usually acknowledged to be the first philosopher, certainly the first in the modern period, to study religion systematically from a philosophical point of view. In his own day, Hume was best known for his six-volume *History of England (1754–1776)*. Although he abandoned philosophy per se when he was relatively young, his impact remains on philosophical discourse to this day. As a result of his empirical analysis of causality, Hume concluded that all arguments for the existence of God fail. But if there is no evidence for the existence of God, then how is one to understand common belief in God and the practice of religion? With the destruction of the rational ground of homage, worship and the things pertaining to worship lose their rationale. Belief in God, in the absence of demonstration, becomes just that, belief. This form of agnosticism must be understood as a radical break with antiquity. The ancients from Plato to Plotinus and beyond had no trouble reasoning to a self-thinking intellect, a *summum bonum*, a first efficient cause, an ultimate final cause and an immaterial intellect. Design in nature hardly had to be postulated; it was taken for granted. Their treatment of religion usually took place in the context of their discussions of the virtue of justice. Religion was considered an act of piety due a provident, unseen higher intelligence.

Recognition of dependence naturally leads to discussions of appropriate ways to acknowledge debt to unseen God. Thus we find Cicero drawing up a set of liturgical prescriptions in legalistic terms, distinguishing between modes appropriate to rural and to urban areas. The manner of acknowledging dependence was open to human invention. The temples of ancient Greece and Rome inspire even to this day.

Given Hume's limitation of knowledge to sensory experience, and without an acknowledgment of the intellect's ability to move from an observed effect to an unobserved cause, there is no way to demonstrate the existence of God, and, one could add from the vantage point of the twentieth century, much of what we today take for granted in theoretical physics. Given Hume's premises, God can no longer be an object of philosophical inquiry, yet religion remains a distinctive social artifact that can be investigated as such. This is what Hume sets about doing in his *Dialogues Concerning Natural Religion* (published posthumously in 1799), and in effect he launches, if not a new philosophical discipline, certainly a discussion that is to reverberate in the decades following. Historically aware of the part played by religion in the life of humanity, Hume is led to examine its nature and power empirically. He is willing to admit that at no time in recorded human history have men been without religion. It is not a happy picture. Religion, as he finds it, is characterized by superstition, fanaticism, bigotry and intemperate zeal. Investigation may disclose that true religion is not to be identified with superstition and fanaticism. Yet, even true religion, to the extent that it is based on the idea of the greatness and majesty of the infinite God, seems to encourage attitudes of abasement and practices of asceticism and mortification, ideas that Hume finds foreign to the pagan mentality which he takes as normative in this case. In fact, with its doctrine of eternal reward, religion impairs morality by encouraging people to act for motives other than love of virtue for its own sake. Continuing his empirical approach to the study of religion, Hume is led to conclude that belief in the existence of God is a natural disposition; one may call it a *property* of our nature. There may be no rational justification for belief in the existence of God, but neither is there a rational justification for our belief in the existence of an external world. Yet we give assent to both. Given that religion is a habit of mind due to our nature, its proper study clearly belongs to philosophical anthropology, and this Hume undertakes at length in his *Dialogues Concerning Natural Religion*. In that work, Hume examines the wellsprings in human nature from which the religious attitude and the religious interpretation of our existence arise. Acknowledging that religion is a complex human phenomenon, Hume's next step is to take it apart analytically and then study its component factors. Hume is not interested in any particular body of teaching but in religion as a characteristic human outlook. His analysis reveals that the elementary roots of religious belief are to be found in the "passional drives of fear and hope," coupled with a lively concern to know the causes affecting our human welfare. By definition religion posits a relational bond between God and man. But what is one to do with the God-pole of the religious relationship since, given Hume's methodology, God is not an object of investigation? Is the philosophical examination of religion thus hopelessly frustrated? Not at all. The religious attitude, answers Hume, involves a belief about some matters that fall within the realm of experience and some that do not. Those that do not fall within the scope of experience can be handled the same way as the problem of the external world, that is, by specifying the grounds in experience which lead men to believe in a powerful, minded-being, existing independently of ourselves. Here we find the groundwork for an interpretation that will be completed in the twentieth century by Sigmund Freud. Hume finds that although religion is a property of human nature, it is not a primary impulse and therefore irreducible and beyond analysis. If religion were a primary impulse and analytically irreducible, nothing could be done about it. It would be an unreformable tendency of man, without a history and without the possibility of reform. It is because the first religious principles are secondary that they may be easily perverted by various accidents and causes. Although religion can be said to be natural to man this carries no guarantee about its human worth or the soundness of any religious conviction. The human heart is notorious for yielding both good fruit and bad.

Hume finds that although man may come to religion under the pressure of deep-seated fear and hope, sheer recognition of a superior power in the world is not enough to constitute the religious attitude. A threefold response must occur. Men must relate themselves to the superior power as agents through some practical striving and not remain merely theoretical observers. This relationship must be suffused with a personal quality—the superior power has to be given a personal form. And finally, the development of the religious attitude requires men to feel a tension between affirming a superior power beyond nature and their seeking to relate themselves practically to it. In short, religious striving must be practical and personally ordered, but it must rest on a definite strain of transcendence.

In spite of his anti-metaphysical epistemology and his rejection of all argument for the existence of God, Hume's interest in religion was not nihilistic. Religious belief, he came to hold, has an intrinsic structure that resists reduction to natural theology, to design speculation, or to moral admonition. He acknowledges the distinctive nature of religious assent. Given that religious belief does not depend on demonstration, can we speak of religious belief as a cognitive act? Hume answers that it can be classified along with other complex ideas involving an imaginative synthesis of many strains of meaning and as a complex idea it can be dissolved into its components. But there is this difference. Here we are dealing with a complex idea that is also a belief. Distinctive of the religious mind is the mind's way of entertaining and interpreting impressions. The mind does not meet a situation impassively—the encounter is active. Man comes to grips with the world through the mediation of his concrete intelligence that moderated by his hopes and fears. Religious belief provides an integration of worldly experience with aspirations for happiness, coupled with a natural propensity to seek divine aid to cope with the world. Religion may be subjected to radical and persistent skeptical treatment, but even after such skeptical treatment, one recognizes that belief in God remains and is not diminished to the extent that one might expect.

To those who expected that upon criticism, religious belief would shrivel up and disappear, Hume maintains that one's assent to God's reality may be deprived of many of its customary supports in argument without being annihilated or reduced to the status of a stubborn social custom. Its persistence may be taken as a sign of its totally noncognitive basis. But that is not all. Even the sophisticated believer inquires about the orderly aspects of the natural world, believing that they represent the powerful presence of a transcendent mind. This believer will not claim that he has demonstrative knowledge of God, but he will recognize some ground within his own questioning nature and within the visible world for believing.

We must conclude that a man formed by Hume's philosophy of nature cannot remain either an untroubled dogmatist or an untroubled skeptic. He is compelled to give a cautious, highly qualified assent to the religious reference of human life. Since the philosopher cannot remain satisfied with the popular forms of religion, he is obliged to determine the conception of religion that will survive the severest form of criticism and, in addition, be compatible with a secularly grounded morality. In sum a philosophic critique of religion frees one from both popular belief and from skepticism. Religion as endorsed by Hume is thus confined to the act of giving a probable speculative assent to a cosmic mind. Hume draws no practical consequences. For Hume, to know God is to worship Him. All other worship is indeed absurd, superstitious and even impious. It is clear that a philosophically reformed religion is viable for only a few reflective minds. As such it does not become a habitual principle of thought and action, nor does it entail religious observance.

Immanuel Kant (1724–1804), following the lead of David Hume, similarly produced a comprehensive philosophy of religion, defending the reasonableness of belief in spite of reason's inability to demonstrate the existence of God. His theory of religion is part of his philosophical system and is governed by his conception of the nature, aim, and method of philosophy. For Kant the task of philosophy is largely therapeutic. Its obligation is to criticize and to reform. Confronted with Hume's empiricism, he faced the question of how mathematical and scientific knowledge are possible whereas metaphysics is not. He takes as axiomatic that method precedes all science. It would be rash to undertake any study before its methodology has clearly been worked out and the precepts of that method clearly established. In his three famous Critiques, he addresses three questions: in the *Critique of Pure Reason*, the question "What can I know?"; in the *Critique of Practical Reason*, "What ought I to do?"; and in the *Critique of Judgment*, What may I hope?"

Kant's theory of religion arises as he attempts to answer the third question. The theme of hope is central to his critical work. Kant read Hume's *Dialogues* in 1780, and, convinced by Hume that we cannot demonstrate the existence of God, Kant opens the way to a practical foundation for belief in the existence of God. Kant's philosophy of religion has to be seen against the backdrop of the seventeenth-century pietist movement, a religious revival that originated in Germany as a reaction to the Lutheran theology of the day. The pietist regarded the Christian faith not as a set of doctrinal propositions to which the believer gives assent but as a living relationship with God. They stressed the power of God to transform the believer's life through a conversion or a rebirth experience. Like orthodox Lutheranism, pietism exalted the authority of Scripture above that of natural reason. It was hostile to the hellenization of Christianity, including the systematic study of Sacred Scripture, insisting that the Bible is to be read for inspiration and moral edification.

Kant's attitude toward his pietist background was ambivalent. He rejected pietism's anti-intellectualism, but much of his conception of morality and religion can be regarded as a rationally purified version of pietism. Following Hume, Kant engages in sustained criticism of what he calls speculative arguments for the existence of God. These he recognizes as three: the ontological, the cosmological, and the teleological argument. In spite of his negative assessment of their value, he finds that a believing philosopher may engage in radical criticism of speculative demonstration without undermining his religious convictions. One must believe, he maintains, even if one cannot demonstrate. If one cannot say, "It is morally certain that there is a God," one can say, "I am morally certain there is a God." While arguments for the existence of God can never have demonstrative force, they can nevertheless serve an incitive role. Such arguments, says Kant, keep our minds alive to the importance of existential questions about God. To believe is to accept as certain and true, and hence to assent to those realities which are implicit in our moral freedom and obligation but which are not available to intuition or demonstration. For Kant, the act of believing is not a step along the way to speculative knowledge. Belief is a cognitive way of its own. It requires a distinctive disposition of the mind. A modern person alive to the challenge of skepticism in religious matters must adopt a distinctive orientation of mind in order to believe. This entails a deliberate process of reflection and gradual orientation. Kant identifies four steps in reflective preparation. First, we must make sure that the object of the search does not fall within the scope of knowledge and opinion; second, that it contains no contradiction and survives the test of internal consistency; third, that it is coherent with what we do know. Only then can we take the fourth step and make a comparison between the limits of human knowing and the drive to increase our cognitive act so that it may somehow include the divine reality lying beyond the range of objective knowledge as such.

To do justice to Kant's theory of religion would require several lectures if not a volume. Kant was not willing, as was Voltaire, to restrict religion to its philosophically elaborated content. The invisible, Kant maintains, needs to be represented through the visible. A religion of pure moral belief is not enough. Religion must develop social forms that take account of the practical mediation of the human community in our movement toward God. Religion cannot consist solely in Hume's mystical flight of "the alone to the alone." Of necessity, religion must realize itself in a social manner, even in visible ecclesiastical institutions. A visible church, among other things, is necessary for its tutorial role.

In a lofty passage Kant writes that man is not only responsible for his own conduct but is obliged to aid others in their quest for moral perfection. In fact, he must share his moral maximum with others in a spirit of love and fellowship. In this context, Kant memorably defines love as "the free reception of the will of another person into one's own maxims." Love opens us out responsibly to the interior struggle of other men to achieve a virtuous life. It is a forceful reminder of our moral interdependence. "What may I hope for?" may be reframed as "What may we hope for together?" In this manner God is seen as the Lord of the ethical commonwealth.

To place these discussions in an historical context, by the mid-decades of the nineteenth century on both sides of the Atlantic, it was recognized that British empiricism and the Enlightenment philosophy originating in France and Germany were posing a threat to the Christian faith. *The Journal of Speculative Philosophy*, the first journal of philosophy to be published in the English language, was established at St. Louis in 1867, among other reasons, to combat the secular philosophies arriving from Europe. The chosen mode of counterattack was that of German idealism, particularly the idealism of Hegel. In its first issue, its editor, William Torrey Harris, gave three reasons for the purpose of the journal. In his judgment, speculative philosophy provides, first, a philosophy of religion much needed when traditional religious teaching and ecclesiastical authority were losing their influence. Secondly, it provides a social philosophy that is compatible with a communal outlook as opposed to a devastating individualism. Thirdly, while taking cognizance of the startling advances in the natural sciences, it provides an alternative to the empiricism that claims to be the proper rationale for scientific inquiry.

Speculative philosophy for Harris is the tradition that begins with Plato, a tradition that finds its full expression in the system of Hegel. The foremost representative of the speculative outlook endorsed by Harris was undoubtedly Josiah Royce, whose Gifford lectures, published as *The World and the Individual*, sought not only to counter Hume's skepticism but to provide a rational foundation for the Christian faith. The problem created by Kant's destruction of metaphysics Royce regarded as fundamental. In 1881, he wrote, "We all live, philosophically speaking, in a Kantian atmosphere." Eschewing the outright voluntarism of Arthur Schopenhauer, Royce sought a metaphysics that would permit him to rationally embrace his Christian heritage. Whereas William James, his contemporary and fellow member of the Harvard University faculty of philosophy, was convinced that every demonstrative approach to God must fail, Royce was convinced that speculative reason gives one access to God. The code words of the day—"evolution," "progress," "illusion," "higher criticism," "communism," "socialism"—he thought evoked a mental outlook that reduces Christianity to metaphor and Christian organizations to welfare dispensaries. At issue for Royce was not simply a philosophical problem. The philosophers, he realized, spoke not only to one another but tutored the architects of the new biblical criticism, the *Redaktionsgeschite* movement. David Frederick Strauss, in his *Das Leben Jesu*, under the influence of the Enlightenment, examined the Gospels and the life of Jesus from the standpoint of the higher criticism and concluded that Christ was not God but a supremely good man whose moral imperatives deserved to be followed. This Royce could not accept: there is no philosophically compelling reason, he maintained, to embrace a purely naturalist interpretation of the Sacred Scriptures. Royce sought in Hegel a defense of Christianity, but such was not to be.

Although indebted to Kant, Hegel takes issue with Kant and with Hume on a number of crucial issues, specifically on what we can know of God. "The doctrine that we can know nothing of God, that we cannot cognitively apprehend him, has become in our time a universally acknowledged truth, a settled thing, a kind of prejudice," writes Hegel. Challenging this prejudice, he says, "I declare such a point of view . . . to be directly opposed to the whole nature of Christian religion, according to which we should know God cognitively; God's nature and essence, and should esteem this cognition above all else." Hegel affirms that philosophy itself has as its object the true, and the true in its highest form as God. "To know this true not only in its simple form as

God, but to know the rational in God's works—as produced by God and endowed with reason—that is philosophy." Religion, Hegel maintains, is a spur to philosophy. Religious faith stirs up the subjective energies in the human existent and impels him on a lifelong quest for the intellectual grounds of his religious interpretation of life and the practical means of bringing this ideal to realization. Gradually, it dawns on the reflective person, says Hegel, that the relationship between philosophy and religion is not an instrumental one but rather one of organic maturation. The theoretical and practical truths that he once held on faith can eventually be held through philosophically motivated judgment. The act of faith and that of philosophical knowing stand related as the implicit and explicit stages of a single growth of awareness. Religion, Hegel is convinced, is philosophy grasped in the mode of groping presentiment, whereas philosophy is religion brought to its internal fulfillment and conscious articulation. Hegel rejects the view that there is only one natural religion. Hegel posits instead that the naturalness of religion consists in its being an appropriate expression of a segment of man's needs and feelings within a particular temporal period and historical stage of development. To understand religion, one necessarily begins with the modern world, but it is a world that embodies the religious heritage of Greece and ancient world religions, especially Christianity in its biblical presentation. But modernity places a unique stamp upon these human materials by reinterpreting them in the light of decisive steps taken in the Reformation, the Enlightenment and the French Revolution. When religious modernity is understood in this historical sense, there is nothing parochial about requiring that the philosophical approach to religion begin with an assessment of the here-and-now actuality of religious life. Hegel continues. The modern student of religion has to take note of the fateful shift in the scales of knowledge and human interest. History teaches that the more our knowledge of and control of nature increases, the more our claim to possess knowledge of God weakens. Man's interest in the practical has led him away from religion and things that pertain to the temple. "There was a time," writes Hegel, when one had the interest, the drive, to know about God, to fathom His nature, when the spirit had found no rest in this occupation. . . . Our time has renounced this need and its toils." One can understand why Royce up to a point found Hegel congenial. With Hegel it remains open for debate whether God is to be viewed as a person or as a process and immortality as universal or personal. Hegel's voluminous writings lent themselves to varied interpretation, and soon there were "left wing" and "right wing" Hegelians. Royce would have been numbered among the right, but clearly the left carried the day. Among Hegel's pupils were Ludwig Feuerbach, David Frederick Strauss, Søren Kierkegaard, and Karl Marx. Each was to author treatises on religion, most challenging traditional interpretations of religion and each in his own way undermining Christian belief. Strauss reduces religion to a freely created myth. In his reduction of Christianity to humanism, Feuerbach comes to the conclusion that the essence of faith is man trusting himself. For Kierkegaard, faith is an irrational leap into the dark. Marx's view that "religion is the opiate of the people" is well known.

To change the scenario, at approximately the same time that the young Josiah Royce entered the intellectual arena, Leo XIII, aware of the secular challenge to the Catholic faith and convinced that philosophy must be fought by philosophy, recommended, not Hegel, but Aquinas. His encyclical, *Aeternae Patris*, by endorsing a fledgling Thomistic movement, gave direction to Catholic philosophy and theology that was to last through most of the twentieth century. Worthy of note, Josiah Royce, in paying tribute to Leo XIII for the Thomistic revival, expressed the fear that a resurgent Thomism might give way to the Kantian legions and to the demand that the epistemological issue be settled first. Etienne Gilson, the French philosopher, who was to influence the direction of Thomistic studies in North America, warned repeatedly that if one starts with the mind, that is, with the problem of knowledge, one is likely to remain forever estranged from the domain of being. It is only through a metaphysics of being, a metaphysics that acknowledges that natures exist independently of the mind and that reason can move from the contingent to the necessary, that we can reach the self-existent cause of being. Without the principles of substance and causality, man is not only estranged from a natural knowledge of God but science is reduced to description and prediction. The metaphysical issues that confronted the late nineteenth century confront the intellectual world today. As Royce feared, there developed a distinctive stream of transcendental Thomism exemplified in the work of Karl Rahner and Bernard Lonergan. On another front, British empiricism as represented by David Hume finds its foremost expression in North America in the legacy of John Dewey and his disciples. That philosophy, known as pragmatic naturalism, became in the last half of the twentieth century the dominant force in American educational circles. As the air we breathe, it is simply taken for granted, the lens through which policy is viewed from school curricula to court appointments. The battle for the soul of America continues.

It must be admitted that David Hume was right about one thing. Men remain religious in the absence of evidence for the existence of God, one can say in spite of the secular outlook that prevails in the halls of the academy, in the media, and among our governing elites. Kant's effort to salvage what we may call a fideistic Christianity was not without influence. One can see this especially in Kierkegaard and in Kant's twentieth-century disciples such as Karl Barth, Rudolf Bultmann, and Paul Tillich. We see here the great divide between mainstream Protestantism and Catholicism. The Catholic mind is not the fideistic mind of Kant's believer, nor the Gnostic mind of Hegel's philosopher. The Catholic mind is at one with the Fathers of the Church who drew upon Hellenistic learning in their efforts to understand and explicate the truths of the Gospels. The inherited Hellenic mind was a confident mind. In the work of Plato, Aristotle, and the Stoics, the West had achieved before the birth of Christ what we may call the rational preamble to the Christian faith, namely, that God is and that we can know something of His nature. The Catholic Church has long claimed that Christ came in the fullness of time when the human intellect was prepared to receive the truths of the Gospels. Revelation, it consistently teaches, builds upon natural reason, not the other way around, as Hegel would have it.

The study of Hume, Kant, and Hegel and the genesis of contemporary attitudes toward religion is not a mere academic exercise. The seemingly academic battles we have discussed have consequences within the social order. One will find within the work of David Hume and his disciples, that is, within the Anglo/French and German Enlightenment the roots of contemporary European agnosticism, the underlying source of the European Union's failure to acknowledge in its proposed Constitution the Hellenic and Christian sources of Western culture. What is at stake is the acknowledgment that this creature, man, is "made in the image and likeness of god" and "nourished by one divine law." Without an acknowledgment of the transcendent, man is reduced to a physical being, to a barren, cold, and temporal existence.

Chapter Ten

Santayana on the Role of Religion in Society

In a 1992 collection, *Essays on Religion and Education*, R. M. Harré reprints his 1973 article, "The Simple Believer," where he writes, the philosophy of religion is "a subject which fastidious philosophers do not like to touch."[1] Equipped by his empiricist progenitors, Hare is not afraid to enter the field to confront what he takes to be an enfeebled Christianity defended only by its simple masses. From the outset he assumes that the educated man cannot believe in the supernatural, a belief which he equates with superstition. He does not argue for this position but regards it as so well established that he, at least, needs to provide no evidence. Harré then asks, "Can religion do without the supernatural? . . . Suppose someone produced an interpretation of Christianity that could be accepted by the best humanists; would this necessarily be a bad thing?"[2] An informed reader might respond, such interpretations are plentiful and have existed from the early centuries of Christianity, and they exist also for Judaism. Santayana, whose thought we will examine in a moment, provides one for Christianity. Lenn Goodman, in a work entitled, *On Justice: An Essay in Jewish Philosophy,* provides a purely naturalistic interpretation of the books of the Torah.[3] Wishing to salvage the moral teaching of the Hebrew prophets, Goodman, nevertheless, cannot bring himself to acknowledge either an immaterial reality or an afterlife. This should give us pause. If Goodman can carve out a role for a secularized Judaism, and Harré is willing to embrace a Christianity which has no reference to the supernatural, what is there about religion that makes even the non-believer reluctant to discard its trappings? "I believe," says Harré, "that matters are so ordered in the world that there is a point in trying to live by the precepts to which Christians subscribe."[4] One may ask, are the biblical religions, Christianity and Judaism, to be respected merely for their moral teaching?

Attitudes toward religion indicate not only personal acquaintance with religious structures and practices but deep-seated metaphysical outlooks as well. Obviously, from the examples offered above, one can be agnostic or flatly deny the existence of God and yet be appreciative of the role of religion in society, although consistency would seem to dictate the opposite. As the intellectual and cultural influence of religion wanes in a nation once thought to be Christian, it may be instructive to examine the thought of two diverse American figures who share a materialistic metaphysics but whose attitude to religion varies considerably. The two, John Dewey and George Santayana, are usually regarded as preeminent in a small band coming to be known as classic American philosophers. I have discussed Dewey's attitude in detail elsewhere and will use him merely to display a difference; it is Santayana who is the principal focus of this brief enquiry.[5]

To the historian of ideas, skepticism with respect to Christian convictions has been forming among the occidental intelligentsia for the last century and a half. Nietzsche's lament of the decline of humanist values and of liberal humanist civilization is well known. For Nietzsche, even in the last century, Western culture no longer possessed the spiritual resources which had formerly justified its existence and without which he believed it could not survive.

What is new is that this loss of moral sense has within the twentieth century made itself felt on the level of the common man. Views entertained in eighteenth and nineteenth century drawing rooms and in the academy of that day have in our own lifetime entered the market place. Diderot set the tone in his famous *Encyclopaediae* when he wrote, "Everything must be examined, everything must be shaken up, without exception and without circumspection." Voltaire urged the eradication of Christianity from the world of higher culture, but he was willing to have it remain in the stables and in the scullery, mainly as a moral force, lest a servant class emancipated from traditional morality might pilfer. Like Diderot, he was convinced that the critical spirit could do its constructive work only after it had liberated man from the shackles of traditional belief. There are times, he says, when one must destroy before one can build. Voltaire readily admitted his intolerance, declaring that his was an intolerance against intolerance. Bentham thought the state should actively work to stamp out religion. His disciple, John Stuart Mill, repudiated Christianity, but not the religion of humanity which he thought to be, from the point of view of the state, a useful thing. Auguste Comte was more benevolent in his attitude toward Christian practice than either Voltaire or Mill. In spite of his denial of all metaphysical validity to religious belief, he was willing to accept as a civic good the moral and ritual traditions of at least Catholic Christianity.

Emile Durkheim was not so positive. For him, a major task of the state is to free individuals from partial societies such as the family, religious organizations, and labor and professional groups.[6] Modern individualism, Durkheim thought, depends on preventing the absorption of individuals into secondary or mediating groups. In antiquity, religious and political institutions were but parts of a larger social fabric into which the individual was introduced without question. Nonconformity was not an option. Only in modern circumstances, brought about by the centralization of government, Durkheim thought, has the individual acquired an untrammeled personal freedom.

Feuerbach, whose materialism was to have a significant influence on both Marx and Freud, assigned to reason the role of destroying the illusion of religion, "an illusion, however, which is by no means insignificant, but whose effect on mankind, rather, is utterly pernicious." Freud took up the theme in his *Future of an Illusion* where he describes the struggle of the scientific spirit against the "enemy" religion. "Criticism," he writes, "has gnawed away at the probative power of religious documents; natural science has shown the errors they contain; comparative research has been struck by the fatal resemblance of the religious conceptions we revere to the mental products of primitive peoples and times."[7] In a letter to Princess Marie Bonaparte, Freud complained that intellectuals had slackened in their attack on religious belief, but understandably. "That comes from the most varied drinks being offered in the name of 'religion,' with a minimum percentage of alcohol—really non-alcoholic; but still they get drunk on it." Showing no respect for the social gospel or for accommodationist religion, Freud wrote, "The old drinkers were after all a respectable body."[8]

In the twentieth century many of these ideas were to find expression on the North American side of the Atlantic in the writings of John Dewey, whose philosophy was to play an influential role in the development of American educational philosophy and social policy. In his educational philosophy, Dewey provided no role for religion or religious institutions, whatever roles they may have played in the past. Religion is an unreliable source for knowledge, Dewey believed, and, in spite of contentions to the contrary, even of motivation. Many of the values held dear by the religious are worthy of consideration and should not be abandoned, but a proper rationale ought to be sought for those deemed commendable. Through his critique of religion, Dewey sought not merely to eliminate the church from political influence, but to eliminate it as an effective agent even in private life. Religion is deemed socially dangerous insofar as it gives practical credence to a divine law and attempts to mold personal or social conduct in conformity with norms which look beyond temporal society.

Etienne Gilson, the historian of philosophy, once ventured the opinion that the fortunes of metaphysics are bound to the fortunes of religion. It may be that the current attack on the Western literary canon is not unrelated to the demise of religion as an intellectual catalyst. Under the banner of multiculturalism the West is challenged to abandon the very standards which have served to make cultural judgment possible. The legacy of Greece and Rome, not to mention Jerusalem, a legacy which provided those time-transcending truths in the light of which religious belief is rendered intelligible and which historically provided the intellectual framework for the emergence of modern science is challenged as if it were one among equals. Of course, calls to look elsewhere, particularly to the East, are not a late-twentieth-century phenomena. Arthur Koestler in his *The Lotus and the Robot* compares East and West and finds little that is viable in the East which has not been imported from the West and much indigenous to the East which can be faulted.[9]

With the ascendancy of the secular outlook as the dominant intellectual force in the university and in the media, religion has effectively been removed as a cultural leaven. The consequence is plain for all to see in the crumbling moral order. Religiously inspired calls to self-restraint, piety and fidelity have not been duplicated by a civic philosophy. As a matter of record, philosophers and even theologians have been in the forefront of the march toward a permissive society. As moral chaos has led to discernible social effects, a number of political observers from Beatrice Ask, Sweden's minister of education, to Richard Neuhaus and Irving Kristol, have called for a re-examination of the role of religion in personal and communal life. It must be acknowledged that religion is such a multifaceted social phenomenon that apart from specific ecclesiastical structures, it may be difficult to identify it as an object of study.

Although George Santayana (1863–1952) was a contemporary of John Dewey (1859–1952) and exposed to many of the same cultural, literary, and philosophical sources, his attitude toward religion was remarkably different. No less a materialist than Dewey, Santayana nevertheless maintained an appreciation (albeit a purely secular one) of the role of religion in society. He could say where Dewey could not, "Religion when seen to be poetry, ceases to be descriptive and therefore odious . . . (and) becomes humanly more significant than it seemed before."[10] In his *Interpretations of Poetry and Religion*, Santayana wrote, "Religion and poetry are identical in essence, and differ mainly in the way in which they are attached to practical affairs. Poetry is called religion when it intervenes in life, and religion, when it merely supervenes upon life, is seen to be nothing but poetry."[11]

Santayana's Catholic upbringing was clearly a factor in his appreciation of the role of religion in society. Born in Madrid, he spent the first nine years of his life in Spain. By his own account, as an adolescent he oscillated between solipsism and the Catholic faith. But John Dewey was no less religious as a youth. One of his first lectures as a young teacher at the University of Michigan was entitled, "The Obligation to Knowledge of God," a lecture delivered to the Student Christian Association in 1884. One cannot say that the difference between Dewey and Santayana is the difference between a New England Puritanism and a Spanish Catholicism since from age nine until his resignation as a member of the Harvard faculty Santayana was a resident of Boston. The difference may lie much deeper in conflicting theories of knowledge, perhaps in conflicting theories of being.

Santayana, as a cultured non-believer, provides for the contemporary reader an interesting witness to the personal and communal effects of religious practice. While denying literal truth to Christian doctrine, his interpretation of religion nevertheless accords it cognitive value. Almost apologetically, he remarked, the believer may not relish his interpretation of religion, but considering what he has said about its rivals, the believer should not be chagrined.

With the possible exception of William James, Santayana wrote more about religion than any other American philosopher of his period. Intelligence, learning, and experience, bolstered by an unflagging honesty and courage, fuse to make him one of the most interesting and perhaps timely philosophers of religion in the twentieth century. He was especially perceptive in writing about Christianity; he even wrote a book, albeit heterodox, entitled, *The Idea of Christ in the Gospels.*[12] He understood the difference between Protestantism and Catholicism and recognized the internal inconsistency of the modernist's claim to authentic Christianity while attacking the Magisterium and the authority of tradition.

It is not difficult to identify the source of Santayana's cultural appreciation of religion. Throughout his life he could recall with fondness his early experiences of religious pageantry, of the many feasts, such as Corpus Christi, celebrated in his boyhood Avila. Strangely in later life, he claimed never to have practiced his faith. His estrangement seems to have occurred during his college years when he began the study of philosophy, particularly the work of Spencer, Hume, Mill, Schopenhauer, and Nietzsche. While he was enrolled at the Boston Latin School he continued to attend Mass, but at Harvard College his faith in the literal truth of Christianity began to fade. After studying with William James and Josiah Royce he subsequently spent two years in Germany and then returned to Harvard for graduate study, eventually joining its faculty. It was Royce who directed his doctoral dissertation on Lotze. Santayana relates that he wanted to write on Schopenhauer, but Royce prevailed.

Santayana's years at Harvard spanned a watershed period, with an inherited idealism sometimes called "the classical period of American philosophy" on the one side and various realisms and materialisms which were to replace it on the other. Idealism of the Germanic variety was at that time thought to be an adequate prop or metaphysical underpinning for a religious outlook. But confidence in Hegel was soon to erode as achievement in the sciences seemed to entail philosophical empiricism, and the critical movement in biblical studies, cast doubt on the supernatural sources of the sacred scriptures. The new realism and the critical realism which soon replaced idealism were materialisms of one sort or another. Although the intellectual biography of John Dewey provides a snapshot of the larger academic terrain, Santayana himself never traversed that terrain. His was a materialism from the outset of his intellectual career. Santayana's reflections on religion were always the reflections of a materialist and therefore of a non-believer. He was appreciative of Catholicism in the same way that he was appreciative of other coherent systems of belief which produce effects in the practical order. In *Persons and Places* he tells us, "I had never practiced my religion, or thought of it as a means of getting to heaven or avoiding hell, things that never caused me the least flutter. All that happened was that I became accustomed to a different *Weltanschauung*, to another system having the same rational function as religion: that of keeping me attentive to the lessons of life."[13] Elsewhere, he said, "I have found in different times and places, the liberal, the Catholic and the German air quite possible to breathe."[14] George Herbert Palmer once said of Santayana that "he had Hume in his bones."

In Santayana's assessment, religion ought to be the highest synthesis of our nature—making room for the gifts of one's senses, of one's affections, of one's country and its history, and of the science, morality and taste of one's day.[15] He admits that the circumstance of time and place account for much. "The Englishman finds that he was born a Christian, and therefore wishes to remain a Christian; but his Christianity must be his own, no less plastic and adaptable than his inner man; and it is an axiom with him that nothing can be obligatory for a Christian which is unpalatable to an Englishman."[16] That observation is followed by another: "Only a few years ago, if a traveler landing in England on a Sunday and entering an Anglican church, had been told that the country was Catholic and its church a branch of the Catholic Church, his astonishment would have been extreme. 'Catholic' is opposed in the first place to national and in the second place to Protestant."[17] What then is Protestantism? I see in it, says Santayana, three leading motifs: 1) a tendency to revert to primitive Christianity, 2) a call to moral and political reform, and 3) the acceptance of the religious witness of the "inner man." Santayana's appreciation of Protestantism is limited.[18] Santayana will say the "inner man," for the Catholic as for the materialist, is apt to be regarded as a pathological phenomenon.

Santayana's interest in Catholicism was far from superficial. He was appreciative of the integrity of its doctrine and recognized the folly of watering down key elements in the attempt to gain secular acceptance. His criticism of the "modernist movement" in the Catholic Church is as severe as any produced by a Catholic apologist. "The modernist," he writes, "wishes to reconcile the church and the world. Therein he forgets what Christianity came into the world to announce and why it is believed. . . . Having no ears for the essential message of Christianity, the modernist also has no eye for its history. . . . The church converted the world only partially and essentially; yet Christianity was outwardly established as the traditional religion of many nations. And why? Because, although the prophecies it relied on were strained and its miracles dubious, it furnished a needed sanctuary from the shames, sorrows, injustices, violence, and gathering darkness of earth."[19] The church, continues Santayana, is not only a sanctuary but a holy precinct where one might pursue sacred learning, philosophy, and theology in the midst of an ordered community life, perhaps within a superior artistic milieu. Speaking of the Catholic Church and particularly of the papacy and its material ambience, he writes, "Much has been added but nothing has been lost." In his palace full of pagan marbles the pope remains faithful to the teaching of Christ, promoting the basic truths of the New Testament. It is within the halls of the papacy that the gospel is still believed, not among the modernists.[20]

Santayana goes on to say that it is open for anyone to say that a nobler religion is possible without the trapping of the papacy. The ancient Greeks, Hindus or Mohammedans might well acquit themselves before an impartial tribunal of human nature and reason. But they are not Christians, nor do they wish to be. Neither are the modernists, "men of the Renaissance, pagan and pantheistic in their profound sentiment, to whom the hard and narrow realism of official Christianity is offensive just because it presupposes that Christianity is true."[21] "They (the modernists) think the weakness of the church lies in not following the inspirations of the age. But when this age is past, might not that weakness be a source of strength again."[22] "In a frank supernaturalism, in a tight clericalism, not in a pleasant secularization, lies the sole hope of the church."[23] "As to modernism, it is suicide."[24]

What civic task does religion perform that obliges Santayana to defend its integrity against those who would dilute its message? The answer lies in Santayana's conviction that poetic knowledge possesses cognitive value both for the speculative insight it provides and for the guidance it offers in the practical order. Religion, when confused with a record of facts or natural laws, is deflected from its proper course, but when seen as poetry it becomes a guide to life.[25]

Religion has the same original relation to life as poetry has to life. "Like poetry, it improves the world only by imagining it improved, but not content with making this addition to the mind's furniture—an addition which might be useful and ennobling—it thinks to confer a more radical benefit by persuading mankind that in spite of appearances the world is really such or that rather arbitrary idealization has pointed it. . . . Religion remains an imaginative achievement, a symbolic representation of moral reality which may have a most important function in vitalizing the mind and in transmitting, by way of parables, the lessons of experience."[26] Santayana saw in Christ an idealization of virtue which men even with all their wayward tendencies still recognize as worthy of imitation. The blessing which Christ bequeathed "was the image of himself upon the cross, whereby men might be comforted in their own sorrows, rebuked in their worldliness, driven to put their trust in the supernatural, and united, by their common indifference to the world, in one mystic brotherhood."[27] "As men learned these lessons . . . they began what they felt to be an imitation of Christ."[28] But religion has its negative side. It is at "the same time an incidental deception; and this deception, in proportion as it is strenuously denied to be such, can work infinite harm in the world and in the conscience."[29] In this judgment Dewey would concur.

Santayana continues, "The feeling of reverence should itself be treated with reverence, although not at a sacrifice of truth, with which alone, in the end reverence is compatible. Nor have we any reason to be intolerant of the partialities and contradictions which religion displays. Were we dealing with a science such contradictions would have to be instantly solved or removed; but when we are concerned with the poetic interpretation of experience, contradiction means only variety, and variety means spontaneity, wealth of resource, and a nearer approach to total adequacy."[30]

"The present age is a critical one," Santayana was saying in 1937, "and interesting to live in. The civilization characteristic of Christendom has not disappeared, yet another civilization has begun to take its place. We still understand the value of religious faith. . . . On the other hand the shell of Christendom is broken. The unconquerable mind of the East, the pagan past, the industrial socialistic, future confront it with equal authority. Our whole life and mind is saturated with the slow upward filtration of a new spirit—that of an emancipated, atheistic, international democracy."[31]

I said a moment ago that I thought Santayana's appreciation of religion might be related to his theory of knowledge. For Santayana, religion as poetry is a way of knowing. As poetry, it is not radically different from other forms of knowing, pre-scientific and scientific, which grope toward but never achieve final adequacy. Santayana acknowledges the distinction between speculative and practical knowledge. Speculative knowledge, as Plato taught, focuses upon the essence of things, but Santayana tempers his Platonic impulse with a bit of realism. Considered abstractly, things have natures which transcend the here and now and our limited awareness of them; concretely no particular instance exhausts the perfection possible to the class. The nature or "class essence" resembles an ideal which things themselves approximate in varying degrees. The things of experience may be said to participate in the eternal essence which our knowledge approximates in varying degrees. Yet it is things considered in their particular concreteness which are the primary object of our scientific knowledge. Santayana stresses the validity of pre-scientific or common sense knowledge. Science builds upon the pre-scientific. The ancients knew that one of its most useful metals—silver—possesses a certain hue, is malleable, is relatively light in weight, and tarnishes. Modern science differs in that it can tell us why silver has all of these properties. Science itself is open ended and is in some sense fragmentary; all human knowledge is approximate. Although these insights may be commonplace, significant is Santayana's conviction that types of knowledge function differently in specific situations.

Religion as cognitive not only unifies various modes of knowing but integrates knowledge with emotion. In religion, cognition, both sensory and intellectual, and appetition are unified and given expression in religious constructs from the Sermon on the Mount to the Gothic architecture of the High Middle Ages. Religion as poetry is at once insight and admonition. It can both lend appreciation to the beauty of nature and direct human activity. In so doing it sanctifies what perhaps otherwise would be humdrum. Through its rituals, it solemnizes the important occasions of life, i.e., birth, puberty, marriage and death and in doing so it gives rise to some of the most delightful feasts of the year. Religion is troubling only when its high priests do not recognize its true character, when they take literally its metaphors, or look upon it as productive of knowledge not garnered from human experience.

Readers unsympathetic to Santayana may find his interpretation reminiscent of the Averroistic one, namely, the view that religion is merely philosophical truth made accessible to the masses. The enlightened know that religion taken literally is a lie; and if one has no taste for metaphor, one must reject it. Thus John Smith could write with perception in the preface to the 1962 edition of his work, *The Spirit of American Philosophy*, "The American mind, as Santayana himself saw, is voluntaristic and not contemplative; it is moral and moralistic rather than aesthetic; it would sooner give up religion altogether than retain it as mere poetry."[32] Was Santayana something of a prophet, perhaps a prophet without honor? In his lifetime, Santayana produced no disciples, nor did he want them. Today, however, there is a Santayana Society and a newsletter, *Overheard in Seville*, and in 1992, there was a major Santayana conference in Avila to commemorate the fiftieth anniversary of his death.

John Smith, one of few historians to exclude Santayana from the American canon, defends his position in his book, *The Spirit of American Philosophy*, a study that examines the thought of Peirce, James, Royce, Dewey and Whitehead, by saying "I have not discussed him (Santayana) in this study, for it seems to me that despite his presence in the 'golden age' of American philosophy his thought is not representative of the main drift of American thinking."[33] And certainly it was not; Santayana himself recognized it. At first opportunity he fled New England for Europe, eventually ending his years in the Eternal City. He loved the labyrinth of the old streets of Rome, the Pantheon, Michelangelo's *Moses*, and the Forum from the top of the Capitoline. He loved to meditate seated in the Basilica of San Giovanni in Laterano, the Pope's own church, amidst the baroque Titans lining its columns. Intellectually he remained a pupil of the Enlightenment philosophy which he learned as a student while at Harvard: he remained steadfast in his materialism, culturally at home only among the artifacts of spirit whose transcendent source he denied. I am certain that he understood and appreciated a statue found in the Borghese Gallery in Rome, a statue carved by the seventeenth-century sculptor, Gian Lorenzo Bernini (1590–1680). In his splendid marble treatise, Bernini captured the ancient reverence for the transcendent as he depicts Aeneas, Anchises, and Ascanius fleeing Troy—Aeneas in the prime of life rescuing his aged parent who holds aloft the household shrines and his son who carries a lamp with the hearth fire. Santayana would have it no other way in spite of his disbelief.

Although Santayana spent his last years in Rome, his philosophy of religion has little in common with classical Latin writers or with their medieval commentators. Cicero, Seneca, and Macrobius all approached religion, not as a cultural artifact, but as a moral virtue. Piety, they commonly held, is a species of justice, the habit of paying one's debt to the gods. The religious act is primarily an act of homage, whatever its specific manifestation in prayer or sacrifice. In the words of Cicero, there is "no nation or tribe so uncultured that it does not acknowledge some sort of deity," and consequently, none without worship. The word "religion" itself implies as much. As Aquinas reminds us, Cicero found the origin of the word in the verb *re legit* (to ponder over, to read again), Augustine in the verb *re eligere* (to re-elect) and Lactantius in the verb *re ligare* (to bind back).

From the classical point of view, religion begins in an acknowledgment of several facets of reality, namely, that there is a god or gods, that reality consists in more than spatio-temporal-physical and mental events, that history is guided and controlled by a non-human force, and that individual existence does not terminate with the cessation of bodily processes. For the enlightened Roman, assent to those propositions is generated by philosophical considerations: for the masses assent is produced either by intuition or by a more or less gratuitous act of faith.

The twentieth century religious mind tends to the conviction, shared by Santayana, that modern philosophy has undermined what was formerly regarded as evidence for the existence of God, and that, consequently, religious faith is a completely gratuitous act. In the eighteenth century, Kant could boast that he has destroyed reason in order to make way for faith. In the nineteenth century, Kirkegaard is anxious to leap into the dark.

But to the mind schooled in the tradition of Plato, Aristotle, the Stoics, and Aquinas, faith cannot be a leap into the dark. Assent must be rational, meaning that what is proposed for belief must be not only internally consistent but must cohere with what is known through experience and demonstration.

Against such a backdrop, the art of paying homage to the divine, its attendant ritual, feasts, architecture, painting, literature, and other fine arts may be appreciated as human artifacts. But they are robbed of their intrinsic intelligibility when the wisdom, philosophical and theological, which generated them is thought to be mere poetry.

Santayana's materialism leads him to deny the existence of God, yet he remains a cultured non-believer. He cannot bring himself to deny the human worth of the religiously inspired literature and other artifacts which he holds to be among the treasures of the world. No iconoclast is he. Yet even from his own vantage point, one may doubt that those arts, deprived of their rationale, will continue to thrive, though art does not have to be created from a religious perspective to be in some sense sacral. That which is driven by an ideological perspective at variance with the spiritual component of human nature is likely to fail. A cursory acquaintance with the proletarian art of the twentieth century suggests that it exists on a much lower plane than the religiously inspired art of the high Middle Ages, or of the Italian Renaissance, or of the Baroque. Experience teaches that materialisms of any variety have an almost built-in debilitating effect on the arts.

One is tempted to ask: What would Santayana say if he were writing today? Would he still adhere to the nineteenth century rationalism which he embraced as a youth. With the methods and assumptions of modern science virtually destroying turn-of-the-century positivistic philosophy, would Santayana adopt a much more comprehensive synthesis, one rationally open to experience, science, philosophy, and revelation. Of course there is no way of knowing.

Perhaps Santayana's greatest contribution as an interpreter of religion is his appreciation of its integrity when it is well crafted and his acknowledgment of the positive role it plays in the lives of many. For the contemporary reader, he remains something of a snob, an enlightened snob, still delightful to read, but not a sure guide.

NOTES

1. R. M. Harré, *Essays on Religion and Education* (Oxford, England: The Clarendon Press, 1992), 1.

2. Harré, *Essays*, 25.

3. Lenn Goodman, *On Justice: An Essay in Jewish Philosophy* (New Haven, Conn.: Yale University Press, 1991).

4. Goodman, *On Justice*, 33.

5. "John Dewey on the Role of Religion in Society" in *The New Scholasticism*, vol. LI, 3, Summer 1977, 303–327.

6. *Leçons de Sociologie: Physique des moeurs et du droit*, trans. as *Professional Ethics and Civic Morals* (Glencoe, Ill.: The Free Press, 1958), 60–61, 93 ff.

7. Sigmund Freud, *The Future of an Illusion*, in The Standard Edition of the *Complete Psychological Works of Sigmund Freud*, 24 vols., ed. James Strackey (London: Hogarth Press and Institute of Psycho-Analysis, 1986), vol. XXI, 38.

8. Freud to Marie Bonaparte, March 1928. Ernest Jones, *The Life and Work of Sigmund Freud*, 3 vols., vol. III, 447. *Complete Correspondence of Sigmund Freud and Ernest Jones, 1908–1939*, ed. R. Andrew Paskaukas (Cambridge, Mass.: Harvard University Press, 1993).

9. The author of *Darkness at Noon* and the *Sleepwalkers* writes at the end of a book length study: "Lilies that fester smell far worse than weeds: both India and Japan seem to be spiritually sicker, more estranged from a living faith than the West. They are at opposite ends of the Asian spectrum, whose center is occupied by the vastness of China, one of the world's oldest cultures; yet it proved even less resistant against the impact of a materialistic ideology. The nation which had held fast for two and a half millennia to the teaching of Confucius, Lao-Tse and the Buddha, succumbed to the atheistic doctrine formulated by the son of a German lawyer, and has become the most accomplished robot state this side of science fiction. To look to Asia for mystic enlightenment and spiritual guidance has become as much of an anachronism as to think of America as the Wild West" (*The Lotus and the Robot* (New York: Macmillan, 1961), 27.

10. Preface to vol. VII, *The Works of George Santayana*, "On the Unity of My Earlier and Later Philosophy" (New York: Charles Scribner Sons, 1937), xiii–xiv.

11. George Santayana, *Interpretations of Poetry and Religion* (New York: Charles Scribner & Sons, 1921), v.

12. George Santayana, *The Idea of Christ in the Gospels* (New York: Charles Scribner & Sons, 1946).

13. George Santayana, *Persons and Places* (Cambridge, Mass.: MIT Press, 1986), 419.

14. George Santayana, *Soliloquies in England and Later Soliloquies*, (New York: Charles Scribner & Sons, 1937), 189.

15. Santayana, *Soliloquies*, 77.

16. Santayana, *Soliloquies*, 77.

17. Santayana, *Soliloquies*, 77.

18. Santayana, *Soliloquies*, 78.

19. George Santayana, *Winds of Doctrine*, in *The Works of George Santayana*, Triton edition, vol. VII (New York: Charles Scribner's Sons, 1937), 45.

20. Santayana, *Winds*, 47.

21. Santayana, *Winds*, 47.

22. Santayana, *Winds*, 47–48.

23. Santayana, *Winds*, 49.

24. Santayana, *Winds*, 49.

25. Santayana, *Interpretations of Poetry*, 289.

26. George Santayana, *The Life of Reason*, vol. IV (New York: Charles Scribner's Sons, 1933), 9–10.

27. Santayana, *Idea of Christ*, 250–251.

28. Santayana, *Idea of Christ*, 251.

29. Santayana, *Idea of Christ*, 10.

30. Santayana, *Idea of Christ*, 10–11.

31. Santayana, *Winds*, 5.

32. John Smith, *The Spirit of American Philosophy*, rev. ed. (Albany: State University of New York Press, 1983), xiii.

33. Smith, *Spirit of American Philosophy*, xiii.

Chapter Eleven

Indestructible Islam

One's attitude toward Islam is likely to be determined by one's attitude to Christianity. Western culture is so bound up with its classical and Christian sources that, given an historical perspective, the two are inseparable. Romantic interpretations of Islam speak of its beneficent presence in the West, overlooking its history of conquest, subjugation, and intolerance. From its inception, that is, from the preaching of the prophet Mohammed, Islam has been willing to use the sword to accomplish its ends, subjecting conquered peoples either to accept Islam or to suffer penalties ranging from taxation to death.[1] A disposition to look upon Islam as just another religion somehow occupying a place in the West on par with Christianity as a component of Western civilization ignores its adversarial character.

It is currently fashionable among the politically insouciant to distinguish between "Westernized moderate" Muslims and "radical" or "extreme" Muslims. The distinction may have some merit, but it blurs a fundamental truth. All Muslims subscribe to the principles enunciated in the Koran (*Qur_A_*), principles, which however interpreted, unite them as brothers in a common cause and which unify them into a spiritual force aimed at world domination, a spiritual force intrinsically hostile to the West and especially to the Christianity which formerly unified the West. One cannot ignore this de facto teaching of Islam throughout the world, nor can one easily overlook the failure of moderate Islam to condemn the rhetoric and violence of the extreme.

Apart from the terrorist actions of September 11, 2001, a contemporary view of Islam must acknowledge its militant character. Mohammedanism stands alone among world religions in sanctioning violence.[2] Only in Islam do we find a fanatical pursuit for converts coupled with a drive to world domination. In Sudan today, Christians are attacked, killed, and butchered in the name of Islam; women and children are sold into slavery. In Nigeria, Muslim majority communities attack Christian communities that resist the imposition of Islamic law. In Saudi Arabia and other Middle Eastern countries, churches are not permitted, and Christian symbols in every form are forbidden, as is Christian literature. Christian artifacts are searched out and destroyed. During the Gulf War American troops were prevented from attending Mass; even the celebration of Thanksgiving Day on the occasion of a visit by the president of the United States was forbidden. During the Iran-Iraq and Gulf wars Saddam Hussein specified that Christians be used as mine sweepers. In Indonesia death that has been inflicted on Christian communities is justified by passages in the Koran that permit militancy against those who reject Allah. These actions are perceived as sanctioned by Shari'ah, that is, Islamic law.

The most comprehensive concept of Islam at the practical level is undoubtedly that of the Shari'ah, "the highway of the righteous life leading to God," the sum of divine commands to man. It includes law, moral principles, and the creed to which every Muslim must subscribe. The Shari'ah is grounded in four sources: the Koran, tradition, consensus of the community, and personal interpretation. Thus it may be misleading to speak of Islamic law in the abstract. Although based on the Koran, Islamic law varies today by country and by geographic region. Attempts to relate the Shari'ah to modern times as a practical system of law are confronted with a chasm between a Westernized, modernist minority and the conservative mass of the Muslim population. The reforms adopted by progressive urban Muslim societies have little significance for traditionalist communities in the rural areas which constitute the great majority of its adherents. Officials interpret Islamic law in the light of their own education and training.

Islamic law is severe in the penalties prescribed for offenses. Shari'ah is broadly divided into duties the individual owes to Allah and those that he owes to his fellow man. For specific crimes the punishment is usually fixed. Traditionally offenses against the person, from assault to homicide are punishable by retaliation, the offender being subject to precisely the same treatment as his victim. Offenses of this type are regarded as a civil injury and not a crime in the technical sense; it is the family and not the state which is entitled to retribution.

For apostasy, extramarital sex, and homosexuality the penalty is death; the same for highway robbery. Amputation of the hand is mandated for theft; 100 lashes for fornication; 80 lashes for unproved accusation of unchastity and for the drinking of any intoxicant.

The Koran preaches equality, yet in most Muslim countries a woman's place is determined by a man's will. In Koranic law, a husband can prevent his wife from traveling abroad; a father can marry off his daughter against her will, and she by law must obey. The Koran gives a husband the right to beat or scourge a disobedient wife. An adulterous woman is subject to death by stoning. Moreover, Muslims refuse to recognize laws that differ from theirs and call other people "infidels" who do not worship as they. To be born into a Muslim society means to be a Muslim for life, subject to the consequences of apostasy.

Reflecting on the militant character of Islam, one cannot easily dismiss statements such as the following: "It is the duty of every Muslim to stand up with the Afghan people and fight against America." When Sheik Hamoud al-Shuabi was asked, "Should all Americans be their target," he replied, "There is no difference between someone who approves of the war or supports it with money and one who is actively fighting."[3] In Saudi Arabia, youth have been taught not only to hate America but that anyone who is not a Muslim is an enemy. They are taught the sanctity of martyrdom as they kill their enemies.[4]

How did this come to be? Is violence inseparable from the teaching of the Prophet? The history of Islam is instructive. The Mohammedan era begins in 622, the date of the flight of Mohammed from Mecca, where he had been persecuted, to Medina. In instructing his followers to pray, Mohammed at first had them turn toward Jerusalem. Later he instructed his followers to turn toward Mecca and to fulfill at Mecca those ancient pilgrimage rites instituted by Abraham and Ishmael. But Mecca was governed by a hostile tribe and not accessible to Mohammed's followers. This situation provided the impetus to subdue Mecca. Mohammed encouraged his followers not only to conquer Mecca but to intercept and raid the caravans of merchants going to and fro. Subsequent military pressure and diplomacy managed to unite disparate tribes throughout Arab lands. Emphasizing confessional pride, communal solidarity, Mohammed taught that brothers in faith are united more closely by religion than they are by blood. They were prohibited from fighting each other, but they could raid non-Muslims. This enabled the community to expand through the subjugation of others.

Among the community of faith there were undoubtedly those who made a sincere conversion and who really believed, but there were many more who, like the Meccan traders, found outward conformity profitable and who then contributed time and effort on behalf of the spread of Islam.

Mohammed preached to a society ripe for reform. The decline of the Roman Empire had left a complicated and fatigued society. In Egypt, Syria, and the East there was everywhere slavery, excessive taxation, and the bureaucratic government interference in the lives of ordinary people. "To all of this," writes Hilaire Belloc, "Islam came as a vast relief and a solution of social and economic strain. The slave who admitted that Mohammed was the prophet of God and that the new teaching had, therefore, divine authority, ceased to be a slave. The slave who adopted Islam was henceforth free. The debtor who 'accepted' was rid of his debts. . . . The small farmer was relieved not only of his debts but of crushing taxation."[5]

Much of Mohammed's teaching consisted of ideas that were peculiar to Christianity, ideas which distinguished Catholicism from paganism—for example, the unity and omnipotence of God, His personal nature, goodness, timelessness, and providence. Mohammed recognized God's creative power as the origin of all things as well as His sustenance (conservation) of all that He had brought into being. In his teaching, he acknowledged good and evil spirits, such as Christendom recognized; the immortality of the human soul; personal moral responsibility and accountability after death, including punishment and reward. Although denying His divinity, Mohammed gave to Christ the highest reverence and venerated His mother, the Lady Miriam.

In the beginning, Islam was regarded by Byzantine Catholics as a Christian heresy, not as a new religion, but soon its vitality and endurance gave it the appearance of a new religion.[6] Christians who were contemporary with its rise saw it not as a denial but as an adaptation and a misinterpretation of the Gospels and the teachings of the apostles.

Within the span of a hundred years Islamic warriors conquered Syria, Mesopotamia, Egypt, the whole of North Africa, and Spain. Within a lifetime after the death of Mohammed, half of the wealth and nearly half of the Christian Roman Empire was in the hands of Mohammedan masters and officials. Arabic military power conferred on its caliphs, who were at once its generals and successors of the Prophet, not only absolute authority but great wealth.

The Arab conquest in the seventh century was the starting point of a new civilization in the southern basin of the Mediterranean. Abu Bakr, Mohammad's first successor during his brief reign (632–634) led the armies of Muslims who reached southern Iraq and Palestine. Umar ibn al-Kattab (634–644), the second successor to Mohammed, conquered Syria, Palestine, Persia, and Egypt as far as the Cyrene and even Tripoli. When the Ommiad caliphs under Mo´awiya took up residence in Damascus in 661, the campaign against Constantinople began. In 672, the city was besieged by land and sea in an attempt that was to last for seven years. In the West, Carthage fell into their hands and was leveled around 698. The conquest of Andalusia followed, with Mohammedan troops reaching as far north as the Loire in 731. Mingling with the peoples they subdued, the Arabs showed an extraordinary power of assimilation. Their culture had nothing original about it, so they were able to reap great benefits from the Hellenistic culture, exploiting the treasures of Greek thought.

In the East the intellectual and artistic legacy of the past, especially as diffused by the highly intelligent Syrians, enabled the Arabs to evolve, in Baghdad, Damascus, Cairo, and Córdoba. Those centers fostered a brilliant culture, one far superior to anything found in the West at the time.

Islam in its early centuries, in the period we call the Dark Ages, particularly in the eighth and ninth centuries, produced the highest material civilization in the world. In that period Islam was far more lettered than was Christendom. It became for centuries the caretaker of the texts of Aristotle, the mathematics and natural science of the early Greek and Roman writers. No one who surveys that period can deny the rich and brilliant society of Moslem Spain, the age of the Fatimid caliphate and the caliphate of Córdoba in the tenth and eleventh centuries. Even the Norman kings of Sicily adopted the outward forms of the court life of the Islamic world and became generous patrons of Moslem scholars and men of letters.[7]

Medieval Europe inherited Greek philosophy indirectly through the channel of Syrian, Persian, and Arabic scholars, scientists, and philosophers. In the early centuries of Christendom, Greek philosophy was imported into Asia by Christian scholars who had studied in Athens before Emperor Justinian ordered the closing of the philosophic schools in 529 A.D. The Christian school in Edessa, founded in 563, taught the philosophy of Aristotle and the medicine of Hippocrates and of Galen. When the Syrians converted to Christianity, they had to learn Greek to read Sacred Scripture. Greek theology followed and with it Greek culture. When the school at Edessa was closed, its professors migrated to Persia. By that time many philosophical and scientific works had been translated from Greek into Syriac, which explains why even such an epoch-making event as the founding of Islam by Mohammed did not stop the spread of Greek philosophy.

The dynasty of the Abbassides caliphs, established in 750 by Aboul-Abbas whose successors were to reside in Baghdad from 762 until the middle of the thirteenth century, became an important catalyst in the transmission of Greek learning. Syrian scholars were soon employed as translators by the Baghdad caliphs. Continuing the same work under their new masters, the Persian scholars began to translate Greek texts into Arabic, sometimes directly from the Greek, sometimes from previously made Syriac translations. Among the authors translated were Aristotle, Euclid, Archimedes, Ptolemy, Hippocrates, Galen, and Theophrastus. Syriac scholars successfully transmitted Greek learning to the Arabs, who passed it on to the Jews and eventually to the theologians of the Christian West. The twentieth-century historian of philosophy Etienne Gilson provides the chronicle.

In his *History of Christian Philosophy in the Middle Ages*, Gilson writes, "Like Christian faith, Islamic faith soon felt the need of an intellectual interpretation, be it only in order to correct the literal interpretations of the Koran upheld by the fundamentalists of those times."[8] There soon emerged a school of Muslim theologians whose use of Greek philosophical insight to interpret the Koran was challenged by other theologians who repudiated the use of

Greek philosophy. This controversy resulted in yet another generation of Arabic thinkers who, without losing touch with their religion, began to pursue philosophy for its own sake. Ibn Rushd (d. 1198), known in the Latin world as Averroes, writing as a philosopher, was careful to leave the door open for revelation, but this did not satisfy the theologians schooled in the tradition of Al Ghazali, who took it upon themselves to challenge Averroes. In both Muslim and Jewish worlds their profoundly religious civilization created for philosophers a new problem unknown in classical antiquity, namely, the relation of faith to reason.[9] Gilson tells us, "A curious consequence of this situation was that, since Islamic theology was progressively separating itself from Greek philosophy up to the point of repudiating it, the great Christian theologians were to become pupils of the Mohammedan philosophers much more than the Mohammedan theologians."[10] Arabic philosophy became a major source of medieval scholasticism. Once Aristotle was translated into Arabic, his influence spread to the limits of Islam's dominion. Joseph Pieper describes this intellectual saga at length. "Within this cultural sphere, then, were written the great commentaries on Aristotle whose authors are mentioned on almost every page of the theological *Summae* of the thirteenth century."[11] Al Kindi, Al Farabi, Avicenna, Averroes are names whose philosophy is known to all contemporary students of St. Thomas Aquinas. To study Aquinas is also to study medieval Arabic philosophy. No major Catholic university is without its specialist in medieval Arabic thought. It remains part of the scholastic curriculum.

One can marvel at the way in which the mind of Western Christendom reconquered the lost world of Hellenic science and annexed the alien world of Moslem thought without losing its spiritual or religious integrity. The cultural historian Christopher Dawson gives an account of the courtly culture of medieval Europe in the second half of the twelfth century, speaking of it as the fruit of the Crusades. He describes the development of "a new aristocratic culture, which traveled in the opposite direction from the Crusades but along the same roads, from the Mediterranean to Northern France and Italy, and ultimately to Germany, England and Wales."[12] The last Norman kings of Sicily adopted the outward forms of the court life of the Islamic world and became generous patrons of Moslem scholars and men of letters. It was through music and poetry and the vision of a new delightful way of life that the influence of the southern Mediterranean penetrated feudal society.

Following the lead of Córdoba, Toledo became a center of translation in the twelfth century. Toledo Archbishop Raymond of Sauvetat (1126–1151) established a school of translators which continued its activity for more than a century.[13] Scholars translated into Latin the whole of the Aristotelian corpus in its Arabic form. They also produced versions of the principal works of the great Moslem and Jewish philosophers, including Al Kindi, Al Farabi, Avicenna, Ibn Gabriol, and Al Ghazali. In a cosmopolitan effort, Jews, Arabs, and Greeks cooperated with Spaniards, Italians, and Englishmen. Averroes, born in Córdoba in 1126, jurist, physician, and philosopher, became for the West in the thirteenth century "the Commentator" on Aristotle. His influence was so great that the philosophy of the Italian Renaissance has with some justification been called Averroism.[14] Moses Maimonides, the great Jewish thinker of the twelfth century, was likewise born in Córdoba (1135). Maimonides, like Averroes, turned to the teaching of Aristotle as he prepared his *Guide for the Perplexed*, a book addressed to those whose faith in biblical revelation had been shaken by philosophy and science. Sometimes called the Jewish scholastic *Summa,* it was written in Arabic.

Josef Pieper provides this comparison between the state of learning at the time in Córdoba and Paris. "Here on the one hand was a great wealth of Arabic-Jewish philosophy; and on the other hand the schools of the West were at the same time producing little of value aside from strictly theological studies. The education available at the Faculty of Arts in Paris around 1200 rested chiefly on the "'cult of law' and 'contained nothing that even remotely resembled a philosophical view of the whole of reality.'"[15]

Why did not the Arabs, in the Middle Ages so far advanced in civilization, so powerful in aims, not eventually attain the leadership of the world's culture? Bernard Lewis, the noted Middle East scholar, pointedly asks: *What Went Wrong?* and writes, "In the course of the twentieth century it became abundantly clear in the Middle East and indeed all over the lands of Islam that things had indeed gone badly wrong. Compared to its millennial rival, Christendom, the world of Islam had become poor, weak and ignorant."[16] From the sixteenth century onward, as Europe advanced in military, economic, and political affairs, Islam's fortunes dramatically reversed. As Lewis remarks, "Middle Eastern technology and science ceased to develop, precisely at the moment when Europe, more specifically Western Europe, was advancing to new heights."[17]

Gustav Schnurer, writing in the early part of the last century, suggests that the reason may be intrinsic. Lacking the fullness of Christianity, Islam lacked the determinant civilizing force associated with the Gospels. "Islam, by its principle of spreading belief with the sword, lacked the calm and organizing force possessed by Christianity, which is bent on developing the intellect and disciplining the will."[18] Christian teaching gave women equal status to men. In preaching not war but peace, it gave a powerful impulse to the social order. Insisting on self-discipline, upon regulation of conscience consistent with the Gospels, Christianity produced a society quite different from Islam, which, devoid of these principles, could form only states with despotic governments.

Christianity laid the foundation for the development of the individual, no less than that of the nation, combining national strength with the greatest possible freedom of the individual consonant with peace and order.[19]

Bernard Lewis does not provide a clear-cut answer to his question, "What Went Wrong?" He is not satisfied with the suggestion that the disparity between Islam and the West is not the result of Islam's decline but of a Western upsurge since that dates to the eighteenth century if not the Renaissance. Addressing a number of factors, economic, military, and political that undoubtedly played a role, he hints that the cause may be much deeper, though he does not reach anything approaching Schnurer's conclusion. "Reading Mr. Lewis's book," Karen Elliot House comments, "one is reminded that there are many reasons for the humbling of Islam and the rise of the West, ranging from superiority at ship building, which allowed small countries like Holland and Portugal to become powers, to Islam's subjugation of women, which squandered the talent of half of its population. But the fundamental reason—best grasped if we read between the lines of *What Went Wrong*—derives from major differences between Christendom and the Islamic world."[20] Those differences cannot be ignored. Islam is a religion that commands obedience, not understanding, one that preaches conversion through force, not persuasion.

Perhaps the most conspicuous but not the most profound difference between Islamic and Christian civilizations lies in the status of women. The Turkish writer, Evliya Celebri, visiting Catholic Vienna in 1665, observed, "They [women] are honored and respected out of love for Mother Mary." The fruit of Islam's subjugation of women is felt not only in the family but in society as a whole. In this as in so many of its prescriptions and prohibitions, Islam is devoid of principled law. Islamic law is positive law. It is not grounded in metaphysics or in a philosophy of nature and of human nature. Its arbitrary character stands at variance with Roman law and British common law, sources of the rule of law as we know it in the West.

Another difference is the role of Islamic clerics in the governance of the state. Christendom from its inception, following Christ's admonition, "Render unto Caesar the things that are Caesar's and unto God the things that are God's,"[21] developed an understanding of the different roles played by church and state. As Augustine made clear in *The City of God*, the church is concerned with worship and with the spiritual and intellectual sustenance of its adherents; the state is responsible for the common good, the material well being of its citizens. Islam accepted no such dichotomy; the church is the state; the state is the church.

These differences are reflected in the discomfort Muslims feel when living among infidels under alien law. While Islam through the centuries was able to accommodate itself to those it conquered, it has proved unable to live with those it could not conquer. Witness its drive to form separate states under its own rule in Bosnia, Greece, the Philippines, and Indonesia and even to form a separate community in cities such as Birmingham, England.

Given its universally acknowledged material failure and its refusal to live peacefully in the West, what does the future hold? In the mid-decades of the last century, Hilaire Belloc warned, "The power of Islam may at any moment re-arise."[22] How could that be? Islam, Belloc tells us, is indestructible:

> It has kept those Christian doctrines which are evidently true and which appeal to the common sense of millions, while getting rid of priestcraft, mysteries, sacraments, and all of it. It proclaims and practices human equality. It avows a commitment to justice and forbids usury. By its own light, it produces a society in which men are happier and feel their own dignity more than in any other [society]."[23]

Never mind the disparity between the Shari'ah of the professors and actual practice. Its doctrines, says Belloc, are "its strength and that is why it still converts people and endures and will perhaps return to power in the near future."[24] Belloc puts the question forcefully, "Will not perhaps the temporal power of Islam return and with it the menace of an armied Mohammedan world which will shake off the dominance of Europeans—still nominally Christian—and reappear again as the prime enemy of our civilization?"[25] Belloc is convinced that we fail to recognize that religion is at the root of all political movements and changes; Dawson would add, "the root of all great cultures." Islam may be physically paralyzed, but morally it is intensely alive. There may exist an unstable equilibrium between its material incapacity and its moral vigor, but that is not likely to remain. No one can deny Islam's vitality. As a body of doctrine it is relatively simple. Its sacred book, its code of morality, and its organized system of prayer attract converts wholesale from those quarters unexposed to Christianity.

Given the universal breakup of Christianity in Europe, the culture based upon it has undergone a similar decay. The same is not true of Islam. The whole spiritual strength of Islam remains, from Egypt to Indonesia.

Belloc's judgment is reinforced by that of George Santayana, who, in the passage quoted earlier, referred to "the shell of Christendom" as broken.[26] Since September 11 we have become accustomed to distinguishing, the "terrorists" and the Taliban from Islam itself, an Islam often romanticized in the halls of the academy. Absent Christianity, we may ask: Is the West able to defend itself against Islam? Within the present cultural context, is the "emancipated, atheistic, international democracy" feared by Santayana any match for a militant Islam which finds abhorrent the new barbarism which the West has willfully embraced. Belloc and others such as Lewis would not count on it.

NOTES

1. See the *Qur_A_*: S_rah 9.5 "And when the sacred months have passed, then kill the polytheists wherever you find them and capture them and besiege them and sit in wait for them at every place of ambush. But if they should repent, establish prayer, and give Zakah, let them [go] on their way." S_rah 9.14 "Fight them; All_h will punish them by your hands and will disgrace them and give you victory over them." S_rah 5.33 "Indeed the penalty for those who wage war against All_h and His Messenger and strive upon earth [to cause] corruption is none but that they be killed or crucified or that their hands and feet be cut off from opposite sides or that they be exiled from the land." S_rah 8.39 "And fight them until there is no fitnah (persecution) and the religion of all of it is for All_h," *The Qur_A_ Arabic Text with Corresponding English Meanings* (English edition, revised and edited by Saheeh International [Jeddah, Saudi Arabia: Abul-Qasim Publishing House, 1997]).

2. Many commentators allude to the Crusades of the Middle Ages as if they had political relevance to the present day. They are often cited as evidence that Islam has a justified grievance against the West, ignoring the fact that the Crusades were an attempt to recover Constantinople and the once Christian lands of Syria, Lebanon, and Egypt, lands that had fallen to Muslim conquest. The religious and other wars of Europe, similarly cited as evidence of violence, find no mandate in the New Testament or in Christian teaching in any period, which teaching, to the contrary, admonishes peace, long suffering, and forgiveness. Just war theory associated with Catholic moral teaching places severe restraint even on warfare undertaken in self-defense.

3. *New York Times*, 5 December, 2001, B1.

4. Cf. Dr. Sahr Muhammad Hatem of Riyahd in the London Arabic-language daily, *Al-Sharq Al-Awsat*, 21 December, 2001.

5. Hilaire Belloc, *The Great Heresies* (Rockford, Ill.: Tan Books, 1991), 45–46.; reprint of 1938 edition.

6. St. Thomas disputed the view that Mohammedanism is a Christian heresy and had some harsh things to say about Mohammed himself. Speaking of Mohammed, he writes, "He seduced the people by promises of carnal pleasure to which the concupiscence of the flesh goads us. His teaching also contained precepts that were in conformity with his promises, and he gave free reign to carnal pleasure. In all of this, as is not unexpected, he was obeyed by carnal men." Lacking any sign of a divine mandate, "Mohammed said that he was sent in the power of his arms—which were signs not lacking even to robbers and tyrants. What is more, no wise men, men trained in things divine and human, believed in him from the beginning. Those who believed in him were brutal men and desert wanderers, utterly ignorant of all divine teaching, through whose numbers Mohammed forced others to become his followers by the violence of his arms. Nor do divine pronouncements on the part of preceding prophets offer him any witness. On the contrary, he perverts almost all the testimonies of the Old and New Testaments by making them into fabrications of his own, as can be seen by anyone who examines his law. It was, therefore, a shrewd decision on his part to forbid his followers to read the Old and New Testaments, lest these books convict him of falsity." Thomas Aquinas, *Summa Contra Gentiles*, trans. Anton C. Pegis as

On the Truth of the Catholic Faith (Garden City, N.Y.: Hanover House, 1995), Book I, chap. 6.

7. Cf. Christopher Dawson, *Religion and the Rise of Western Culture, Gifford Lectures, 1948–1949* (London: Sheed & Ward, 1950), 184 ff.

8. Etienne Gilson, *History of Christian Philosophy in the Middle Ages* (New York: Random House, 1955), 182.

9. In addressing the faith/reason problem in his *Book of Religion,* Alfarabi held that religion is dependent on philosophy. He looked upon religion as political in character, having more to do with rulership than creed. The founder of a religion is referred to as a supreme ruler rather than as a prophet. "Religion is opinions and actions, determined and restricted with stipulations for a community by their first ruler." A virtuous ruler directs the community to its ultimate happiness, not to the goods of this world. Alfarabi, *The Political Writings*, trans. and annotated by Charles E. Butterworth (Ithaca, N.Y.: Cornell University Press, 2001), 93ff.

10. Gilson, *Christian Philosophy,* 183.

11. Joseph Pieper, *Scholastik,* trans. from the German by Richard and Clara Winson as *Scholasticism: Personalities and Problems of Medieval Philosophy* (London: Faber & Faber, 1960), 104.

12. Dawson, *Religion and the Rise,* 185.

13. Córdoba and Toledo were not the only centers of translation. The first rendering of the Koran into a Western language was made by Robertus Retenensis in 1143 at the request of Peter the Venerable, Abbot of Cluny. Cf. Arthur J. Arberry, *The Koran Interpreted* (London: George Allen & Unwin, 1955), 7.

14. Paul Oskar Kristeller, following certain French scholars, refers to it as "Paduan Averroism," tracing its origin to Salerno at the beginning of the twelfth century and then to other Italian universities in the thirteenth century. He finds it flourishing at Padua in the fifteenth and sixteenth centuries, where it continued to develop until the first part of the seventeenth century.

15. Pieper, *Scholasticism,* 105.

16. Bernard Lewis, *What Went Wrong* (New York: Oxford University Press, 2002), 151.

17. Lewis, *What Went Wrong*, 125.

18. Gustav Schnurer, *Kirche und Kultur im Mittelalter* (Paderborn: F. Schoningh, 1936), trans. George J. Undreiner (Patterson, N.J.: St. Anthony Guild Press, 1956), 440.

19. Schnurer, *Kirche*, 440.

20. *Wall Street Journal,* January 1, 2002, W-10.

21. Luke 20:25.

22. Belloc, *Heresies*, 42.

23. Belloc, *Heresies*, 55.

24. Belloc, *Heresies*, 5.

25. Belloc, *Heresies*, 73.

26. George Santayana, "Winds of Doctrine," in *The Works of George Santayana,* vol. VII (New York: Charles Scribner's Sons, 1937), 5.

Chapter Twelve

Science and the Shaping of Modernity: The Reciprocal Influence of Science and Culture

Cultural historians necessarily deal in broad generalizations. Whatever is affirmed of a period, a people, or a nation, no matter how well grounded by factual study and reflection, is subject to qualification. Exceptions to broad characterizations may always be found without mitigating the value of the broader insight. We grasp something when an author refers to the Greeks, to Roman civilization, to the Hellenic period, to Christendom, to the Benedictines, to the Renaissance, or to the Enlightenment. These designations, all generalizations formed by an examination of a host of particulars, indeed refer to something intelligible, something quite apart from the mind.[1] Generalization, of course, can be misleading or false as well as perceptive and true. There is always the danger of unscrupulous forces manipulating history for present purposes. Then, too, in the study of history there is always the propensity to judge the past in the light of contemporary categories of experience. It is axiomatic that one must banish from the mind the customary conceptions of one's own period before one can rightly understand the past. With that caveat in mind, this essay purports to examine with the aid of a host of distinguished twentieth-century scholars the reciprocal influence of science and culture with particular attention to the role of religion at the birth of modern science.

Detached narrative is rare, yet, for example, those acquainted with the lifelong work and studied objectivity of Christopher Dawson are likely to give credence to his insight when he speaks of the great movement of thought which passed over the ancient world about the middle of the first millennium B.C. "that turned away men's minds from the world of human experience to the contemplation of absolute and unchanging Being, from Time to Eternity."[2] There are few readers who are in a position to render the same judgment unaided. Similarly, Dawson is convincing when he writes that with the advent of Christ, "the Absolute and the Finite, God and the World were no longer conceived as two exclusive and opposed orders of being standing over and against one another in mutual isolation. The two orders interpenetrated one another."[3] Dawson's judgment is an invitation to reflection. He makes a like generalization about the advent of modern science and its medieval antecedents. Scholars are nearly unanimous in recognizing that something dramatic occurred in the culture of Europe around the turn of the eleventh century. Explanations vary, with some emphasizing technological advancement, others the recovery of Greek learning, still others the practical influence of Christianity.

In 1925 the distinguished American philosopher Alfred North Whitehead delivered the prestigious Lowell Lectures at Harvard University, lectures subsequently published as *Science and the Modern World*.[4] Those lectures were significant because Whitehead, for a predominately American audience, challenged the Enlightenment view that only with the repudiation of a religious world view could modern science have emerged from a dark age. Whitehead, it must be noted, was writing a generation before the in-depth studies of Marshall Clagett, A.C. Crombie, and Anneliese Maier, and before the monumental work of Pierre Duhem became available in English translation. Examining the relation between science and culture, Whitehead put to himself a fundamental question: Why did modern science emerge in the West during the sixteenth and seventeenth centuries when all the conditions required for its birth were seemingly in place in classical antiquity. That question has entered public consciousness again with the reemergence of militant Islam. Contemporary scholars in their attempt to understand an adversarial Islam ask why the scientific revolution that we associate with Europe bypassed Islam when for centuries Islam was in many respects at the forefront of human civilization and achievement. Bernard Lewis, in the volume previously cited, asks "Why did the great scientific break through occur in Europe and not as one might reasonably have expected in the richer, more advanced, and in many respects more enlightened realm of Islam?"[5]

Putting aside for the moment Lewis's somewhat romantic view of the "Golden Age of Islam," his question has been addressed, perhaps never more authoritatively, than by A.C. Crombie.[6] In the same vein, a more recent account of the development of modern science, one that we will subsequently discuss, is that of Stephen Gaukroger.[7] Crombie's research led him to the conclusion that the new science which began to percolate into Western Christendom in the twelfth century, although largely Arabic in form, was founded on the works of the ancient Greeks. The Arabs, Crombie relates, preserved and transmitted to medieval Europe a large body of Greek learning, adding to it to be sure, but what they added to its content was perhaps less important than the change they made in the conception and purpose for which science ought to be studied. The speculative or theoretical aspect of science interested them less than its application. In the judgment of Crombie, the most important and original contributions that the Arabs made to the history of European science were those of alchemy, magic, and astrology. This was due partly to the Arabic approach to the study of nature where power over nature, rather than rational explanation of fact, led enquirers to seek "the Elixir of Life," the magic properties of plants and minerals, instead of the causes of the properties of the things they experienced.[8]

It has been well documented that the Arabs themselves acquired their knowledge of Greek science from two sources: initially from Syriac intermediaries, but later directly from the Greeks of the Byzantine Empire. Their first encounter with Greek learning came from the Syriac-speaking Nestorian Christians of Eastern Persia.[9] The role which the Arabs played in the transmission of Aristotle to the West is an interesting and complicated story in itself and cannot be recounted here, but this much needs to be said: with the rapid expansion of Islam after Muhammad's death in 632, regions where Greek learning had previously been deposited came under Islamic domination. Under the Abbasid caliphs after 749, Muslims established contact with both Christians and Hellenized Persians. The Abbasid caliphs and other patrons of translating activity were primarily interested in works of immediate practical utility, i.e., technical treatises on medicine, astrology, logic, and the mathematical sciences.[10] "Partly through the growth of scholastic theology," David Lindberg tells us, "Islamic interests quickly expanded to encompass the whole of Platonic and Aristotelian philosophy. Texts already available in Syriac, the language of the Nestorian Christian community, were translated into the Arabic. Works not available in Syriac were rendered directly from Greek into Arabic."[11] The high-water mark of translations from Arabic to Latin came during the twelfth century. Lindberg finds that the story of the transmissions of Greek learning to the West is largely a tale of individual scholars responding in personal ways to unique historical circumstances. Yet there were important centers, such as Toledo and Palermo, where significant if not cooperative work was being done. In 1250, for example, the provincial chapter of the Dominicans in Toledo sent eight friars to the *studium arabicum* in Tunis. By that time the works of Aristotle were diffused and understood throughout the Latin West. Interest in Aristotle was accompanied by interest in the philosophical works of the great speculative thinkers al Kindi, al-Farabi, and Avicenna, all Persians. The most influential Arabic thinker of the period was undoubtedly Averroes (1126–1198) who was regarded as the interpreter of Aristotle par excellence and was frequently referred to simply as the "Commentator."

Perhaps the better focus, unlike that of Lewis, should be not upon what went wrong in Arabia but what went right within Christendom. Whitehead provides this insight: "My explanation is that the faith in the possibility of science, generated antecedently in the development of modern scientific theory, is the unconscious derivative from medieval theology."[12] "The Middle Ages," Whitehead claims, "formed one long training of the intellect in Western Europe in the sense of order. There may have been some deficiency with respect to practice. But the idea never for a moment lost its grip. It was predominantly an epoch of orderly thought, rationalistic through and through."[13] Yet for science, something more is necessary than a general sense of the order of things. Equally important is the habit of definite and exact thought, which Whitehead attributes to the Greek philosophers, a legacy carried through the Middle Ages. Whitehead, in this passage, is less interested in the metaphysics that undergirds induction than he is in the impact of technological advance and the reciprocal influence of the theoretical and the practical. "We owe to St. Benedict," he writes, "that the monasteries were the homes of practical agriculturalists, as well as saints, and artists and men of learning. The alliance of science and technology, by which learning is kept in contact with irreducible and stubborn facts, owes much to the practical bent of the early Benedictines. Modern science derives from Rome as well as from Greece and this Roman strain explains its gain in an energy of thought kept closely in contact with the world of facts."[14]

The medieval historian, Lynn White, Jr., later develops this theme in an article entitled "The Dynamo and the Virgin Reconsidered." Like Whitehead, he calls attention to the significant role that the Benedictines played in the history of Western technology, saying of St. Benedict that he was probably "the pivotal figure in the history of labor."[15] White, in comparing the status of labor in ancient Greece with its status in the later Middle Ages, finds that in the classical tradition, there is scarcely a hint of the dignity of labor. The civilizations of ancient Greece and Rome had rested on the backs of slaves. Reversing this Greek attitude toward labor was St. Benedict, by making labor part of the corporate life of his monastery, by adopting it not merely as a regrettable necessity but rather as an integral and spiritually valuable part of monastic discipline. White suggests that the Benedictine regard for the dignity of labor "marks a revolutionary reversal of the traditional attitude to labor: it is the high peak along the watershed separating the modern and ancient world. . . . Moreover, although St. Benedict had not intended that his monks should be scholars, a great tradition of learning developed in the abbeys following his *Rule*: for the first time the practical and the theoretical were involved in the same individual. The monk was the first intellectual to get dirt under his fingernails. He did not immediately launch into scientific investigation, but in his very person he destroyed the old artificial barrier between the empirical and the speculative, the manual and the liberal arts, and thus helped to create a social atmosphere favorable to scientific and technological development."[16] What Whitehead dimly saw, Crombie makes explicit in his well-documented *Medieval and Early Modern Science*,[17] a history of science from Augustine to Galileo, from its decay after the collapse of the Roman Empire in the West to its full flowering in the seventeenth century. He emphasizes what he believes are the two most significant results of twentieth-century scholarship: the essential continuity of Western scientific traditions from Greek time to our own, and the significance of medieval discussions of scientific methodology. Crombie's wide study has convinced him that the most significant changes in the history of science are always brought about by new conceptions of scientific procedure. It is Crombie's thesis that if modern science owes most of its success to the use of inductive and experimental procedure, then it owes a great deal to the philosophers of the thirteenth and fourteenth centuries who first produced an understanding of that experimental procedure. He credits them with transforming the Greek geometrical method into the experimental science of the modern era. Although the conception of scientific explanation accepted by Galileo, Harvey, and Newton is a theory of formal proof developed by Greek geometers and logicians, the distinctive feature of the seventeenth century, Crombie writes, is non-Greek in origin. It is a scientific method based on "a conception of how to relate a theory to observed facts it explained, the set of logical procedures . . . for constructing theories and for submitting them to experimental tests."[18] Whereas Aristotle distinguished natural science on the basis of subject matter, deriving three orders of abstraction—physics, mathematics, and metaphysics—the medieval mind tended to look upon this distinction as not one of subject matter but method of inquiry. The philosophers of the thirteenth century distinguished clearly among the kinds of questions to be asked under each level of enquiry. Crombie likens this to the role of linguistic analysis in our own time. The object of the experimental method worked out during this period was to discover and to define the conditions necessary and sufficient to uncover the experiential data. It was recognized that a theory defining these conditions could never be certain: it was necessary to "save the appearance" but it may not be "necessarily true" in the sense of being a *demonstrated* conclusion. The effect of this tendency to regard mathematics as a method rather than a domain or province of study was to change the kind of questions asked. Interest gradually shifted from the physical or metaphysical to the kind of question that could be answered by a mathematical theory within reach of experimental verification. The history of medieval science shifts to the working out of the consequences of this new approach to nature. Examples of this shift are seen in the sciences of statics, optics, and astronomy.[19]

Crombie is not alone in his view. Whitehead and Dawson imply as much.[20] Lynn Thorndike[21] and W.C. Bark[22] take similar views. Dawson makes much the same point when he compares the utilitarian view of science propounded by Roger Bacon in the fourteenth century with the speculative view of science entertained by the Greek mind. Bacon is obviously closer to the modern mind than to the Greek when he makes science an instrument of world conquest and exploitation. Dawson suggests that both the utilitarian view and the Greek view of science contributed to the European scientific tradition: "The pragmatic experimentation of the Baconian ideal could have borne no fruit apart from the intellectual training and discipline which were provided by Aristotelian scholasticism"[23]

Other scholarship suggests that it is from Robert Grosseteste[24] that Bacon derived his distinctive philosophical and scientific views. Both Dawson and Crombie accord Grosseteste a major role in the history of scientific theory using Grosseteste as a symbol of the fusion of two traditions. Crombie writes: "From the almost pure empiricism of such practical sciences of the twelfth century as practical mathematics, astronomy, and medicine, and the almost pure rationalism of theoretical speculation in contemporary philosophy on scientific method, he [Grosseteste] produced a science in which he tried to show the principles according to which the world of experience could be experimentally investigated and rationally explained."[25] Other important elements of Grosseteste's thought are his conception of physical nature, in which the essence or "form" is mathematically determined, and his conception of the immediate objective of inquiry as mathematical and predictive laws instead of Aristotelian essential definition. These concepts, Crombie maintains, were not without their effect for in the fourteenth century we find developments of mathematical technique designed to take advantage of the new methodology and conceptions of explanation. At the same time, extension of the use of experiment and mathematical abstraction had begun to produce results so striking that this movement in itself could well be called a "scientific revolution." Benjamin Farrington similarly attributes the success of Renaissance science to the technological revolution of the Middle Ages.[26] According to Farrington, when the classic works arrived in the West, the West was prepared. Medieval man had learned the use of natural resources and upon this had built a society in which humans were free from a large part of their former drudgery. Technical advance had led to social change. The slave had been replaced by the serf and the craftsman.[27] Concerning the relation of the new technology to slavery there are a number of theses. Lynn White, who has directed considerable attention to the subject, suggests that the development of medieval technology owes its impetus to the Christian teaching of the infinite worth of the individual and the Church's opposition to slavery. In his article, "Dynamo and Virgin Reconsidered" White notes that whereas Henry Adams can symbolize an age by the concept of "dynamo," the early Middle Ages can be characterized by the devotion shown to Our Lady. "St. Bernard's Cistercian monks were so devoted to the Virgin that every one of their hundreds of monasteries was dedicated to her; yet these White Benedictines seem often to have led the way in the use of power."[28] In a seminal article, entitled "Technology and Invention in the Middle Ages," White argues: "The chief glory of the later Middle Ages was not its cathedrals or its epics or its scholasticism: it was the building for the first time in history of a complex civilization which rested not on the backs of sweating slaves or coolies but primarily on non-human power. . . . The labor saving power machines of the later Middle Ages were produced by the implicit theological assumptions of the infinite worth of even the most degraded personality, by the intrinsic repugnance towards subjecting of any man to monotonous drudgery which seems less human in that it requires the exercise neither of intelligence nor choice. It has often been remarked that the Latin Middle Ages first discovered the dignity and spiritual value of labor—that to labor is to pray. But the Middle Ages went further: they gradually and very slowly began to explore the practical implications of an essentially Christian paradox: that just as the heavenly Jerusalem contains no temple, so the goal of labor is to end labor."[29] In defending this thesis, White is developing Lefebvre des Noëttes's argument that the new inventions destroyed slavery by making it unnecessary and undesirable.[30] On the other hand, the French medieval historian Marc Bloch[31] has argued that the end of slavery came first and created a necessity to which such devices as the new harness and water mill were the response. Both Crombie and Bark nevertheless defend the view that the Church, although it never succeeded in completely stamping out slavery, was greatly aided in its opposition to slavery by the new labor-saving devices.

In the opinion of Pierre Duhem (1861–1916), author of the classic ten-volume history of the physical sciences from Plato to Copernicus, *Le Systeme du monde*,[32] if we had to assign a date to the birth of modern science, we would be compelled to choose the year 1277, when Etienne Tempier, Bishop of Paris, solemnly condemned 219 philosophical and theological propositions then currently entertained within the Arts Faculty and the Faculty of Theology of the University of Paris. His example was followed in the same year by the Archbishop of Canterbury, John Pecham. From the vantage point of Duhem, it was significant that the condemnations undermined the authority of Aristotle insofar as they condemned the Peripatetic theory of place, and everything that Aristotle's *Physics* asserted about infinity, place, and time and the possibility of a void.

It is to be remembered that Aristotle arrived in Paris with considerable baggage, imperfect translations, to be sure, but more damaging were the often misleading commentaries of Averroes. Of the 219 theses condemned by Tempier, many were Averroistic in nature. Although no names were mentioned in the condemnations,[33] many were presumably held by Siger of Brabant and Boethius of Dacia. Some of the condemned theses were held by Albertus Magnus and Thomas Aquinas. Just how many of them were clearly Thomistic depends, Gilson remarks, on whether the list "is compiled by a Franciscan or a Dominican."[34] William A. Wallace provides a cautionary note when he writes, "It is generally agreed that Duhem's thesis is extreme, for there is no indication of a spurt in scientific thought or activity following 1277, and it is doubtful whether any authoritarian restriction on cosmological teachings could have stimulated that free spirit of inquiry that is generally seen as characteristic of modern science."[35] Yet Wallace concedes, "It is undeniable that the condemnation of 1277 had an effect on the development of medieval science, although not as profound as was maintained by Pierre Duhem."[36] Clearly the condemnation did not seriously affect the study of Aristotle. With Albert and Thomas, scholars began to sort out what in Aristotle was merely outmoded science or cosmology from the time-transcendent value of his philosophy of nature and its supporting metaphysics. It is not an exaggeration to claim that Aristotle's philosophy of science remains viable in the twentieth century. Whereas Gilson speaks of the 1277 condemnation as a "landmark," Stephen Gaukroger employs the notion of a "paradigm shift" to suggest the magnitude of the change.

The investigation of the physical world, or natural philosophy, until the thirteenth century was regarded as part of a single philosophical activity. Its purpose was to discover the enduring and intelligible reality behind the changes perceived through the senses. With the condemnation of the deterministic (Averroistic) view of Aristotle, the authority of Aristotle was challenged, thus undermining confidence in his entire system. In the judgment of Crombie, the natural philosophers of the thirteenth century, "because of the skepticism of Christian theologians," were freed from the authority of Aristotle and thus free to develop the empirical habit of mind but within a rational framework.[37]

Cultural historians agree that since classical antiquity there have been a number of civilizations that have witnessed a scientific revolution. Stephen Gaukroger,[38] whose work we will now consider, speaks of the "rich productive scientific cultures, in which fundamental and especially intractable, physical, medical, astronomical, and other problems are opened up and dealt with in an innovative and concerted fashion, producing cumulative results over several generations."[39] Besides Greece and the Hellenic diaspora, he identifies these as the Arab/Islamic North Africa/Near East/Iberian Peninsula in the ninth, tenth, and eleventh centuries, Paris and Oxford in the thirteenth and fourteenth centuries, and China from the twelfth to the fourteenth century[40] The scientific revolution of seventeenth- and eighteenth-century Europe is something different, he thinks, insofar as the uninterrupted and cumulative growth of the early modern period breaks with the boom/bust pattern of earlier cultures. Not only that, but the scientific revolution was so spectacular that it not only displaced competing accounts but was extrapolated to all cognitive disciplines. In a relatively short period of time, Copernicanism and Darwinism came to replace firmly held philosophical and theological views concerning nature and the order in nature that had persisted since biblical times.

Stephen Gaukroger, like Whitehead, takes exception to what he calls the "Enlightenment interpretation," namely, that the scientific revolution occurred as a result of Western science's ability to disassociate itself from religion. Vigorously challenging that "self-serving account," he writes: "Far from science breaking free of religion in the early modern era, its consolidation depended crucially on religion being in the driver's seat: Christianity took over natural philosophy in the seventeenth century, setting its agenda and projecting it forward in a way quite different from that of any other scientific culture."[41] Gaukroger's strong claim is defended in what promises to be a multi-volume study, the first of which is entitled, *The Emergence of a Scientific Culture: Science and the Shaping of Modernity, 1210–1685.*

In demonstrating the continuity of science and technology through the later Middle Ages into modernity, Gaukroger contrasts the progress of science in the *West* with that in the cultures of Islam and China. "Arab-Islamic science," he writes, "had two distinctive features. The first is that there was no institutional support available for scientific work that was not motivated by extra-scientific concerns. . . . Second, the way in which the achievements of Greek philosophers, and Greek and Alexandrian mathematicians, were 'naturalized' in the Arab-Islamic culture is distinctive. They were domesticated, incorporated into an indigenous culture and philosophical system, rather than being institutionalized in such a way that they carried 'their own specific gravity of autonomy and legitimacy, independent of the moral and religious scruples of the surrounding culture.' The consequence of these two institutional features of Arab-Islamic civilization is that while it was occasionally possible for innovations to be made in astronomy, optics, and even metaphysics, there was no way in which they could be followed up in a systematic manner."[42]

With respect to China, the situation was almost the reverse. "If Arabic-Islamic culture could initiate scientific developments but not follow them up, China had an extensive network of communication, and this acted in such a way as to foster scientific and technological achievement. In the Sung and Ming dynasties we find inventions such as mechanical clocks, moveable type, and seismographs that predate developments in the West by a couple of centuries, and we find significant advances in observational astronomy and medicine."[43] Yet there were serious obstacles to innovation that were not practically oriented. The bureaucratic structure of Chinese society was a crucial factor. Then, too, traditions of philosophical disputation are relatively marginal in Chinese intellectual culture. Adherence to tradition plays a crucial role in all artistic and intellectual pursuits, with the result that there was a strong sense that scholarship rather than innovation is the path to wisdom. This was reinforced by the Confucian tendency to self-effacement and avoidance of contentiousness, as well as a strong commitment to outward obedience to public authorities. This Chinese respect for authority formed a sharp contrast with Greek models of confrontational debate.[44]

Crombie's study is reinforced by Gaukroger when he writes that, "In the thirteenth century, natural philosophy was transformed from a marginal enterprise into one that was to provide the principal point of entry into understanding of the natural world and our place in it."[45] The engine of transformation was Aristotle's natural philosophy in spite of the condemnations. Gaukroger thinks the significant event is not Etienne Tempier's condemnation of 1277 but the much earlier Paris condemnation of Aristotle in the year 1210. He uses that date as a starting point as he traces the development of natural philosophy from the scholasticism of the early thirteenth century, through the copuscularism and atomism associated with Gassendi and Mersenne, to Descartes' cosmology and to Hobbes's mechanism. The year 1685 Gaukroger uses to mark the twilight, if not the demise, of Aristotelian natural philosophy and the ascendancy of a period dominated by the works of Locke, Newton, and Leibniz. He maintains that from the thirteenth to the sixteenth century two models had provided the unity of knowledge: one was the Aristotelian notion of *scientia*, the other the Christian idea of a universe designed and created *ex nihilo* by a single God as an abode for human beings. In the seventeenth century both were confronted by nominalistic and mechanistic interpretations of nature. Copernicus was thought to displace a man-centered universe, Darwin to displace *Genesis,* and Hobbes's mechanism to displace the recognition of design in nature.

The shift from an Aristotelian world view to modernity, although gradual, was radical. Pagan philosophers had made natural philosophy the basis of moral philosophy. Aristotelian categories had been employed by the early Church Fathers as they interpreted the texts of the Gospel. Justin Martyr, Marius Victorinus, and Clement of Alexandria recognized that Aristotelian natural philosophy, while not intrinsically Christian, was nevertheless not inherently pagan. Aristotelian natural philosophy, although not without rivals, notably those of the neo-Platonic and Augustinian schools, held sway until it gave ground to mechanistic interpretations of nature in the seventeenth century, notably that advanced by Pierre Gassendi (1592–1655). It is Descartes and his artificially created "mind-body problem" that stimulated Gassendi to address the age-old problem of universals and the relation between sense and intellectual knowledge.[46] In his criticism of Descartes, he writes, "When you say that you are simply a thing that thinks, you mention an operation that everyone was aware of but you say nothing about the substance carrying out this operation: What sort of substance it is, What it consists in, how it organizes itself in order to carry out its different functions."[47] Gassendi's atomism in its pre-Newtonian form is an attempt to explain macroscopic phenomena by means of the microscopic. Presented as a matter theory inspired by the Greek atomists, when combined with the doctrine of primary and secondary qualities, it undermined the Aristotelian concept of "nature" and with it, teleology. But those implications and others are not what he intended. It is a small step from Gassendi's atomism to Auguste Comte's positivism.

Science in the Aristotelian sense and above all an acknowledgment of its scholastic roots suffers greatly at the hands of Renaissance humanists. A number of scholars are of the opinion that the fifteenth-century humanism that arose in Italy and spread northward was an interruption of the development of science. The so-called revival of letters deflected interest from content to literary style, and in turning back to classical antiquity, many humanists affected to ignore the progress of the previous three centuries. Unaware of how much they owed to their immediate predecessors, these humanists, by their contempt of scholasticism, did much to initiate the Dark Age myth which the *philosophes* of the French Enlightenment were happy to perpetuate. Crombie suggests that: "The same absurd conceit that led the humanists to abuse and misrepresent their immediate predecessors for using Latin constructions unknown to Cicero and to put out the propaganda, which in varying degrees has captivated historical opinion until quite recently, also allowed them to borrow from Scholasticism without acknowledgment. The habit affected almost all the great scientists of the sixteenth and seventeenth centuries, whether Protestant or Catholic, and it has required the labors of Duhem and Maier to show that their statements on matters of history cannot be accepted at face value."[48]

Whitehead is convinced that the natural scientists of the sixteenth and seventeenth centuries were anti-intellectualists in the same way as the religious reformers were anti-intellectualists.[49] Herbert Butterfield recalls how the humanists of the Renaissance, Erasmus included, were accustomed to complaining of the boredom of scholastic lectures and suggests that this was due to the ignorance of the humanists more than anything else.[50] The humanists derided their scholastic teachers, but these despised scholastic disciplines now hold a remarkable key position in the story of the evolution of the modern mind. Butterfield writes: "Perhaps the lack of mathematics or the failure to think of mathematical ways of formulating things was partly responsible for what appeared to be verbal subtleties and an excessive straining of language in these men who were yearning to find the key to the modern science of mechanics."[51]

The Renaissance attitude took hold and has held sway since. As we have seen in a previous chapter, positivism, for complex reasons, has come to be associated with modern science. Positivism, insofar as it restricts knowledge to that attained by physio-mathematical methods, in effect reduces science to description and prediction. With remarkable insight, Christopher Dawson, writing three-quarters of a century ago, commented, "The disease of modern civilization lies neither in science nor in machinery but in the false philosophy with which they have been associated. . . . Though these ideas accompanied the rise of the machine order, they are in reality profoundly inconsistent with that order and with scientific genius."[52] Elsewhere he remarks that "we cannot be sure that the world which science has made will be as favorable to the production of scientific genius as the world that made science."[53]

Karl Popper likewise indicts the positivistic attitude toward science in which the emphasis is placed on description and practical results: "Instrumentalism," Popper maintains, "is unable to account for the importance to pure science of severely testing even the most remote implications of its theories since it is unable to account for the pure scientist's interest in truth and falsity. In contrast to the highly critical attitude requisite in the pure scientist, the attitude of instrumentalism (like that of applied science) is one of complacency at the success of application. Thus it may well be responsible for the recent stagnation in theoretical physics."[54]

We began not with Bernard Lewis's question of what went wrong in the Islamic world but shifted the discourse to what went right within Christendom. As contemporary Europe struggles with its identity, Dawson's work is there to remind us: "Europe is not a group of people held together by a common type of material culture; it is a spiritual society that owes its existence to the religious tradition which for a thousand years molded the beliefs, the ideals, and the institutions of European peoples."[55] Dawson adds a frightening thought: "If modern Europe falls either through internal revolution or through loss of her world leadership, modern civilization falls with her. For that civilization was entirely a European creation, and there is no force outside Europe today capable of carrying on her work, whatever the case a century or two hence."[56]

NOTES

1. Lynn White, Jr. reminds us of the Herculean task awaiting the cultural historian. He writes "History is being made faster than we can absorb it. . . . As yet no mind, not even Arnold Toynbee's, has really digested the new material," "The Changing Past," in *Frontiers of Knowledge in the Study of Man*, ed. Lynn White, Jr. (New York: Greenwood Press, 1969), 68.

2. Christopher Dawson, *Progress and Religion* (Garden City, N.Y.: Doubleday Image Books, 1960), 23.

3. Dawson, *Progress*, 126–27.

4. Alfred North Whitehead, *Science and the Modern World* (New York: Macmillan, 1925); also published as a Mentor Book, 4th printing, 1953.

5. Bernard Lewis, *What Went Wrong?* (Oxford, England: Oxford University Press, 2002), 156.

6. A.C. Crombie, *Medieval and Early Modern Science, 2 vols.: vol. I, Science in the Middle Ages: V–XIII Centuries: vol. II, Science in the Later Middle Ages and Early Modern Times: XIII–XVII Centuries (*Garden City, N.Y.: Doubleday Anchor Books, 1959).

7. Stephen Gaukroger, *The Emergence of a Scientific Culture: Science and the Shaping of Modernity, 1210–1685* (Oxford, England: Clarendon Press, 2006).

8. Crombie, *Medieval and Modern*, 52.

9. Cf. David C. Lindberg, "The Transmission of Greek and Arabic Learning to the West," in *Science in the Middle Ages,* ed. David C. Lindberg (Chicago: University of Chicago Press, 1978).

10. Lindberg, "The Transmission," 56. For an alternative account, one written from an Islamic perspective, see George Saliba *(Islamic Science and the Making of the European Renaissance,* Cambridge, Mass.: MIT Press, 2007). Saliba confirms with considerable textual evidence Crombie's account of the westward transmission of astronomical data from the world of Islam and makes the case that Copernicus's heliocentric view of the universe was largely indebted to Arab sources.

11. Saliba, *Islamic Science.*

12. Whitehead, *Science and*, 14.

13. Whitehead, *Science and*, 12.

14. Whitehead, *Science and*, 16.

15. Lynn White, Jr., "The Dynamo and the Virgin Reconsidered," *American Scholar* 27 (1958): 187.

16. White, "The Dynamo," 188–189.

17. Crombie, *Medieval and Modern*, 52.

18. A.C. Crombie, *Robert Grosseteste and the Origins of Experimental Science, 1100–1700* (Oxford, England: Oxford University Press, 1971), 1.

19. Crombie, *Robert Grosseteste*, 2–3.

20. Whitehead, *Science and*, 12.

21. Lynn Thorndike, *A History of Magic and Experimental Science, 1923–1958* (New York: Columbia University Press, 1923–1958, 8 vols.).

22. See especially W. C. Bark, *Origins of the Medieval World* (New York: Doubleday Anchor, 1960), 115 ff.

23. Christopher Dawson, "Origin of European Scientific Tradition." *The Clergy Review*, 2 (1931): 203.

24. Cf. Pearl Kibre and Nancy Sirasi, "The Institutional Setting of the Universities," in *Science and the Middle Ages*, ed. David C. Lindberg (Chicago: University of Chicago Press, 1978), 128–29.

25. Crombie, *Robert Grosseteste*, 43.

26. Benjamin Farrington, *Greek Science* (London: Penguin, 1952), 307ff.

27. Farrington, *Greek Science*, 307ff.

28. White, Jr., "The Dynamo," 190.

29. Lynn White, Jr., "Technology and Invention in the Middle Ages," *Speculum* 15 (1940): 156.

30. The medieval contribution to technology gained recognition as a result of the researches of Commandant Lefebvre des Noëttes, a one-time cavalry officer, who upon retirement from military life, turned his professional attention to account by making a historical study of animal power. This work, published in the early 1930s eventually led him to accumulate an impressive body of evidence on medieval technical developments and their social consequences. The result of his work has been praised as one of the capital historical discoveries of the early twentieth century. Cf. *l'Attelage et le cheval de selle à travers les âges* (Paris, 1931); *De la marine antique à la marine moderne* (Paris, 1935).

31. Cf. Marc Bloch, *Feudal Society*, trans. L. A. Manyon (Chicago: University of Chicago Press, 1961).

32. Pierre Duhem, *Le Systeme du monde: Histoire des doctrines cosmologiques de Platon à Copernic* originally published in French by Hermann, éditeurs des sciences et des arts (Paris). Selections from Duhem's massive work have been translated and made available by Roger Ariew, *Medieval Cosmology: Theories of Infinity, Place, Time, Void, and Plurality of Worlds* (Chicago: University of Chicago Press, 1985); cf. also Stanley Jaki, *Uneasy Genius: The Life and Work of Pierre Duhem* (Dordrecht, Netherlands: Martinus Nijhoff, 1984).

33. For an authoritative account of the condemnation, cf. John F. Wippel, "The Condemnations of 1270 and 1277 in Paris," *Journal of Medieval and Renaissance Studies* 7 (1977): 169–201; also "Thomas Aquinas and the Condemnation of 1277," *Modern Schoolman* 72 (1955): 233–72.

34. Etienne Gilson, *History of Christian Philosophy in the Middle Ages* (New York: Random House, 1955), 728.

35. William A. Wallace, "Philosophical Setting of Medieval Science," in *Science in the Middle Ages*, ed. David C. Lindberg (Chicago: University of Chicago Press, 1978), 105–106.

36. Wallace, "Philosophical Setting," 105.

37. Crombie, *Medieval and Early Modern Science*, vol. I, 64.

38. Gaukroger is writing some eighty years after Whitehead and fifty years after Crombie. Specialized studies subsequently written abound, yet the basic facts as well as most interpretations remain unchanged. Cf. Stephen Gaukroger, *the Emergence*

of a Scientific Culture: Science and the Shaping of Modernity, 1210–1685 (Oxford, England: The Clarendon Press, 2006).

39. Gaukroger, *The Emergence*, 17.
40. Gaukroger, *The Emergence*, 18.
41. Gaukroger, *The Emergence*, 23.
42. Gaukroger, *The Emergence*, 33.
43. Gaukroger, *The Emergence*, 33.
44. Gaukroger, *The Emergence*, 33.
45. Gaukroger, *The Emergence*, 33.
46. Cf. the excellent study of Antonia Lolordo, *Pierre Gassendi and the Birth of Early Modern Philosophy* (Cambridge, Mass.: Cambridge University Press, 2006).
47. As quoted by Lolordo, 228.
48. Crombie, *Augustine to Galileo*, 268–269. Cf. Also Charles B. Schmitt's extended treatment, *Aristotle and the Renaissance* (Cambridge, Mass.: Harvard University Press, 1983).
49. Whitehead, *Science in the Modern World*, 12.
50. Herbert Butterfield, *Origins of Modern Science* (New York: Macmillan, 1957), 2.
51. Butterfield, *Origins*, 2.
52. Christopher Dawson, *Christianity and the New Age* (London: Sheed and Ward, 1931), 102.
53. Christopher Dawson, *The Modern Dilemma* (London: Sheed and Ward, 1933), 49.
54. Karl Popper, *Contemporary British Philosophy* (New York: Macmillan, 1960), 381.
55. Dawson, *Progress and Religion*, 173.
56. Dawson. *Progress*, 171.

Part Three

CONTEMPORARY MORAL ISSUES

Chapter Thirteen

The Use and Abuse of Analogy and Metaphor in Scientific Explanation

Aristotle observed that even the most abstract of thought is necessarily accompanied by a sensory image. This notion came to be expressed by the scholastic dictum, "There can be no intellection without accompanying sensation." The function of images in scientific explanation will be addressed, but the immediate focus of the paper is the use of metaphor in communicating insight into natural phenomena. Models employed in the sciences are a kind of metaphor in which a familiar structure or mechanism is used as an analogy to interpret a natural phenomena.

Historians of science tell us that scientific models are often suggestive in the development of new theories and in the modification of existing ones. Niels Bøhr said of his own work that he could not understand anything unless he could make a model of it. In my school days, the Bøhr model of the atom was to be found in every science classroom. That model, of course, gave way as we learned more about atomic and subatomic structure. New models introduced us to electron orbits, quantum leaps, and similar constructs. Maritain complained in his *Philosophy of Nature* that in the domain of mathematical physics it is sometimes difficult to distinguish fact from theory. Pierre Gassendi, an early seventeenth-century mathematician and philosopher cautioned: "It is not permitted to transfer into Physics something abstractly demonstrated in Geometry," an admonition often forgotten. Myanna Lahsen, an anthropologist who spent several years interviewing staff at the National Center for Atmospheric Research, reports that a member of the staff once confided, "It is easy to get caught up in it: you start to believe that what happens in your model must be what happens in the real world. And often it is not true."[1] Yet even mathematical physics, though seeming confined to the world of abstract necessity, must return to the empirical for confirmation. A physicist may formulate his findings in the language of laws and express these by means of equations, but he still thinks in terms of things that govern his work.

From an Aristotelian point of view, every scientific explanation is necessarily a realistic explanation, not nominalistic one. Even Kant, who separated the world of logic from the ontological, assigned to metaphysics the role of preventing the employment of reason beyond its limits. He conceded: "*Intellectualia* as objects serve only as *modo cognoscendia* for the sensitive *dabilium*."[2] Theoretical physicists who have had some training in classical philosophy readily identify themselves as Aristotelians. Mathematical description, they acknowledge, is not scientific explanation.

Pursuing a point made above, if the investigator himself sometimes fails to distinguish fact from theory, how much more difficult it is for the layman to do so. Popular accounts of scientific reports come laden with metaphor, often colorful but not helpful. We are puzzled by the metaphor, "wrinkle in space time," and equally mystified when we hear someone speak of gravity as "warped space time." We read of "anti-matter," "drops of electricity," "black holes," "right- and left-handed spin of K-mesons," "backward causation," and "strong locality." And I haven't even mentioned "string theory." What, if anything, is conveyed to the layman by these terms? When the concept "anti-matter" was first introduced, the news was reported in ominous terms on the front page of major newspapers across the country. One of my classmates was called upon by a reporter for Washington's *Herald Tribune* for an explanation. The upshot was that a graduate student in physics at Catholic University was depicted as having refuted a prominent physicist at Berkeley. Of course he had done no such thing; he was merely unpacking a simile or metaphor. My friend endured quite a bit of ribbing from his colleagues, but within a relatively short time he was teaching at Princeton and later became chairman of the physics department at Vanderbilt. We know the mischief that can be created through the improper use of terms such as "evolution," "indeterminacy," and "relativity." In a given scientific community metaphor may be a shorthand way of referring to certain data, to a theory, or to a working insight. Thus, although a metaphor may have a meaning within a specific context, employed outside of a cognizant community as, for example, when it is thrust upon a newspaper reader by a flamboyant reporter, it can be mystifyingly vague and convey no information at all. It is true that context confers meaning, but that is not the whole story. Our sympathy is with Alice when she confronts Humpty Dumpty who insists that "words mean just what I want them to mean." As a good Aristotelian, Alice could have said the meaning of a term is determined by its referent, the ontological structure to which it is applicable, Aristotle took it for granted that the way we think and talk about natural entities is, for the most part, the way they are, but he does not go so far as to suggest that language directly mirrors nature. Language certainly provides some indication of the structure of reality, but it can be a source of error.

Historians of science provide numerous accounts of how interesting metaphors enter the vocabulary of physics. Ernest (Lord) Rutherford in proposing a mental model of the atom in 1911 drew an analogy between the solar system and the hydrogen atom. The nucleus of an atom, he found, is more massive than the electron, just as the sun is more massive than the planets. The nucleus attracts the electron in a relationship that causes the electron to revolve around the nucleus. A year later, Bøhr, utilizing information drawn from quantum mechanics offered an alternative model in which he suggested that electron orbits were not like planetary ones; they were more like the rungs of a ladder, with electrons only at the rungs and not in between. Another famous example followed the calculation by Lisa Meitner and her nephew, Otto Frisch, who determined, based on a report by Strassmann and Hahn, that the uranium nucleus had indeed been split. Frisch remembered that Niels Bøhr once remarked that the nucleus of an atom behaved something like a drop of liquid. With that metaphor in mind, Frisch asked one of his colleagues, a biologist, what biologists called the splitting of a cell. "Fission," came the reply, and the concept "nuclear fission" entered the common vocabulary.[3] Max Black, who has written at length on models and metaphors, saw a tight connection between the two, concluding that a model is nothing other than the explanation of a metaphor. Black was convinced that the first level of scientific activity, to the extent that it culminates in a hypothesis, begs to be complemented by an image. The image need not be concrete to be suggestive enough to guide research.[4] To use another example, this one offered by Giorgio de Santillana who in a passage entitled, "The Embarrassment of Reality," tells us that Maxwell's highly mathematical theory of gases assumed the reality of hard elastic particles. As Giorgio de Santillana comments, "Real representations fight their way through progressive abstraction and the all embracing theorems of physics and chemistry." Theory begs to be complemented by the physical image.[5] Metaphors can, of course, be inappropriate and misleading as well as suggestive. As a form of analogy, metaphor is the weakest form, lacking the clarity of proper proportionality and the force of analogy of attribution. In the natural sciences nothing can be proved by analogy, suggestive though some analogies may be. An egregious use of analogy is provided by a front-page article in the *New York Times* of April 6, 2006, entitled "Fossil Called Missing Link from Sea to Land Animals." The report tells us that the fossilized skeleton remains of a giant fish has features that anticipate the emergence of land animals and, in the words of the report, "is thus a predecessor of amphibians, reptiles and dinosaurs, mammals and eventually humans."[6]

The poet can speak of "the yellow fog that rubs its back upon the window pane," and the metaphor is suggestive, conveying an image and creating a mood. The ancients referred to the "heaven of fixed stars" and spoke of the planets as "wanderers," descriptions that anyone who has spent a sleepless night under the stars can appreciate. In a poetic mood, Copernicus spoke of the sun as "the lantern of the universe, at rest in the middle of everything . . . for in this beautiful temple [the universe] who would place the lamp in another or better position than that from which it can light up the whole thing at the same time."[7] We delight in the images conveyed and recognize their merit or their appropriateness, but the intellect remains aware that reality differs from that poetically suggested. Apart from its poetic value, metaphor as employed in the sciences can suggest or focus attention on reliably attained information or systematically acquired observation. Robert Sokolowski, writing from a phenomenological point of view, tells us. "Metaphors are enlightening precisely because they would be incoherent if taken literally. The fact that they don't literally fit what we are talking about makes us scrutinize the object more carefully than we have been accustomed to; we let it manifest itself in a new way."[8] Discussions of metaphor inevitably lead to deeper issues addressed in the philosophy of science.

Reflections on the nature and capacity of human knowledge did not await the eighteenth century or the advent of modern mathematical physics. Plato's discussion of science and claims to knowledge by the Greeks will forever remain the starting point of the philosophy of science. It was Plato who bequeathed to Western philosophy the insight that all science is of the universal. Aristotle concurred, finding the universal not in some unseen realm of archetypes but in the nature common to members of a species. Aristotle taught that by a process of abstraction we come to know the essence, nature, or quiddity of a thing, prescinding from its accidental features, which it may or may not have while remaining the thing that it is. Such is the object of science, a knowledge of the nature of things or the structure of a process as known from their properties and potentialities. Yet to have scientific knowledge is not simply to know what is, not simply to have uncovered a law of nature. For Aristotle to have scientific knowledge is to know the entity, process, or property in the light of its cause or causes. To have achieved a scientific explanation is to have rendered intelligible something that was not self-intelligible. The ancients, for example, knew well the properties of metals such as copper, gold, and silver, and they knew how to form alloys with them for specific purposes, but why those metals possessed certain properties and no others had to await the twentieth century. Why is copper malleable, a conductor of heat, a conductor of electricity, and relatively light in weight? Any attempt at explanation must first acknowledge that there is such a thing as copper, must recognize that "copper" is not a name we give to a bundle of properties but a natural structure or substance, the source of those properties. For an empiricist, such as Auguste Comte, to advance theories concerning the why or what of phenomena is to commit a cardinal sin, the vice of a mind wholly alien to the true scientific spirit. Following the lead of David Hume, Comte would reduce science to description and prediction. Ever since the Pythagoreans, Western science has tended to view nature in purely mathematical terms. Galileo looked upon mathematics as the instrument by which man is enabled to understand the script God employed in creating the universe. Kepler shared this view when he wrote, "Just as the eye was made to see colors, the ear to hear sounds, so the human mind was made to understand Quantity."[9] But the natural sciences consist in more than measurement, more than an account of quantitative relations and variations. It is true that much of the activity we associate with the natural sciences is indeed an attempt at description, an attempt to get straight the data or the facts under consideration. But the mind is not so easily content. It seeks to know the intrinsic nature of things, why things are as they are. Much of that knowledge is by inference. The knowledge we have of the submicroscopic, for example, is by inference. The mental mechanisms by which we hold that knowledge entail the creation of models, plausible mechanisms responsible for the phenomena observed. Models may be either sentential (an equation, for example) or iconic, (a mental picture or a diagram). Thus in the history of theoretical physics, we find successive schema depicting the atom as our knowledge increases. We are led to recognize that our knowledge of nature is open ended, the focus of an intellectual quest that is never satisfied. In 1933 the state of particle physics was such that it seemed necessary to postulate the existence of a particle as yet undetected. The Italian physicist, Enrico Fermi, assuming its existence, built his theory of beta decay upon it and gave the undetected particle a name: "neutrino," Italian for "little one." In spite of support from Niels Bøhr, he was subjected to remarks about his "poltergeist" since no one had empirically shown it to exist in spite of its "theoretical necessity." It remained a hypothetical entity until Clyde Cowan, a colleague when I joined the faculty at Catholic University, who with access to a particle accelerator at Handford, Washington, performed an experiment that confirmed the neutrino's existence. He duplicated the experiment in 1956 at the Savannah River Laboratory in Georgia. And, as they say, the rest is history. I use this example as an illustration of the principle of sufficient reason, sometimes called the principle of efficient causality where an explanation is sought for something otherwise unintelligible.

Analogy or metaphor sometimes plays a role when researchers trained in one area or in one method attempt to apply that method beyond its capacity. Emile Durkheim, Auguste Comte, and their American disciple, John Dewey optimistically thought that if the method that had been successfully employed in the natural science were utilized in the sciences of man, we could expect there a similar success. Unavoidably, no matter how useful mathematical techniques may be in the study of nature, subject matter yet determines method. The way we ordinarily talk of mind and human agency does not fit well with our understanding of the world derived from the physical sciences. The realm of reason, the realms of judgment, of belief, and of desire are independent of physical facts about human agency. We may be every bit a part of nature, as are the inanimate elements that surround us, but there are facts about what we think and what we do that have no counterparts when the subject is a plant or animal. To explain human behavior in the language of physics or chemistry, or by causal accounts that cast human beings as a collection of physical particles, is to miss that which is distinctive about human beings.

A frequent mistake in this area of research is to confuse mind with brain activity, assuming that the nervous system and the brain are the cause of what goes on in "consciousness." From an Aristotelian point of view, mind is clearly bodily and as such cannot be discussed apart from brain activity. Discussions of the intellect are something else. While intellection cannot take place apart from sensation, the two are not the same. How one discusses the relationship depends first on a clear distinction between sensation and intellection. Sense knowledge provides the material for the intellectual formation of concepts that transcend sensory experience. Yet there is more in the sensory report than the senses themselves are able to appreciate. Recognition of the transcendent or non-material aspects of human knowing entails a modeling of human nature that finds a prototype in Aristotle in contrast to reductionist accounts that ignore or falsify data in the interest of simplicity.

Perhaps the most serious consequence of a failure to understand the nature of scientific explanation is what may be called a "failure of misplaced expectations." The notion of progress, taken for granted in physics, chemistry, and biology, cannot be predicated of the sciences that depend on our knowledge of human nature, what Charles Taylor calls "the sciences of man." Christopher Dawson makes the case that "faith in progress" is one of the most dangerous ideas to find its way into modernity. No one can fail to notice that there is a certain linear progression in our knowledge of nature, cumulative and ever more precise, enabling its application to achieve feats undreamt of even in a previous generation. With respect to our knowledge of human nature, such progress does not exist. This holds consequences for the social and political sphere. Whereas our knowledge of nature increases almost day by day, there is no similar increase in our knowledge of human nature. True, we know more about the human body and its functioning than was known even in the last century, let alone in ancient times, but knowledge of the human body is not the same as a knowledge of human nature. There is a difference between mathematical description and mechanical explanation, on the one hand, and philosophical refection, on the other. The natural sciences advance on the back of technology and are directly traceable to the use of instruments, i.e., telescopes, microscopes, particle accelerators, and other specialized investigative tools, but there are no instruments available today that were not available in antiquity when the subject is human nature. Governments may have the technical resources to explore the solar system, but those same governments cannot with confidence set out to eradicate poverty, improve education, or devise immigration policy without taking into account certain time-transcending facts about human nature. In setting norms for collective action, policy makers must resort to a higher order of learning, namely, that wisdom that finds its source in the classics of Western culture, sources identified with the work of Plato, Aristotle, the Stoics, Augustine, Boethius, the Fathers of the Church, and their commentators through the ages.

NOTES

1. *Wall Street Journal*, 1 February, 2006, A-15.

2. Immanuel Kant, *Fragments*, 17:533, ed. By Guyer, 13.

3. Cf. Ruth Moore, *Niels Bøhr: The Man, His Science, and the World They Changed* (Cambridge, Mass.: MIT Press, 1985), 227.

4. Max Black, *Models and Metaphors: Studies in Language and Philosophy* (Ithaca, N.Y.: Cornell University Press, 1962).

5. Giorgio de Santillana, *Reflections on Men and Ideas* (Cambridge, Mass.: MIT Press, 1968), 251.

6. The research was first published in *Nature* by Erik Ahlberg of Uppsala University and Jennifer Clark of the University of Cambridge. The scientists offered their description of the forward fins of the 375-million-year-old fish as evidence of limbs in the making. The fins, it is claimed, are the beginnings of digits, proto wrists, elbows and shoulders.

7. As quoted by Fernand Hallyn, *The Poetic Structure of the World* (New York: Zone Books, 1995), 127.

8. Robert Sokolowski, *Husserlian Meditations: How Words Present Things* (Evanston, Ill.: Northwestern University Press, 1974).

9. Johannes Kepler, *Opera I*, 31 as quoted by Christopher Dawson.

Chapter Fourteen

Morality with and without God

Historically considered, Western morality, since the advent of Christianity, has been characterized by an acknowledgment of God's existence, by the belief that union with God is the end of man, and by the conviction that man is morally free in the sense that he is not totally controlled by his desires and passions or by social forces, and that he is possessed of a soul immaterial in nature which permits him to enjoy life in God. From the time of the Stoics until the eighteenth century, moral reflection, for the most part, took God and an immaterial order for granted. In the eighteenth century dramatic changes occurred. Hume freed morality from creed; Kant plucked it from its roots in natural theology. These deeds are well known, and there is no need to chronicle them here, but certain features of the moral theory of Hume and Kant are relevant to the present enquiry and may be briefly recalled. Perhaps one ought to begin with Hobbes, but it was Hume who drove home the point that religion and morality are distinct and even disparate in their respective bases and ultimate references, their motivations, and their consequences for human existence. Morality, says Hume, cannot afford to wait on the efforts of natural theology. Mankind must have some commonly available principles and grounds for moral judgment. Hume believed that as a matter of experience, a natural inclination to humanity and benevolence has a more constant and reliable effect on man's conduct than even the most pompous view suggested by theological theories and systems. In this as in other matters, Kant was to accept too much from Hume.

In his first *Critique,* Kant denies that our theoretical reason can provide evidence for the existence of God or for freedom or for immortality, but he is nevertheless convinced that these notions are required for morality. For Kant, it is axiomatic that moral law requires justice, defined as a measure of happiness in proportion to virtue. Because happiness may elude the virtuous in this life, Kant must posit the existence of God and a future life to ensure that virtue will be properly rewarded. He writes, "There is only one possible condition under which . . . there can be a God and a future world. I know with complete certainty that no one can be acquainted with any other conditions which lead to the same unity of ends under the moral law. Since therefore the moral precept is at the same time my maxim (reason prescribing that it should be so), I inevitably believe in the existence of God and in a future life, and I am certain that nothing can shake this belief, since my moral principles would thereby be themselves overthrown, and I cannot disdain them without becoming abhorrent in my own eye." Kant will go on to say that even though no one can demonstrate the existence of God, one can still say, "I am morally certain." He admits, "My conviction is not logical, but is morally certain, and since it rests on subjective grounds, I must not even say 'It is morally certain there is a God, etc.' I can only say, 'I am morally certain.'"[1]

For many Jewish and Christian thinkers who come after Kant, the only genuine basis for morality is religion. This is true of theologians such as Brunner, Barth, Niebuhr and Bultmann, who hold that without belief in God, there is no ground or reason for being moral. Elizabeth Anscombe has similarly argued that only if we believe in God as a lawgiver can we come to believe that there is anything a man is categorically bound to do on pain of being a bad man.[2] Anscombe maintains that the moral use of obligation statements makes no sense apart from a divine law conception of ethics. Anscombe's judgment focuses on an issue that must be faced by anyone who takes up the problem of moral obligation. When in the eighteenth century God was removed as a source of moral law, something happened to the notion of obligation. It required a different sort of grounding. Enter the notion of "social contract" brought in to impose obligation and legitimate coercion by virtue of consent given to some hypothetical primitive state. Since the eighteenth century, the societal contract theory has been the prevailing one and perhaps the only modern rival for the doctrine that power proceeds from the barrel of a gun. The social contract is the keystone of John Rawls's celebrated examination of "justice."[3]

Leaving modernity aside for the moment, my topic, "Morality with and without God," demands at least a cursory examination of some pre-Christian or pagan codes of morality. To begin with the Greeks, we note that classical civilization had its gods and took for granted an immaterial order. Every schoolboy knows the names of Greek and Roman gods. An immaterial order needed little defense in classical antiquity. Plato reasoned to a *summum bonum*, worthy of veneration; Aristotle reasoned to a self-thinking intellect, a first efficient cause, and an ultimate final cause. Cicero believed that the universe is governed by a divine plan and held that the mind or soul of each individual is a reflection, indeed, a part of the divine mind.

I take Cicero (106–43 B.C.) to represent the noblest expression of the Roman mind, indeed of the Hellenistic mind, on the subject of the moral life. Cicero claimed no originality but thought of himself as transposing Greek ideas about public life, specifically those of Plato and Aristotle, into a Roman context. In the *Discussions at Tusculum*,[4] drawing upon both the Stoics and the Peripatetics, and making use of Plato's *Gorgias*, and his *Phaedrus*, *Republic*, and *Laws*. Cicero begins: "If, my son, we adopt moral goodness as our guide—in each and every one of its forms, it will follow automatically what our practical duties or obligations must be. . . . The next step is to go to the various kinds of obligations which have a direct bearing on people's daily lives and needs." This is something that he does elsewhere in *De officiis*.[5]

In the *Discussions at Tusculum*, he examines the essentials for a happy life. In the first four books of that treatise he concludes that death is not to be feared, that pain is endurable, that sorrow can be alleviated, and that disturbances of the mind can be conquered. Book Five is given to the thesis that moral goodness by itself is sufficient to make one happy. "But just suppose, on the other hand, that the good way of life lay at the mercy of a whole lot of unpredictable accidents, so that if appropriate accidents were not forthcoming this goodness would lack sufficient strength to maintain itself independently by its own account. If that were really so, all we could do to achieve a happy life, it seems to me, would be merely to hope for the best and pray heaven that happiness might somehow come our way."[6] "The happy are the ones who are alarmed by no fears, anguished by no cravings, dissolved into no voluptuous languor by fatuous transports of delight."[7] But is there such a man "who is capable of regarding all the hazards and accidents of human life as endurable, a man who moreover is troubled neither by fear nor by distress nor by passion, a man whom all empty pleasures of whatever kind leave utterly cold—then if such a person exists, there is every reason why he should be happy."[8] The issue is not resolved by Cicero although one is left with the impression that in the absence of complete self-control there may be degrees of happiness.

In *De officiis*, Cicero discusses the nature of responsibility and obligation. Given that all mankind is one brotherhood, Cicero infers that we should not be indifferent to the happiness and well being of others. Recognition of brotherhood implies a tremendous social and communal obligation. From the very fact that every human being possesses a spark of the divinity, an essential and indissoluble bond is created with all his fellows. He must therefore treat them with respect and dignity. In fact we incur an obligation to the other, indeed, a responsibility for the other. Nature's law, says Cicero, promotes and coincides with common interest.

In *De re publica III*, 33, we find Cicero's famous definition of natural law, "True law," he says, "is right reason, consonant with nature, spread through all the people. It is constant and eternal; it summons to duty by its orders, it deters from crime by its prohibitions. . . . There will not be one law at Rome and another at Athens, one now and another later, but all nations at all times will be bound by this one eternal unchangeable law and the God will be one common master and general (so to speak) of all people. He is the author, expounder, and mover of the law."[9]

Justice, Cicero finds, is the crowning glory of the virtues, and close akin to justice is charity, which may also be called "kindness" or "generosity."[10] Like the law of nature, to which it is essential, justice is absolute, eternal, and immutable. He extends this concept even to punishment, "There are certain duties that we owe even to those who have wronged us; for there is a limit to retribution and to punishment."[11] It is no wonder that Petrarch could say of Cicero, "You could sometimes fancy that it is not a pagan philosopher but a Christian apostle who is speaking."[12]

Turning to the Orient, we find that Confucianism represents a way of life that was followed by the Chinese people for well over 2,000 years. Although regarded by some people as a religion, it is non-theistic. Within its moral code there is no reference to God or to a teleological conception of nature.[13] Ethical issues, for the Confucian, are not determined or formulated apart from the social setting in which they arise. One does not find in Confucian ethics any clear demarcation between moral rules and other sorts of rules. There are no rules that are functionally the equivalent of the Mosaic Decalogue. One finds rather in Confucian ethics a theory of virtue rather than a theory of obligation. The sage follows his desires, satisfies his emotions but at the same time is restrained by a sense of propriety. That which is proper is that which is in accord with reason. The "reasonable" is a product of experience, both personal experience and that of the community. Yet classical Confucian ethics contains no division among the rational, the emotional, and the appetitive tendencies of man, comparable to their distinction in Greek morality.

Where difficult questions for ethical decision arise in a particular setting, their solution is to be found in the individual's sense of rightness. Whereas the exercise of the individual's sense of rightness in normal cases may well be the simple application of a rule, in complex issues that judgment may be challenged by a fellow agent. In such cases the agent proposing a solution must be prepared to offer a reasoned justification for his proposed course of action.

Confucius, like Plato, would have the ruler be a sage. Moral qualities, he maintained, are indispensable for leadership. To govern is to set things right, but he who would govern must first set himself right. He who would lead is the man who has cultivated, above all, the virtues of filial piety, magnanimity, loyalty, reciprocity, courage, and wisdom. Added to that list is the requirement that the superior man who would govern is one who loves his fellow man joyously from the innermost recesses of his heart. The superior man stands in awe of the ordinances of Heaven. He stands in awe of great men, and in awe of the "world of sages." A just ruler derives his authority from and rules by the Mandate of Heaven, a mandate conferred upon him by reason of his virtue and talent.[14]

It is said of Confucius that he prayed and fasted, that he attended sacrifices, and that he once even swore by "Heaven." Heaven is to be understood here, not simply as the regularities found in nature, as it is understood by a later disciple, Hsun-tzu,[15] but as a cosmic-moral power. Obedience and trust in Heaven are said to have given Confucius courage in times of disappointment and physical danger and to have provided him with a sense of a Heavenly mission in a troubled time.[16] The Way of Heaven, Confucius held, should serve as the model for the way among men. The ruler is something like a schoolmaster whose purpose is to help his charges become better men.

Buddhism, like Confucianism, is sometimes regarded as a religion, even though there is no reference to God, to a transcendent reality or to personal immortality. Like most traditions, Buddhism is complex and to a significant degree heterogeneous. Buddhist ethics from the very beginning has been committed to a middle way between asceticism and hedonism but is perhaps best considered as asceticism. Gautama Buddha (b. about 563 BC) condemned all attempts to enquire into or to define the supreme good of life. Salvation is not to be found in theoretical speculation but in a strenuous moral endeavor which aims at the destruction of desire, the root of all suffering. The path to deliverance is the extinction of desire, a turning away from human life and the external order. It is such a path that leads to Nirvana, the eternal beatific silence. How sweet, he taught, would it be to be freed of all craving and of all passion? The path to such freedom is a life of virtue, the habitual choice of the mean. The ethical ideal thus becomes one of quietism and spiritual detachment. The wise man will take no part in the life of the state or in the business of human affairs. He will live in solitude, perhaps as a monk, conforming his spirit to the Absolute.

Although the Buddhist commits himself to a certain way of life, on the whole Buddhism eschews mandatory dogmas and specific injunctions to which the adherent must conform. There are, nevertheless, traditional precepts that are to be observed. There are five precepts for the layman, precepts that prohibit killing, stealing, engaging in sexual misconduct, lying, and the drinking of intoxicating liquor. There are an additional five precepts for monastic novices, i.e., not to eat during prohibitive hours, not to take part in festivals and amusements, not to use luxurious furniture and beds, not to accept money for oneself, and not to use garlands, perfumes, or ornaments. There is within the many strands of Buddhism a recognition of the obligatory nature of charity, of hospitality, and of love for every living thing. Thus the life of the fetus is to be protected, whereas Confucian ethics would permit its destruction in the early stages.

Viewed from a Greek perspective, that is, from classical Western philosophy, one is inclined to see in Confucianism and Buddhism intimations of a natural law philosophy, even though both lack an ontological foundation. There is no doubt that the transition from either Buddhism or Confucianism to Christianity is relatively easy to make, in the sense that little has to be given up. Though both Confucianism and Buddhism are godless, the humanism characteristic of both is evident in their common admonition to self-restraint, charity and, in the case of Confucianism, its sense of propriety. We also find in both an appreciation of custom and tradition, and judged from a Christian perspective we have a sense of the fulfillment possible to both if only they were completed by the acceptance of divine revelation. Yet such "conversion" or fulfillment rarely happens. Confucianism and Buddhism are not a prelude to Christianity in the same way as Hellenic philosophy. It cannot be said of the East something we say of the intellect of the West—namely, that "Christ came in the fullness of time when the intellect of the West was prepared to receive the truths of the Gospel." Although one is compelled to admire the humanism found in Confucian and Buddhist moral codes, neither can be thought of as an expression of natural law morality. Natural law is distinctively Greek in origin and cannot be affirmed except in the Western context which gave it birth. It is the distinctive features of the Greek mind that I will attend to in a moment.

The Enlightenment, we know, challenged not only Christianity but the underpinnings of the moral philosophy characteristic of Aristotle and of those Stoics who followed his lead, notably by denying the reality of nature and human nature along with the principle of final causality or teleology in nature. Our topic compels us to ask: Is a systematic ethics possible without the implicit acknowledgment of those principles? Though he could not reason to either God or to personal immortality, Kant needed to posit both to ground his moral code. His ethics remains theistic, though it is not what we would call a natural law ethics. Affirmation of the intelligibility of nature, itself the product of intelligence, is the key to a natural law philosophy.

In both Aristotle and Aquinas there is the common affirmation that things have natures that are indicative of tendencies that beg to be fulfilled. Aristotle, for example, maintained that from a consideration of what a thing is in its tendential aspects, one can determine what is suitable for it, in other words, its good. From a consideration of what man is, one can determine what ends he ought to pursue. For Aristotle, the supreme end of man is happiness, which consists primarily in intellectual activity, all other pursuits being subordinate or instrumental to that one. Aquinas adds principally that ultimate fulfillment consists in an eternal beatitude in which man's intellectual and appetitive faculties will find complete satisfaction. For Aquinas, ultimate beatitude is possible even if temporal beatitude of the Aristotelian sort escapes one by reason of chance or the poverty of the human organism. This is the natural foundation for the theological virtue of hope.

The foregoing conception of natural law rests upon two ontological pillars: one, the conviction that there are intelligible natural structures, and two, the conviction that the processes of nature are purposive—in the language of Aristotle, upon the principles of essence and finality. But do these principles exhaust the intellectual commitments necessary to support a natural law outlook? We come back to the question, "Is it possible to subscribe to a natural law basis for morality without first establishing the existence of God?" The answer at first blush seems to be in the affirmative. We seem to find the rudiments of a natural law outlook in Confucian and Buddhist codes of conduct. Furthermore, in the West we find many who are agnostic with respect to the question of God's existence and yet who agree that arbitrary will is not final, that civil law and conscience are to be measured against an independent scale.[17] How account for this?

The Confucian, the Buddhist, and the neo-pagan of the West have in common a humanistic ethic but one that is not supported by an acknowledgment of God's existence or by a systematic philosophy of human nature. A difference between ancient moral codes associated with the East and those proclaimed in the contemporary West is this: Confucian and Buddhist moral codes were developed without any knowledge of Christ, whereas much of contemporary Western philosophy has known but has rejected Christ. Yet the moral outlook characteristic of Christianity has not been culturally eradicated and remains to a considerable extent, although unacknowledged, in Western secular philosophy. Dorothy Sayers made this point succinctly in her 1947, Oxford lecture, "The Lost Tools of Learning."[18] "The truth," she says, "is that for the last three hundred years or so we have been living on our educational capital. . . . Right down to the nineteenth century, our public affairs were mostly managed, and our books and journals were for the most part written, by people brought up in homes, and trained in places where the Scholastic curriculum with its emphasis on the Trivium and Quadrivium was still alive in the memory and almost in the blood. Just so, many people today who are atheist or agnostic in religion are governed in their conduct by a code of Christian ethics which is so rooted that it never occurs to them to question it." She then adds this cautionary note, "But one cannot live on capital forever."

Accumulated capital or tradition obviously plays a large role in how a people conduct themselves. St. Thomas, in discussing the role of tradition, gives it almost the force of law. Within Confucianism tradition plays an all-important role. It represents the collective wisdom of a people as they confront their daily affairs. For Mao, to complete his socialist revolution, the Confucian tradition had to be eliminated. To that end, he was aided by an intellectual class, tutored by John Dewey, who held that the function of education is to challenge rather than to perpetuate the inherited.[19] Within the West we know full well what happens when a theistic-grounded morality is repudiated in favor of an outright materialism. We have only to recall the atrocities committed in the name of communism and national socialism. More recently, given the ascendancy of the materialist, secular outlook within the West, we find a renewed threat to Western civilization itself, as biblical and traditional moral standards have been called into question at all levels of society.

The cultural effects of atheism cannot be denied. Absent an acknowledgment of God's existence, worship and the things pertaining to worship have no basis, and the consequence of their being lost within a secular culture portends the loss of Western culture itself. No one can deny that the great achievements of Western art, i.e., in painting, architecture, music, and literature, have been motivated by a sense of the sacred. It is true that Kant's abstract and moralistic interpretation of religion attaches little value to visible manifestations of piety and worship. His pietistic upbringing may have led him to deprecate the cultural effects of communal religious practice, a position that is consistent with his purely moral religion, but contemporary atheism has gone much further, insofar as it seeks to suppress all public manifestations of religion—that, in spite of the fact that European culture has thrived on, and can almost be defined by, its feasts and pageants in celebration of sacred events.

By way of a concluding comment, it may be argued that a theistic natural law theory is best construed as a meta-ethic. Although a natural law outlook is purely philosophical, it opens one to religious testimony, testimony that may have some additional things to say about life's goals, about happiness, and about the norms by which they ought to be pursued. An important feature is its empirical character, that is, its fidelity to evidence drawn from common experience and the sciences of man, insofar as that evidence bears on human fulfillment. Often when natural law is invoked, it is both presented and criticized as a set of normative propositions, which, because of their universality and necessity, in some fashion, transcend periods and cultures. It has that feature, to be sure, but it is best understood as a meta-ethic. It can easily be shown that natural law theory, in addition to its openness to the transcendent has a contribution to make on several fronts, notably as they are discussed in contemporary literature. In providing a theory about the determination of moral norms, it speaks to topics such as ethical reasoning, the movement from descriptive to normative assertions, the extra-legal grounds for judicial decision, and the societal basis of law. Natural law when so understood is seen less as a code than as a metaphysics or philosophical anthropology that calls attention to certain time-transcending facts about human nature and society, facts that must be taken into account as the race grapples with ever more complex moral issues arising notably from the biological and natural sciences and the recent phenomenon of globalization.

The "Universal Declaration on Bioethics and Human Rights," adopted by the General Conference of UNESCO, October 19, 2005, is perhaps the closest one can come to a transcultural declaration of moral objectives. Drafted by an international committee representing the major cultures of the globe, it deliberately eschews any reference to a divinely ordained moral order or even acknowledges that there are "laws of nature." Laudably it promotes the value of human dignity, human rights, and fundamental human freedoms. It insists on honesty and the value of cooperation, dialogue, social responsibility, and the priority of the interest of the individual over that of the state. In the practice of medicine, it emphasizes the importance of consent to any medical intervention and speaks to the patient's right of privacy. The list goes on, but what is missing is an ontological grounding of the principles assumed. Although it speaks of human dignity and human rights, their derivation is not addressed. Omitted, too, is any reference to an important setting of human life—the family—and of that which contributes to its stability. There is no recognition of the destructive force of practices such as adultery, divorce, contraception, abortion, and euthanasia. In fact nothing is condemned; only the laudable, by universal consent, is affirmed. The genius of the document is that it is bland enough for the atheist, the theist, the Christian, Moslem, Buddhist, or Confucian to sign onto. Clearly for the West, this "Declaration" is no substitute for the Mosaic Decalogue. Furthermore, in substituting vague aspirations for tradition, it is, for example, less a guide than Confucianism. One is left with the unintended thought that morality is specific to a culture, with or without God.

NOTES

1. Immanuel Kant, *Critique of Pure Reason*, trans. Norman Kemp Smith (New York: Macmillan, 1929; reprinted, New York: St. Martin's Press, 1965), 650.

2. Elizabeth Anscombe, "Modern Moral Philosophy," *Philosophy*, XXXIII, no. 6.

3. John Rawls, "*A Theory of Justice* (Cambridge, Mass.: Harvard University Press, 1972).

4. Marcus Tullius Cicero, *Discussions at Tusculum* in *Cicero: On the Good Life*, trans. Michael Grant (London: Penguin Books, 1971).

5. Marcus Tullius Cicero, *De officiis*, trans. Walter Miller (Cambridge, Mass.: Harvard University Press), 1913.

6. Cicero, *Tusculum,* 52–53.

7. Cicero, *Tusculum*, 61.

8. Cicero, *Tusculum*, 61.

9. Marcus Tullius Cicero, *De re publica III*, trans. D.R. Shackelton Bailey (Cambridge, Mass: Cambridge University Press, 1977).

10. Cicero, *De officiis, I*, 7.

11. Cicero, *De officiis, I,* 9.

12. (As quoted by Walter Miller in his introduction to *Cicero: On Duties* (Cambridge, Mass.: Harvard University Press, 1913), xiv; numerous reprintings.

13. For a brief overview of Confucian ethics, see Anthony S. Cua, "Confucianism: Ethics," in A. S. Cua, *Encyclopedia of Chinese Philosophy* (New York: Routledge, 2003), 72–79.

14. May Sim, in a valuable study of Aristotle and Confucius, makes the point that Confucius' defense of propriety by an appeal to nature or to the Mandate of Heaven is thin and inexplicable (May Sim, *Remastering Morals with Aristotle and Confucius* [Cambridge, Mass.: Cambridge University Press, 2007], 3).

15. Cf. Antonio S. Cua, *Ethical Argumentation: A Study in Hsun Tzu's Moral Epistemology* (Honolulu: University of Hawaii Press, 1985).

16. Yi Pao Mei, "Confucianism," in *Encyclopedia Britannica*, 15th ed. (1973), 1091–1099.

17. An absurd exception is to be found in a passage from a U.S. Supreme Court ruling supporting a woman's right to abortion that declared: "At the heart of liberty is the right to define one's own concept of existence, of meaning of the universe and the mystery of human life." (*Planned Parenthood of Southeastern Pa.* v. *Casey,* 505 U.S. 833).

18. Available online at: www.cambridgestudycenter.com/articles/sayers1.htm.

19. Cf. Zhixin Su, "A Critical Evaluation of John Dewey's Influence on Education," *American Journal of Education,* 103 (May 1995).

Chapter Fifteen

Responsibility: Recognition and Limits

Acknowledging that global economic integration is moving at an unprecedented pace, the chairman of the U.S. Federal Reserve System, Ben S. Bernanke, in a 2006 address urged policy makers to ensure that the benefits of globalization are widely shared. Although his statement was almost a literal quotation from John Paul II, Bernanke's motive was purely financial, a desire to stem protectionist sentiment in the disadvantaged trading partner.[1] One cannot fault his reasoning, exploitation may not pay in the long run. When F. A. Hayek addressed the phenomenon of globalization almost seventy-five years ago, he feared the power and exploitation that usually flowed from foreign investment.

Economic and other data show clearly the gap between the "developed world" and the so-called "developing world," between rich nations and poor nations. The poverty and misery characteristic of the latter are shown daily on worldwide television. The data recognized, the moral judgment is made; those that have should do something to alleviate the lot of the have-nots. Churchmen talk about a fair distribution of the earth's goods without reference to how those goods are produced, let alone how they might be distributed. Responsibility of the first world to the third world is taken for granted. "Rich nations," "first world," "developed world" are abstractions, yet they support the notion that somehow one collective is responsible for or to another collective.

On the occasion of the 2006 meeting of the G-7, the Center for Global Development released data to show that the commitment of rich countries to the world's poorest nations is slipping. The center maintains a "Commitment to Development Index" and ranks nations according to a set of criteria that reflects national policies and the amount of aid proffered in proportion to the size of the donor's economy. In the judgment of Dennis Roodman, designer of the Index, all nations including the highest could do better. The United States judged in absolute terms with respect to the amount of aid rendered ranks last on the environmental component of the Index because of low gasoline taxes that purportedly encourage consumption and because of per-capita greenhouse gas emission that are second only to Australia's among rich nations. Speaking of the G-7, Roodman says "From what was needed to what was promised, the results are disappointing."[2] Whatever one thinks of Roodman's index, the underlying assumption is that the rich nations have a responsibility vis-à-vis the poor nations of the world and should feel guilty for not doing more.

Readiness to accept the notion of "collective responsibility" and its correlative "collective guilt," no doubt, stems from discussions following a number of egregious cases where societies taken as a whole seem accountable. The twentieth century provides numerous examples of societies' acting, if not as a whole, at least with sufficient unity, to implement morally unacceptable policy, i.e., Germany under Hitler, the Soviet Union under Stalin, both governments systematically eliminating so-called "enemies of the state." One thinks also of South Africa's limiting full civic participation to whites, of the ante-bellum American South enslaving the black, and the post-bellum American South enacting segregation laws. To what extent are we willing to blame the German or Soviet peoples for the atrocities committed within the borders of their nations? Can the nineteenth century immigrant cooper working within his shop in Minneapolis be blamed for slavery or for post-bellum statutes enacted with the South? The way we talk about these matters may contribute to misunderstanding. We speak of "sharing in the greatness of a nation," we may say that "we take pride in belonging to a scholarly family," but we must be careful not to hypostatize abstractions or make them bearers of a value. Linguistic devices that make for succinctness of expression are to be recognized for their metaphorical and elliptical meaning and not taken for literal truth.[3] A family group or nation, I am willing to argue, cannot be the bearer of guilt: in neither is there sufficient unity or participation in the deliberative process to warrant accountability.

Corporations are different. They are not mere aggregates of people but have a metaphysical-logical identity. Otto van Gierke has suggested that the law in conferring on the corporation the status of a legal person is merely recognizing a prelegal, social condition. The corporation is the result of certain social actions and possesses a de facto personality that the law declares to be a juridical fact.[4] Brian Tierney traces the notion of corporate personality to medieval canon law and its doctrine of agency. "In Roman law," writes Tierney, "an individual or group could appoint an agent to negotiate with a third party, but the result of the transaction was to establish an obligation between the third party and the agent, not directly between the third party and the principal. In canon law, when a corporate group established a representative with *plena potestas,* the group was directly obligated by the representative's acts even when it had not consented to them in advance."[5] The ancient Roman principle, *Quod omnes tangit ab omnibus approbatur* (what touches all is to be approved by all), was to be replaced by one that allowed a representative to act on behalf of all. Thus commitments made in the name of an organized group may persist even after the composition of the group or its will changes. If a group reneges on a commitment, the fault may be that of no individual member, yet the liability for the breach of contract, falling on the group as a whole, will distribute burdens quite unavoidably on faultless members.

Peter A. French, in an extended analysis of corporate responsibility, maintains that for a corporation to be treated as a moral person, it must be possible to attribute to it a corporate intention. This is different from attributing intentions to biological persons who comprise its board of directors or its top level management.[6] Corporations, at least major corporations, have internal decision-making structures, and this arrangement is reflected in their organizational charts and in their established methods of reaching corporate policy. French believes that in many cases one can infer the basic beliefs of a corporation by examining its actions over a period of time. The moment policy is sidestepped or violated, it is no longer the policy of the company. Maverick acts cannot be described as having been done for corporate reasons. Thus it is possible to distinguish between individual staff negligence and corporate negligence. Executives voting to adopt certain objectives when required by the corporate structure to vote, in fact, constitute the corporation's deciding to do something. A corporate officer who ignores corporate policy, possibly in the name of expediency, may be morally accountable without moral blame's being attached to the corporation, although corporate civil accountability may be unavoidable. These principles apply to the military occupation of Iraq and to famous cases such as the *Exxon Valdez* oil spill and more recent oil spills off the coast of France and Spain. In the aftermath of the *Exxon Valdez* oil spill, the U.S. National Wildlife Federation urged prosecutors to go after the individual at the top of the corporation who was responsible for the accident. In due course the former skipper of the Valdez and its owner Exxon itself were criminally charged.

It is not surprising to find that following the close of World War II there were numerous discussions of collective responsibility and guilt as the Allied officials debated humanitarian policy vis-à-vis a fallen foe. The literature, of course, is enormous, but a few examples will illustrate the dominant American position at that time that has some bearing on the present discussion.

Judge Robert H. Jackson, the American member of the team prosecuting the Nazis at Nurnberg, in his address at the opening of the trial, repudiated the notion of collective responsibility.[7] "Jackson, made it clear, writes Suzanne Brown-Fleming, that "it would be unjust to indict all German people, women and children who had no voice in domestic politics, as well as to indict the countless number of anti-Nazis, many of whom suffered years in concentration camps."[8] General Robert A. McClure took a similar approach. The U.S. Army, he thought, should approach the German people not on the basis of guilt and punishment, but rather on the basis of cause and consequence.[9] General Dwight Eisenhower condemned a policy of vengeance and called for a fair dealing with a fallen foe.[10] Bernard Baruch, an advisor to Franklin D. Roosevelt, had taken the opposite view. Many thought that a distinction had to be made between guilt and responsibility, one that would permit a claim for reparations without the necessity of establishing guilt on the part of the German populace as a whole. I will return momentarily to the distinction between responsibility and guilt.

Other examples imputing collective guilt may be offered. When the New World was celebrating the 500th anniversary of Columbus's 1492 voyage, dissident voices emerged to condemn the colonization that followed. It was not uncommon to find not only Christopher Columbus but European civilization as a whole condemned for all the ills that befell the native population in the years following the discovery of America. The "affirmative action" movement in the United States may be taken as an example of one generation's assuming responsibility for the sins of another. Peoples, generations, classes, races, industries and religious bodies are often held accountable, not in some vague, "public opinion sort of way," but before courts of law. From tort law as practiced in the United States to affirmative action policy, blame is often assigned to groups no longer in existence and sometimes to mere conceptual entities. Restitution is not infrequently extracted from groups or from heirs of groups without any responsibility for harm's being established.

To cite one notorious example from the United States that may have its counterpart in Europe, consider the concept "market share" where corporate defendants may be assessed damage even after proving that they could not possibly have caused the harm. Courts in several states have employed market share in cases where several corporations that are marketing essentially the same product are held responsible for harm done to a plaintiff who does not remember whose product was used. Damages are in such cases distributed among the manufacturers on the basis of their percentage of the market, with no concrete responsibility having been established.

Broad notions entertained in the framing and implementation of law are almost always the byproduct of previous academic discussion. Before the concept of market share could have become current, certain philosophical discussions of collective guilt, collective responsibility, and punishment had to take place. While this is not the place to examine the history of all of these concepts, little inquiry is needed to show that the notion of collective guilt is an ancient one. In fact, discussions of that notion can be found in ancient and medieval texts as well as modern and contemporary literature. The ancients no less than we recognized that societies are generated out of collective beliefs and traditions that are passed unconsciously by individuals. Emile Durkheim, the influential social theorist of the late nineteenth century, was convinced that traditions can exist in groups even when they are not instantiated by any individual. In his *Rules of Sociological Method* (1895) he even accords ontological status to social traditions and social relations independent of individual members of the group.[11] In an influential volume written shortly after the close of World War II, Karl Jaspers attempted to deal with guilt of the German nation.[12] The horrors perpetrated in the concentration camps were by then generally known. What was suspected had become graphically illustrated. Jaspers raised the question of guilt in the context of demands for restitution. To what extent were the German people as a whole culpable, and to what extent could one expect atonement? The issue was not that of the responsibility of the German state. No one questioned national accountability or the requirement of "reparations." Jaspers was probing much deeper. In a section entitled "Scheme of Distinctions," Jaspers, like the Allied Command, was aware that the vast majority of German-speaking peoples were not morally responsible for the atrocities committed under the Third Reich. If the vast majority of the German people were neither legally nor morally guilty, could the German-speaking peoples yet be held accountable? In an effort to sort things out, Jaspers introduced the notion of "collective guilt at the psychic level." He reasoned that insofar as the German people shared a common language and a common culture and insofar as they were nourished by a common literature, common music and distinctive patterns of civic behavior, they could be said to be a collective. In Jaspers's analysis there existed enough solidarity to produce a national psyche that in some sense could be held accountable such that one generation could make claims on another. Jaspers recognized the difficulty of defending a notion of psychological guilt apart from criminal, political, or moral guilt. He preferred to call it "metaphysical guilt." Having distinguished the four concepts of guilt,[13] Jaspers writes in the concluding pages of his book, "A crime is atoned for; a political liability is limited by a peace treaty and thus brought to an end. . . . But moral and metaphysical guilt, understood only by the individual in his community, are by their very nature not atoned for. They do not cease. Whoever bears them enters into a process lasting all his life."[14] "There exists," he believed, "a solidarity among men as human beings that makes each co-responsible for every wrong and every injustice in the world, especially for crimes committed in his presence or with his knowledge. If I fail to do whatever I can to prevent them, I too am guilty. If I was present at the murder of others without risking my life to prevent it, I feel guilty in a way not adequately conceivable either legally, political or morally."[15] Elsewhere in a puzzling remark, that undermines his theses, he concedes, "There is no such thing as a people as a whole."[16]

Jaspers was only one among many theologians who in the aftermath of the war began rethinking the notions of "responsibility," "guilt," and "restitution." On the American side of the Atlantic, Aloisius Muench, Bishop of Fargo, South Dakota, devoted his Lenten Pastoral Letter in 1946 to the European situation.[17] In his pastoral letter entitled "One World in Charity" Muench objected to official policy, "official inhumanity," he called it, "which does not permit the United Nations Relief and Rehabilitation Administration to ship relief supplies to either Germany or Japan, and besides does not even allow private relief agencies to send and distribute food, clothing, and medicine to war-stricken people living a pitiable life in the ruins of their bombed-out cities."[18] In Europe, policy dictated that refugees from the East were to be taken care of first. The needs of the German people were to be considered last, and only then was aid to be given to avoid disease or the possibility of insurrection.[19] Muench was equally critical of Nazism and Communism, as well as the Allied bombing responsible for the holocaust inflicted on the German populace.

Reflecting on the issues raised by the foregoing, we have laid bare a number of distinctions and assumptions. No one denies that guilt implies responsibility. Responsibility in turn presupposes freedom to act or not to act. In speaking of freedom, it is necessary to distinguish 1) between freedom in a moral sense and freedom under the law, and 2) between the legal sense of guilt and the moral sense. One can be accountable before civil law without being morally responsible for harm. Civil law itself recognizes this when it takes into consideration motivation and extenuating circumstances and sometimes allows them to mitigate guilt. The continuity between the moral and the civil is so connected that in practice the distinction is often blurred or ignored. Moral outrage is not infrequently thought to be immediately translatable into law. Appeals for the creation of law typically invoke danger to health or damage to the environment or cite other material or social disadvantage if action is not taken, but they are, nonetheless, appeals to the moral order.

Another aspect to keep in mind is that action follows judgment and that judgment is made necessarily within a cultural context. How one views a proposed course of action is in part dependent on one's education, i.e., the distinctions one has learned to make and the principles one invokes habitually.

Certain courses of action may be acceptable in the West that are unthinkable in the East. In the West some may see nothing wrong with the merchandising of pornography, with divorce, or with abortion. The same is not true in a strict Islamic society. It would be precarious to attribute moral guilt to those who act in the light of conscience, even if that conscience, when judged by a time-transcending moral code, seems to be ill informed. But this does not mean that holders are unaccountable for their beliefs in all respects. From any point of view one has an obligation to form a correct conscience.

Also recognized is the principle that not all law binds in conscience. Good civil law, as we have suggested, tends to explicate or elaborate the moral order. Thus building codes, traffic regulations, and rules governing securities trading are in some sense moral dictates before they become statutes. Law that flouts common perceptions of right and wrong is not regarded as morally binding. The distinction between civil law and moral law, although sometimes challenged from the academy, is universally recognized. The distinction cuts both ways. A corporation that operates wholly within the law may be guilty of moral infraction. The sale of pornography, the creation of advertising that deliberately manipulates the truth, or media distortion on behalf of partisan causes are examples to the point. One can make the claim that the manufacturing of faux merchandise, merchandise that mimics the genuine article and is usually marketed to the ill-educated or unsuspecting, is a kind of moral infraction. Some would extend guilt to those who manufacture tobacco products or distilled spirits or make clothing from animal pelts. No one would hesitate to attribute moral guilt to a corporation that knowingly manufactures a defective and potentially dangerous product, quite apart from any civic penalty that might be inflicted.

To come to the point: granted immorality on the part of a corporation, where does moral guilt lie? Are all who are associated with the corporation collectively guilty? If not, how far down the corporate ladder does responsibility extend? To the worker on the assembly line? To the wholesaler? To the retailer? To the shareholder? If guilt follows knowledge, it may be that only a few in the testing laboratory or in the executive suite are privy to the information that a given product is potentially troublesome or could be modified with additional cost to diminish risk. Although the corporation before the law can be held accountable for negligence, it is difficult to believe that the average worker in the plant or billing office, unless the company has a record of dubious performance, has the knowledge that would imply criminal complicity. There are exceptions of course. Complicity may be much more widespread or deeper than is sometimes thought. We have all read stories of whistle blowers who, rather than be complicit, have brought to light questionable practices, sometimes to the gratitude of management. Where corporate guilt is determined, it is not likely that all workers would be held accountable either by an irate group of shareholders or before a court of law. When a specific individual, in violation of corporate policy, has been guilty of harm, it makes little sense to hold the corporation criminally liable, subject to punitive damages that are ultimately shared by innocent shareholders.

Jaspers, in his treatise on German guilt, would likely recognize all of these principles, yet he held that the German-speaking populace could not avoid what he called "metaphysical guilt." The currency of this notion does not date to antiquity, and it is certainly not found in the tradition of Aristotle and Aquinas. Psychological or metaphysical guilt in Jaspers's sense is something self-inflicted, subjectively generated, known only to God and to the sinner. It is not accountable to some universally recognized moral order. Theologians may speak of the "stain of sin," but the Calvinist and the Catholic may have different things in mind when talking about punishment due to sin. If there are no outside standards by which the conscience can be measured, metaphysical guilt becomes an indelible ontological disposition that not even therapy can remove. The Catholic may confess, repent, do penance and leave it all behind. Subjectively imposed guilt is indelible and can be exploited by others to gain concessions both of an ideological and material sort.

Returning to the notion of responsibility apart from the guilt question, in what sense are "those who have" responsible for "those who have not?" Indeed, what are the obligations or responsibility of rich nations to poor nations? As I write, one encounters daily appeals for the poor of Somalia and Darfur. The Christian may recognize an obligation in charity that the agnostic may not. Cardinal Muench, in condemning allied policy in the aftermath of World War II, could explicitly invoke Christian principles of compassion, mercy, and charity to positive effect. The vengeful Morgenthau Plan was rejected by President Truman, and Morgenthau's resignation was immediately accepted when precipitously offered on the eve of the Potsdam Conference.[20] Social philosophers, such as Emile Durkheim and John Dewey, have long recognized the motivating power of religion in confronting the difficult good. In a largely secular milieu, are appeals to charity possible? Dorothy Sayers would answer, "yes." In her 1947 Oxford lecture, "The Lost Tools of Learning," she noticed "that many people today who are atheist or agnostic in religion are governed in their conduct by a code of Christian ethics which is so rooted (in the culture) that it never occurs to them to question it." She then adds, aware of the Enlightenment's influence on Western intellectuals, "But one cannot live on capital forever."[21]

When "obligation in charity" cannot be invoked, we find pragmatic appeals on the basis of self-interest; that and emotional appeals accompanied by graphic depictions of need that beg for remedy. Acknowledging that both pragmatic and emotional appeals often fail, the United Nations has sought the power to tax to alleviate recognized need. Whereas charity is rational, imposing its own limits, emotional appeals tend to be unrestrained and often impulsively lead to inappropriate action and squandered resources.

The gap between the "developed world" and the "developing world" is not likely to be bridged anytime soon. Chairman Bernanke's call to avoid exploitation is nothing other than a call for justice, a call for responsible behavior, but apart from treating them justly, the question remains: does that make rich nations responsible for poor ones? In spite of the social determinism favored by the political left, we still recognize the principle of self-reliance, a principle that analogically may be applied to nations.

If we have reached any conclusion, it is this: responsibility cannot be assigned willy-nilly. There is an objective, ontologically grounded moral order in the light of which responsibility is both recognized and limited. All responsibility is determined on the basis of causality. Of the various senses of responsibility, that fostered by charity is not to be equated with legal or moral responsibility. And finally, no sense of responsibility can engender, as Jaspers would have it, an indelible metaphysical guilt.

NOTES

1. *Wall Street Journal*, 26 August, 2006, A-3.

2. News release, Southasia.oneworld.net, September 4, 2006.

3. Cf. Hywel David Lewis, *Philosophy* XXII (84) (January 1948): 47. See also Joel Feinberg, "Collective Responsibility," *Journal of Philosophy* LXV (21) (November 1968): 674–688 and Virginia Held, "Can a Random Collection of Individuals be Morally Responsible," *Journal of Philosophy* LXVII, (July 1970): 471–481.

4. Otto Von Gierke, *Political Theory of the Middle Ages*, trans F.W. Maitland (Cambridge, Mass.: Cambridge University Press, 1900).

5 Brian Tierney, *Religion, Law and the Growth of Constitutional Thought, 1150–1650* (Cambridge, Mass.: Cambridge University Press, 1982), 23.

6. Peter A. French, *Collective and Corporate Responsibility* (New York: Columbia University Press, 1984), 39.

7. Jackson said, "We know the Nazi party was not put into power by a majority of the German vote. We know that it came to power by an evil alliance between the most extreme of the Nazi revolutionaries, the most unrestrained of the German reactionaries and the most aggressive of the German militarists," in: Suzanne Brown-Fleming, *The Holocaust and the Catholic Conscience: Cardinal Aloisius Muench and the Guilt Question in Germany* (South Bend, Ind.: University of Notre Dame Press, 2006), 149.

8. Brown-Fleming, *The Holocaust.*

9. Brown-Fleming, *The Holocaust,* 16.

10. Brown-Fleming, *The Holocaust*, 148.

11. Emile Durkheim, *Rules of Sociological Method*, trans. S. Soloway and J. Mueller (New York: Free Press, 1964), 7.

12. Karl Jaspers, *The Question of German Guilt*, trans. E. B. Ashton (New York: Capricorn Books, 1961). (First published by Dial Press, Inc., 1947.)

13. Jaspers, *The Question*, 31–32.

14. Jaspers, *The Question*, 117.

15. Jaspers, *The Question*, 32.

16. Jaspers, *The Question*, 41.

17. Muench was subsequently named Apostolic Visitor to Germany in 1946 at the request of the American occupation forces, and in 1959 he was appointed Papal Nuncio to Germany. In 1959 he was named Cardinal. Cf. "The Cardinal Muench Papers," Catholic University of America Archives.

18. "One World in Charity," A Pastoral (Lent 1946) 9. Text provided courtesy Jordan Patty, Archivist, The Catholic University of America.

19. Secretary of State, James F. Byrnes, in his statement of December 11, 1945, defining official policies for Germany. "In terms of world supply, liberated areas must enjoy a higher priority than Germany throughout this first postwar winter," quoted by Muench, p. 9.

20. Margaret Truman, *Harry S Truman* (New York: William Morrow & Co., 1973), 265.

21. Dorothy Sayers, "The Lost Tools of Learning," 1947 Lecture at Oxford University, p. 12. Available at www.brccs.org/Sayers.

Chapter Sixteen

National Identity

The present generation, for the first time in history, is experiencing a unity of mankind such that nothing essential can happen anywhere that does not concern all. The Stoic understanding of the unity of mankind, the framework of the *polis*, has been expanded to include the whole of mankind. The growing interdependence among nations seemingly has ended the days of absolute national sovereignty. Almost imperceptibly a new attitude has developed regarding interdependence, so much so that a United States of Europe is regarded as an imminent possibility. As Europeans debate a constitution, the loss of national sovereignty looms with unacknowledged consequences.

This eradication of national identity is occurring at the same time that there is a widespread awareness that the West has lost some of the spiritual resources which animated its past. When George Santayana wrote nearly a century ago that "the civilization characteristic of Christendom has not disappeared, yet another civilization has begun to take its place,"[1] he was not alone in his assessment. Philosophers and theologians as diverse as Nietzsche and Leo XIII addressed the new intellectual climate shaping nineteenth-century European thought. Old patterns of thought were losing the allegiance of the European intelligentsia. Lost was a confidence that the inherited could withstand the assault of the new science and technology and the progress it implied. Nietzsche and later Husserl and Heidegger, each in his own way, called for a return to classical Greece as the source for an understanding of Western culture. Leo XIII recommended Aquinas as the antidote to the nihilism and anti-Christian spirit which animated the intellectual climate in the mid-1800s. Discussion in philosophical circles tended to focus on the meaning of the concept "Europe." Hilaire Belloc could confidently assert that "Europe is the Faith, the Faith is Europe," but that view was not widely shared in the intellectual circles of his day, notably by the philosophers of Enlightenment parentage who thought they had eradicated Christianity. The classical sources of Western culture could not be denied, but was that the whole story? Paul Valéry, we shall subsequently see, would answer with an emphatic "no."

In his 1935 lecture, "Philosophy and the Crisis of European Humanity," Edmund Husserl offered an analysis of Europe's spiritual and intellectual crisis that looked to ancient Greece as a way out of the crisis facing the West. Husserl found in the Greek spirit of philosophical inquiry the sources for "free and universal theoretical reflection" that would serve as a model for a "supranational" ideal of reason. In Husserl's words, "There are only two escapes from the crisis of European existence: the downfall of Europe in its estrangement from its own rational sense of life, its fall into hostility toward the spiritual into barbarity; or the rebirth of Europe from the spirit of philosophy through a heroism of reason that overcomes naturalism once and for all."[2]

Like his mentor Husserl, Martin Heidegger similarly attempted to show that a revival of the Greeks was essential to the future of the West. Heidegger looked upon Germany as the privileged nation whose historical mission is to save the West "when the spiritual strength of the West fails and the West starts to come apart at the seams."[3] Notably, in his several speeches on the Hellenic patrimony of the West, Heidegger omits any reference to Roman Catholicism and Roman humanism.

Historians remind us that cultures do not develop in a linear order of historical growth but grow sporadically, unlike the causal determinism characteristic of science and technology. By the third century B.C. Greece was on the threshold of modern science, but that science had to await the sixteenth century before the intellect of Western man had achieved the necessary understanding of the relation of science to technology. Distinctive cultural patterns arising from religious, social, economic, and political factors provided the necessary condition.

The well-known historian of science and technology Lynn White, in a colorful phrase, reminds us that "the [Benedictine] monk was the first intellectual [in the history of the West] to get dirt under his fingernails."[4] Speaking of the Benedictine, White goes on to say, "He did not immediately launch into scientific investigation, but in his very person he destroyed the old artificial barrier between the empirical and the speculative, the manual and the liberal arts and thus helped create a social atmosphere favorable to scientific and technological development."[5] White offers his observations in the context of his essay, "Dynamo and Virgin Reconsidered," noting that "St. Bernard's Cistercian monks were so devoted to the Virgin that every one of their hundreds of monasteries was dedicated to her; yet these White Benedictines seem often to have led the way in the use of power. Some of their abbeys had four or five water wheels, each powering a different workshop."[6] He then makes the important point that

> the Virgin and the dynamo are not opposing principles permeating the universe; they are allies. The growth of medieval power technology . . . is a chapter in the conquest of freedom. More than that, to those who search out "why it happened," it is a part of the history of religion. The humanitarian technology which in later centuries had grown from medieval seeds was not rooted in economic necessity for such 'necessity' is inherent in every society, yet has found expression only in the Occident, nourished in the tradition of Western theology. It is ideas which make necessities conscious. The labor-saving power machines of the latter Middle Ages were harmonious with the religious assumptions of the worth of even the most seemingly degraded human personality.[7]

Modernity since the European Enlightenment has acquired an implacable faith in progress. Success achieved in science and technology fostered the belief that a similar success is possible in economics, politics, and the social order. Defects in human institutions were to be approached with confidence that they, too, could be remedied with time as if they were problems in physics or mechanics. Lost was an awareness of the distinctive culture and its sources which made Western achievement possible. Those sources lie in classical antiquity, in the Hellenism and Christianity which gave us confidence that the human intellect is powerful enough to ferret out the secrets of an intelligible and purposive nature. This confidence is at once the root of science and technology and the rule of law as reflected in Western social and political institutions. Those laws and institutions create "a people" to the extent that they are lived, not simply recorded on parchment or engraved in marble or bronze but are instilled in the minds and dispositions of citizens.

Just as looking into the past is an essential route to finding oneself, so too a people or a nation needs to understand its past. The German word "Bildung" is useful insofar as it signifies a process, a process which is a continuum of impressions and evaluations which cumulatively give one a sense of belonging to a collective with a distinctive heritage. Only in such a Bildung in which family ties, fostered and perpetuated by love and reverence for forefathers, is it likely that freedom and the rule of law will prevail. Social cooperation depends on national identity. To respect one's people is not tantamount to respecting whatever repressive government may have been thrust upon them in the past.

A point that needs to be underscored is the distinction between political and cultural nationalism. Hilaire Belloc could proclaim, "Spiritually we are all Semites." Despite a certain common spiritual and cultural affinity, rendered increasingly evident as Islam rises in opposition to the West, cultural differences within Europe exist and define national identity. The European Union notwithstanding, there is a German national character, an Italian character, and a French character, and the world is richer for it. An outsider would not want these traits to disappear. It is more difficult to define an American character since until recently it was an amalgam of the many strains found in Europe. Immigration policy and the failure to integrate the black into what is essentially European culture has eroded not only educational standards but the manner and morals of a people. Standards of behavior have been shifted to the lowest common denominator. There is little doubt that the identity of the American people is being further eroded as a result of a political emphasis on diversity and multiculturalism. Moreover, the campaign for inclusion points to a more insidious form of diversity, that which exists between the culture of the intellectuals and the culture of farmers, manufacturers, and tradesmen, sometimes referred to as the difference between middle America and the eastern seaboard intelligentsia.

National identity is a challenge to be faced both in Europe and North America. Absent a common bond in the people, absent a cultural identity, can the laws, let alone those customs and transactions which depend on virtue in the people, long survive? England, as a result of its immigration and asylum policy, is losing its identity, to the chagrin of native Englishmen. The newcomers, in bringing their own culture with them, eschew British traditions and create enclaves of their own to the detriment of the larger society. Some say the Englishman we know from history, literature and film is becoming extinct, with the sovereignty of the country itself in jeopardy as the European Union erodes Britain's self-governance and national identity.

Perhaps we should more properly speak of European identity. Paul Valéry, writing in the first quarter of the twentieth century, gives us a very broad definition of Europe. Europe is more than a geographical designation, he insists. "There is a certain trait, quite distinct from race, nationality, and even language which unites the countries of the West and Central Europe making them all alike."[8] "Wherever the names of Caesar, Caius, Trajan, and Virgil, of Moses and St. Paul and Aristotle, Plato and Euclid have had simultaneous meaning and authority, there is Europe."[9] Again, "Every race and land that has been successfully Romanized, Christianized and as regards the mind, disciplined by the Greeks, is absolutely European."[10] Shakespeare, he points out, is an integral part of French, Italian, and German culture; so, too, Goethe and Dante. If Valéry were part of the commission drafting a European Constitution,[11] he would insist that it contain reference to both Christianity and the character of Europe,[12] for Christianity introduced a universal moral law that took its place alongside the juridical unity contributed by Roman law. Christianity, Valéry is convinced, in taking all it could from Rome gave us a common law, a common God, one and the same temporal judge, and one and the same judge in eternity. Valéry continues:

> Christianity proposed to the mind the most subtle, the greatest, and indeed the most fruitful of problems. Whether it were a question of the value of testimony, the criticism of texts, or the sources and guarantees of knowledge; of the distinction between faith and reason, and the opposition that arises between them or the antagonism between faith, deeds, and works; a question of freedom, servitude, or grace; of spiritual and material power, and their mutual conflict, the equality of men, the status of women—and how much else?—Christianity educated and stimulated millions of minds, making them act and react, century after century.[13]

Having acknowledged the influence of Christianity, Valéry turns to the role of classical learning. He speaks of the "subtle yet powerful influence to which we owe the best of our intelligence, the acuteness and solidity of our knowledge, as also the clarity, purity, and elegance of our arts and literature: it is from Greece that those virtues came to us."[14] What we owe to Greece, he maintains, is perhaps what has most profoundly distinguished us from the rest of humanity. Europe is above all the creator of science. While there have been arts in all countries, there has been true science only in Europe. Valéry's assessment may be contrasted with Heidegger's, whose analysis placed the emphasis on Greece and ignored two of Europe's most fundamental traditions, Roman Catholicism and Roman humanism.

With such a sweeping definition of Europe, can there be national identity within Europe or even a distinction between Europe and North America? What Valéry means by Europe is almost identical to what is referred to today to as the "West," a term used sometimes to designate not only Europe and the Americas but Japan and other parts of Asia that are indebted to Western science and technology, if not religion.

It is not easy to define clearly what a nation is. A line traced on a map and on the ground, constituting a frontier, is the result of a series of historical incidents sanctioned by treaties. It may separate countries that are alike and join others that are very different. There is a tendency to generalize characteristics that are far from indicative of the whole. Few have difficulty speaking of "the Italian," "the German," "the Englishman." These broad, imprecise designations may serve a purpose in colloquial speech and may be indicative of certain prejudices, positive and negative. Yet they do have some foundation in reality, indicative of national or cultural traits. It may be easier to differentiate between oriental traits and occidental ones than between Polish and Czech. Color, custom, and culture differentiate; so also do opinions, prejudices, and evaluations.

Is a rapprochement among the different peoples of Europe, say between Eastern and Western Europe, inevitable? With the creation of the European Union many are now face to face who had never looked on each other as anything but radically foreign. No doubt contact has resulted in the acknowledgment of certain virtues in the other or some superiority, some strength, agility, industry or other virtues we identify with national character.

National character is difficult to define. The history of most countries of Europe is a chronicle of extremes, a chain of peaks and abysses. Some seem fated by geographical structure, water resources, climate, soil, flora and fauna to play a pivotal role on a grand scale. Germany rises, staggers, falls, rises again, retrenches, recaptures her greatness, is rent in two, reunites, displaying by turn qualities of pride, resignation, unconcern, and ardor, standing out from other nations by a distinct character. A certain natural discipline is apparent in the German character which comes to the fore when needed. Sometimes the nation is suddenly united when one would expect it to be divided. Moreover, the simplest and broadest features of any nation are likely to go unnoticed by the inhabitants themselves since they tend to be oblivious to what they have always experienced. It is the foreigner who notices those features and may make too much of them. One must also realize that whereas the effects of man's labor with respect to his surroundings are clearly recognizable, the modifications in man himself brought about by his place of residence are likely to be obscure. A summer travel advertisement tells us that the Greek island, Santorini, was shaped by its natural cataclysms, but its villages and landscapes seem chiseled by the island's stark light. Out of that light came not only the great statues of ancient Greece and the long clean lines of the Parthenon but the precise vocabulary for ideas that gave birth to Western philosophy.

The reader may miss a middle term connecting land, sky, and philosophy, but the words are worthy of some reflection. The effects of sky, the water, the air he breathes, the prevailing winds, what one eats, are physiological and psychological. Manners, ideals, politics are the incalculable effects of subtle causes. The Bavarian is not an Englishman and not simply because of language. The contours of a land that nourishes its people are but one aspect of a complex whole. Location, ethnic composition, and psychological constitution equally contribute to national identity.

To understand a nation, be it England, France, Germany, or Italy, we must attend to what each has created in the realm of the mind, expressions of intelligence or knowledge. The total intellectual and artistic treasure, the accumulated beauty of great works of art—written, sculpted, painted, and constructed—is constitutive of a culture that would not exist apart from its roots in a particular national setting.

Every nation of Europe is a composite, the result of the different ethnic elements that came to be mixed within her territory, and in none of them is a single tongue spoken. Thus, Paul Valéry can say of France, "The French nation resembles a tree several times grafted, the quality and flavor of whose fruit are the result of a happy wedding of very different saps and humors combining in a single and indivisible life."[15] Stretching a bit, he continues, "Whether we speak of the Capelins, of Joan of Arc, Louis IX, Henry IV, Richelieu, the Convention, or Napoleon, we are referring to one and the same thing, an active symbol of our national identity and unity."[16]

Does the preservation of national identity matter? It matters to hosts of immigrants in both Europe and North America who seek to retain not only their inherited customs but even their native language in their adopted country. It matters because traditions, the components of what we call a culture, are specific. One cannot be a citizen of the world. Identity is local; it is the characteristic of a people who have inhabited a land over a period of time, who have developed certain collective habits, evident in their manners, their dress, the feasts they collectively enjoy, their religious bonds, the premium they put on education, and their attention to detail and precision. These are not universal traits but are rooted in centuries past and depend upon a historical consciousness, an attention to the deeds of ancestors past.

National identity is threatened from two sources, the immigrant who refuses to assimilate and the secular, aggressively anti-Christian international socialist whose mentality permeates the major media, the entertainment industries, and the universities. The nation that is conscious of its past may be the only bulwark against the neopaganism which seeks to replace Christianity throughout the West. Cultural and moral standards are specific and cannot be held *in vacuo*, apart from particular peoples, periods, and places. Even the universal works of the mind, philosophy and science are subject to the hidden influence of race, local habit and milieu. In fact, nothing seems to define a nation or region better than the philosophy it has produced or the adherence to the rule of law under which it functions. We speak of classical metaphysics, French literature, nineteenth-century German philosophy, and in the United States of the Southern Agrarians.

A nation or people can only be energized internally, by the goals it sets for itself in the light of a shared perception of the common good. These social and political modes of life cannot be imposed from without as the United States has discovered in Iraq. So-called emerging nations cannot be expected to embrace lock, stock, and barrel the social and political modes of life that are urged on them from without. Anthropologists have, of course, realized all along what policy makers have been slow to acknowledge. In spite of the craving for economic advancement, who does, in fact, want to live in a "world culture"? Given media-driven amoral standards, such a culture would be beneath the dignity of human nature. In talking about declining moral standards, perhaps no one has put the matter more succinctly than John M. Rist in his book, *Real Ethics*.[17]

Rist foresees a bleak future for the West. In losing its grip on its Christian past and in the absence of a clear sense of civic virtue, Western society is preparing itself for a totalitarian democracy. Unable to choose between conflicting claims to the good and the resulting propensity to tolerate all, it is subverting the principle of toleration itself. Unfortunately, recovering a sense of the past may not be an easy task. The past can be clouded by the authoritarian or ideological mentality of academics and humanists or be rewritten or invented to promote a political agenda. Moreover, history is only one vehicle for transmitting the inherited. Whatever wisdom a society has acquired can be passed on only if it is instantiated in institutional structures designed to maintain inherited practices, beliefs, and intellectual acumen. As for the individual caught in an unrooted modernity, those apt to keep their wits in a godless future are those who possess a knowledge—however acquired—of their roots, that is, their own past and traditions.

It is through inherited literature in our native language that we become aware of our collective roots, develop collective attitudes, and develop a political culture. The Frenchman becomes a Frenchman not merely by reason of birth in a particular geographic territory but by reason of the literary tradition to which he is introduced early on. One develops a Catholic mind by reading the Church Fathers, Justin Martyr, Clement, and Augustine, the medieval doctors of the Church, and modern commentators thereon.

In a 1934 essay, "The Sources of Cultural Change," the English historian Christopher Dawson offered this definition: "A culture is a common way of life—a particular adjustment of man to his natural surroundings and his economic needs." In its development it resembles a biological species. "Just as every natural region tends to possess its characteristic forms of vegetable and animal life, so too will it possess its own type of human society."[18] Dawson identifies the three main influences which form and modify human culture. They are the same as in the formation of animal species. "They are (1) race, i.e., the genetic factor; (2) environment, i.e., the geographical factor; (3) function or occupation, i.e., the economic factors. But in addition to these there is a fourth element—thought or the psychological factor—which is peculiar to the human species and the existence of which frees man from the blind dependence on material environment."[19]

Although the intimate linkage of science, technology, and commerce with rapid material progress and change typifies only a minor part of the world, it has assumed the status of a world culture with "globalization" as its hallmark. Leaders of emerging nations are urged to embrace globalization and to become part of the civilized world. If those leaders sense that the diffusion of a scientific world culture may threaten their indigenous cultures, they are sometimes assured that world culture is a purely material culture incapable of impairing the spiritual content of a nation's heritage.

The American journalist Robert Locke makes a suggestive distinction between "globalization" and "the globalists." Globalization as he defines it is an ongoing historical process, a factual description of how things are. Globalism, by contrast is an ideology, a set of political opinions about how things ought to be. Ideological globalists, in Locke's characterization, look upon the existence of separate nations as unacceptable because it fosters inequality. "Separate nations give peoples with histories of brilliant political and economic achievement . . . the free and prosperous lives that their forebears have earned while at the same time consigning peoples of inferior ancestral achievement to lesser existences."[20] The leftist egalitarian project aims to erase borders in order that mass immigration to the first world from the third will force citizens of the first to share their "superior" way of life. National cultural identity gives people an attachment to their land and history and consequently fosters global inequality. Locke may be guilty of some exaggeration, but the globalist spirit he detects is a reality all too often confronted.

I am not suggesting that the problems facing Europe and North America are identical. Both have to deal with the consequences of their permissive immigration policies. The United States has the additional problem of an educational system that tends toward the lowest common denominator at all levels. The universities have become politicized in a leftward direction. One can detect in the publications of major university presses a tendency to rewrite Western history, leaving out Christianity. The media on both sides of the Atlantic are uncompromising in their drive to undermine biblical morality, promoting deviant behavior at every turn, no matter the social consequences.

Many who view the situation in the broad manner suggested here end with an unrelieved pessimism. In fact, it is often difficult to find one who does not come to a pessimistic conclusion. Charles Murray, in offering a preview of his recent book, concludes, "I write at a time when Europe's run appears to be over. Bleaker yet, there is reason to wonder whether European culture as we have known it will even exist at the end of this century."[21]

Husserl and Heidegger in their calls to return to the Greeks for a renewal of European political philosophy are not without warrant. The Greeks understood well the interdependence of *polis* and *oikos*, of public and private. In praising the *polis* as the highest level of human achievement, Aristotle did not ignore the private realm, nor did he undervalue the ties of family for the sake of an abstract polity. Rather he recognized that the city survives only as long as the private particular world of the family does. And for Aristotle that included piety of a religious sort as well as piety toward one's ancestors and one's state.[22]

This fundamental Aristotelian position has been a constant theme of the Papacy, reiterated in the nineteenth century by Leo XIII in his anti-socialist encyclical *Rerum Novarum* (1891) and again by Pius XI in *Quadragesimo*

Anno (1931) and more recently by John Paul II in *Centisimus Anno* (1991). Known in its modern form as the "principle of subsidiarity," the principle calls upon states to foster personal freedom and intermediate institutions for the sake of efficiency as well as the common good. In the words of *Quadragesimo Anno*, "Just as it is wrong to take away from individuals what they can accomplish by their own ability and effort and entrust it to a community, so too it is an injury and at the same time both a serious evil and a disturbance of right order to assign to a larger society what can be performed successfully by smaller and lower communities"[23] Given the contemporary drive to concentrate power in central government, the principle remains relevant in both Brussels and Washington, D.C.

NOTES

1. George Santayana, *The Winds of Doctrine* (New York: Charles Scribner's Sons, 1913), 1.
2. Edmund Husserl, *The Crisis of European Sciences and the Transcendental Phenomenology*, trans. David Carr (Evanston, Ill.: Northwestern University Press, 1970), 299.
3. Martin Heidegger (Rector's Address, 1933–1934), "The Self-Assertion of the German University," in *The Heidegger Controversy*, ed. Gunther Neske and Emil Kettering (New York: Paragon House, 1990), 19.
4. Lynn White, *Machino ex deo: Essays in the Dynamism of Western Culture* (Cambridge, Mass.: MIT Press, 1968), 65.
5. White, *Machino,* 65.
6. White, *Machino*, 67.
7. White, *Machino,* 72–73.
8. Paul Valéry, *Collected Works*, vol. 10, trans. Denise Folliot and Jackson Mathews (New York: Bollingen Foundation, 1962), 322–23.
9. Valéry, *Collected Works*, 322.
10. Valéry, *Collected Works*, 322.
11. Even President Vladimir V. Putin, in discussing the role of his country vis-à-vis the European Union, speaks of the value of Russian identity (*New York Times* 6 October, 2003, 1, 4).
12. It may be observed that Valéry Giscard D'Estaing and the Commission he heads to draft a European Constitution is, in its failure to note the Christian sources of European unity and culture, closer to Heidegger than to his French namesake.
13. Valéry, *Collected Works*, 319.
14. Valéry, *Collected Works*, 319.
15. Valéry, Collected *Works*, 407.
16. Valéry, *Collected Works*, 408.
17. John M. Rist, *Real Ethics* (New York: Cambridge University Press, 2002).

18. Dawson, *Dynamics of World History*, ed. John J. Mulloy (Wilmington, Del.: ISI Books, 2002), 4.

19. Dawson, *Dynamics*, 5.

20. *The American Conservative*, 2 June, 2003, 13–14.

21. Charles Murray, "Measuring Achievement: The West and the Rest," American Enterprise Institute, *News & Commentary*, posted 6 August, 2003, 12. That judgment is not uncommon.

22. For an extended treatment of the role of the family and its religion (cult) in creating the cohesiveness of society necessary for political stability and avoidance of tyrannical rule, see W. K. Lacey, *The Family in Classical Greece* (Ithaca, N.Y.: Cornell University Press, 1968).

23. Pius XI, *Quadragesimo Anno* (1931), 79.

Chapter Seventeen

The Fragility of Democracy

It is reported that as the delegates to the Constitutional Convention trudged out of Independence Hall in Philadelphia on September 17, 1787, an anxious person in the crowd inquired of Benjamin Franklin, "Well, Doctor, what have we got, a republic or a monarchy?" "A republic," Franklin replied, "if you can keep it."[1] The keeping of it is the subject of this essay. The democracy brought into being on that historic day in 1787 was not judged to be imperishable, even in the eyes of its framers. This essay will first examine the commonplace meaning of the term "democracy" and some of the pre-political conditions for its establishment and then consider some of the perennial threats to its perpetuation.

In common usage, the word, "democracy," is far from a univocal term.[2] "The Peoples Democratic Republic" is not what Woodrow Wilson had in mind when he led a crusade to make the world safe for democracy. For John Dewey, the leading American philosopher of Wilson's day, democracy is more than a form of government. It is a way of life, a creed directed to a social ideal.

While it is customary to distinguish among democracy's several forms, i.e., direct, representative, constitutional, and social or economic, what is usually meant by democracy is representative or constitutional democracy. Direct democracy is identified with political life in ancient Greece where policy decisions were made directly by the populace as a whole, the majority determining the outcome. Apart from New England town meetings, initiated in the colonial period and continued through today in some states, notably in Vermont and New Hampshire, the procedure is otherwise unknown in the United States, and those town meetings that survive take place only where the body of citizens is small enough to enable participation by all. Referenda as employed in the United Sates in some way resemble the direct democracy of ancient Greece insofar as they seek the counsel of the populace as a whole, but they are not binding and can be ignored by political authorities or reversed by the courts.

Today when we call a form of government a democracy, we usually have in mind representative democracy in which citizens exercise their right to form policy, not in person but through representatives elected by them. In a constitutional democracy, such as those that prevail in Europe and the United States, the powers of the majority are exercised within the framework of a written constitution designed to guarantee the rights of minorities and the protection of other rights governing speech, press, and religion. A constitution need not be a single written instrument or even a legal document. It may be nothing more than a commonly accepted set of fixed norms or principles that are recognized as the fundamental law of the polity. The essence of a constitution is that it formalizes a set of fundamental norms governing the political community and fixes a limitation on the exercise of power. Political parties are the chief instrument through which the electorate is involved in both the exercise and transfer of power. The political party is at once the means of representing the diverse interests of the electorate in the exercise of power and also a device for allowing a replacement of one set of power holders with another.

Greek democracy was a brief historical episode and is not to be taken as the exemplar of modern democratic governments. Modern democratic ideas were shaped to a large extent by medieval ideas and institutions, notably by the concept of divine, natural, and customary law as a restraint on the power of kings, including the right to levy taxes. Accordingly, the king was obliged to consult the several "estates" or group interests in the realm. Gatherings of representatives of these various estates were the origins of modern parliaments that first appeared in America, Great Britain, and France. Representative parliaments, freely elected under universal franchise, became the key institutions of Western democracy in the late nineteenth and early twentieth centuries. As a matter of fact, few states in the modern world have constitutional arrangements that are more than a century old. Great Britain and the United States are almost alone in possessing constitutions that predate the twentieth century.

Contributing to the development of modern democracy was the introduction into political discourse of a number of profound intellectual ideas, notably the concepts of "natural rights" and the "equality of all mankind," ideas that played an important role in the American War for Independence and in the French Revolution. The liberal notion of democracy that prevails in intellectual circles today presupposes not only the concepts of natural rights and equality but the acceptance of all cultures on an equal footing with obvious consequences for morality and religious observance as well as immigration and educational policy. Given what seems to many contemporary observers as a radical departure from its early intellectual moorings, the time is ripe to examine anew the concept of democracy and its undergirding rationale.

As the United States, like Europe, drifts from its Christian past into an unknown secular future, discussions of the pre-political foundations of democracy gain importance. The principles both implicitly assumed and denied by the European Constitution are worthy of extended study, but I will limit my study to the American founding.[3] The history of that founding is significant because it addresses the pre-political conditions of democracy. The pertinent literature is extensive and divides scholars who write on the subject. Many historians betray a personal disposition by the emphasis they place on the sources of certain key ideas enshrined in the founding documents. Some give primacy to the secular Enlightenment sources represented by John Locke, while others give weight to the religious milieu in which the Declaration of Independence and the Constitution of the United States with its Amendments were actually written. The latter acknowledge the influence of Richard Hooker, Roger Williams, and other Puritan leaders who are often overlooked by those who insist on viewing the founding from an entirely secular perspective.

Richard Hooker (1554–1600), is not to be confused with Thomas Hooker (1586–1647), the founder of the state of Connecticut, who is sometimes called the "Founder of American Democracy." Richard Hooker is the author of *On the Laws of Ecclesiastical Polity,* one of the most influential works in the development of political theory from medieval thought to contemporary natural rights theory.[4] *On the Laws* attempted to reconcile the Thomistic doctrines of transcendence and natural law with the authority of the Elizabethan Anglican Church.[5] That work was not only widely read in the colonies but had a profound influence on Locke, as can be seen from Locke's many quotations of Richard Hooker.[6] But there is a major difference between Locke and Hooker, especially in their understanding of "contract" and "rights." The "contract" for Hooker is an expression of the corporate disposition of the whole, not the consent or disposition of the individual taken one by one. "Equality" for Hooker refers not so much to an individual's status as it does to the individual's equal obligation to the community. Hooker's arguments for the democratic organization of Church governance with its emphasis on consent were to serve the Founding Fathers of the new American republic. Those scholars of the left who tend to ignore the Christian sources of the founding emphasize the influence of Locke on writers such as Thomas Paine, Benjamin Franklin, and Thomas Jefferson. It may be that liberalism in America owes more to the theologies of Richard Hooker, Roger Williams, and John Wise than to the Enlightenment philosophy espoused by Thomas Jefferson. Widely read in the colonies, Hooker anticipated the political philosophy of Locke by more than a generation when, emphasizing the element of consent, he defined the church as "a company of people combined together by covenant for the worship of God."

Many of the notions, especially the idea that although fundamental authority may stem from God, power rests upon the consent of the governed, find concrete expression in Thomas Hooker's *The Fundamental Orders of Connecticut.* Drafted in 1639, the *Fundamental Orders* has been called the first written constitution of modern democracy.[7] The orders dispense with the then-usual property and religious qualifications for voting and provide for town-meeting government and for popular elected assemblies. It was due to the influence of Thomas Hooker that Puritan theocracy gradually gave way to liberal constitutionalism, with the idea of "consent" replacing the strict Calvinist notion of "foreordination" and doctrine of the elect. Implicit in the doctrine of consent is the idea that the church is an instrument of the people created for purposes shared by each, an idea which when carried into the civil order fosters "government of the people, by the people, for the people." Established by mutual agreement for definite ends, government is consequently limited in what it can do. Its primary purpose is to conserve the peace and protect people's bodies and goods.

Some would delve further into history to find the source of these doctrines in what Brian Tierney calls the "theological jurists," who by his account were the first to formulate a theory of natural rights. No one would look to Suarez, Bellarmine, Vitoria, and Las Cassas as the immediate source of the principles assumed in these founding documents, yet their discussions of "natural rights" and "equality" laid the foundation for what was to come. These ideas played an important role in the American and French "revolutions." A full accounting, no doubt, would acknowledge a distinctive Western intellectual tradition, extending from Aristotle and the Stoics through the medieval canonists to their impact on English common law.[8] Harry Jaffa, in a book on the American founding, sees the Declaration of Independence as interpreted by Lincoln to be based on a kind of Aristotelian Christianity.[9]

John Stuart Mill, like Richard Hooker but writing from an entirely different perspective, acknowledged the people as the source of all civic authority, yet he feared what he called "social tyranny." The will of the people, he warned, is not alone an adequate safeguard of liberty. "Self government" and "the power of the people to rule themselves" do not express the complete picture. The will of the people practically means the will of the most numerous or the will of the most active part of the people. Mill consequently advocated measures to thwart the tyranny of the majority. Mill also addressed the possibility of a small group of like-minded people seizing the levers of power to achieve their own ends quite apart from the disposition of the people and even the elected government.[10]

Jacques Maritain, in a short work entitled *Christianity and Democracy*[11] reflecting on the relationship between the two suggests, "The democratic impulse has arisen in human history as a temporal manifestation of the Gospel." He speaks of Christianity as "a leaven in the social and political life of a nation." Yet Maritain recognized that Christianity is not linked to democracy. To be a Christian, he held, does not compel one to support a democratic form of government. He reminds us that it was only after the Second World War that the Vatican declared in favor of parliamentary democracy. Looking to the recent history of the Continent, no one can deny that Christianity played a central role in the formation of the new European democracies in the post-war period, in the drafting of their basic law, and in the drafting of the United Nations Declaration on Human Rights.

Maria Mitchell, in her essay, "Antimaterialism in Early German Democracy," tells us that at its formation there was no agreement in the CDU as to the meaning of "Christian Democracy."[12] Sufficient for the time was the unity of Catholics and Lutherans in their endorsement of a democratic form of government and in their opposition to materialism and secularism. Conservative Protestants as well as Catholics recognized the link between materialism and national socialism, and in the post-war years Protestants joined Catholics in portraying the task of politics as the transformation of secular society. "Inherent in political activity," explained Paul Bausch, a former member of the Christian Social People's Service (CSVD), "is the responsibility to subordinate every aspect of political life to the demands of Christian laws. . . . 'The Ten Commandments of God' delineate the iron foundation for state life. . . . The task for us today is to replace a Godless government with a government that respects God's commandments and makes them principles of life for the Volk and of the state."[13] Bausch implied that if we are not ready to organize in the light of Christian principles, the opposition would organize society for us on utilitarian principles. Mitchell concurs:

> Despite their agreement that only a Christian Germany could prevent the return of the evil of materialism, Catholics and Protestants grounded their critiques in two fundamentally different world views. . . . The dissimilarities, although conceptual and seemingly abstract, would nevertheless govern the dynamics of early Christian Democratic policy making. Even on such a fundamental level as the Protestant and Catholic understandings of the Christian individual, theologically based differences within the CDU shaped profoundly interconfessional cooperation.[14]

Drawing upon the work of Wilhelm Simpfendorfer and Otto Heinrich von Gablente, Mitchell locates the difference between Protestant and Catholic in the Reformation's emphasis on "the freedom of the individual," as contrasted with the Catholic emphasis on *Gemeinschaft*. Emphasis on the individual inevitably leads to a political liberalism at variance with the recognition of responsibility to a higher moral order. Catholic leaders in the CDU, she notes, only felt comfortable with the liberal position when it was willing to accommodate personal freedom to that higher moral responsibility.

The social and political influence of the Christian democratic parties remains, sometimes in ersatz form where the Christian roots are not openly acknowledged. The continued secularization of the masses obscures the pre-political values that gave rise to an inherited political order. It may be plausibly argued that to survive, European democracy must acknowledge its pre-political roots, roots that may be difficult to recover without reference to the Hellenic and Christian sources of Europe itself. Neither source can be understood apart from its common realistic—in the classical metaphysical sense—conception of human nature and human destiny, one that includes the transcendent as well as the material. Western liberalism and Marxism alike ignore the spiritual dimension of human striving. The fatuous optimism of the contemporary left, underestimating human passion and mistakenly believing that man's needs are limited and easily satisfied, can only lead to hopeless despair.

Having called attention to the pre-political conditions of democracy and the unity provided by a common faith or civic creed, it is necessary to acknowledge that democracy is vulnerable from a number of interior threats. The benefits of self-governance can be lost by the indiscriminate awarding of suffrage to illegal immigrants, by a politically biased media that limits access to vital information, by the excessive toleration of deviant behavior and the concomitant failure to punish, by the surrender of basic freedoms in the name of safety, and by the docile acceptance of a bureaucratic imperium and a politicized judiciary. Undoubtedly the list could go on.

In contemporary political discourse we hear much about the value of diversity, multiculturalism, and globalization. Yet diversity under the rule of law presupposes an accepted order of society. In the United States the nineteenth century melting pot successfully blended elements of Christian Europe, but in the twentieth the melting pot has become a cauldron of unmeltable—not simply ethnics—but cultures. The contemporary Western liberal concept of democracy assumes uncritically that men are naturally and morally equal, an assumption that does not bear empirical scrutiny. Wide disparity as a result of parental upbringing and education leaves the populace polarized in a way that is more fundamental than disparity of income. That is only one among many divisive factors. In many American states the electorate is likely to contain undocumented aliens as well as lawful immigrants. Both groups are likely to be deficient with respect to the English language as well as ignorant of American history and the Western political tradition. Universal suffrage, given that it rests on the doctrine that all men are naturally equal, may be the undoing of modern democracy. It is not simply a matter of recognizing that however unequal citizens are with respect to their actual condition that their inequalities can be ignored or at any rate made irrelevant through their equal standing before the law and the abolition of privilege. That doctrine rightly asserts that whatever differences exist in race, language, religion, political opinion, or personal and social conditions, all citizens are peers in human dignity and before the law. Equality, thus construed, means nondiscrimination, a positive value that no one disputes. But equality as a principle is distorted and perverted when used to confer on the illegal immigrant a claim equal to that of the citizen with respect to public benefits and when used even to give the convicted felon voting rights equal to those of the law-abiding. Equality so construed is unjust insofar as it ignores the greater economic and social contribution of the law-abiding citizen and his rightful claim on the common wealth.

Access to information is another factor that can undermine the electoral process. With both academic and media elites at war with the intellectual tradition that brought the nation into being, it would take a well-informed public, better educated than that which seems to prevail, to resist the political demands of the same academic and media intelligentsia that control the major media. It remains to be seen whether the electorate can withstand the unrelenting assault on its inherited beliefs and still make good decisions. Informed decision rests upon the availability of information. The deconstructionists with their rewriting of history, abetted by the willing assistance of major university presses, have obscured if not expunged the Christian sources of Western civilization. We witness a cultural war between a militant atheism confronting a weakened Christianity, a conflict that many are reluctant to acknowledge. John Rawls, in his celebrated volume, *A Theory of Justice*, raises the relevant question: "How is it possible that there may exist over time a stable and just society of free and equal citizens profoundly divided by reasonable though incompatible religious, philosophical and moral doctrines?"[15] The answer from Rawls's perspective is that all sides need only embrace the principle of tolerance. But is toleration really the answer? Presumably a tolerant society would be obliged to protect if not cultivate immorality as well as morality. Under such circumstances those who reject such indifference to the good would eventually desire to form a society of their own, where their own laws and customs would be honored, thus repudiating or undermining the goal of a single, stable society. In fact, we see religious and ideological differences rending societies from Indonesia to Ukraine.

Toleration insofar as it implies acceptance by society of any and all goods proposed by its member, is more an abstract goal than a practical solution. It is unavoidable that some individual goals will be destructive of the goals of others such that they cannot exist side by side without regulation whereby the state curbs some for the benefit of others. But by such curbing, the principle of toleration is breached. The state will necessarily act in the light of some norm that is dependent on some concept of fairness. Either the state offers equal opportunity to all, or it adjusts opportunities in the interest of certain courses of action deemed fair.

In fact, the promotion of tolerance as a virtue is often self-serving or indicative of a political agenda. Tolerance is not mentioned as a virtue by Aristotle or by the Stoics. Nor does Aquinas speak of tolerance as a virtue. To the contrary, Roget's venerable *English Language Dictionary of Synonyms and Antonyms* gives as synonyms for tolerance: leniency, clemency, indulgence, laxity, sufferance, concession, and permissiveness, terms generally regarded as designating questionable behavior. When tolerance is advocated in contemporary political discourse, it is usually religious tolerance that the speaker has in mind, and the admonition is usually singularly directed; it is the Christian who is asked to be tolerant. Religious tolerance, though not confined to Christianity, seems to have a particular appeal to the Christian conscience, perhaps for reasons intrinsic to Christianity itself. The classical and Christian sources of Western civilization, although under attack for the past two hundred years, still remain the unacknowledged basis of Western culture. Appeals for tolerance may resonate within that culture, if within no other. Unfortunately, respect for intellect, for the rule of law, and for the rational foundation of religious faith is not characteristic of all who would have their views tolerated. If the classical and biblical roots of Western culture are not respected by the immigrant who seeks shelter within the West, and if, furthermore, those sources are ignored in the common schools, can the freedoms grounded in their unacknowledged source long survive? The answer seems obvious. The call for a tolerance that ignores or abuses those foundations is inconsistent and self-destructive of its own warrant. It remains to be seen whether the West is able to defend its intellectual and cultural patrimony while yet accommodating the other.

Throughout history, political entities have recognized the need for unity of outlook among their peoples.[16] At times in classical Greece and Rome, atheism could be punished by death. Modern socialist regimes, wherever they come to power, recognizing the influence of ideas, work to suppress religious education, if not religion itself. Within the Western democracies, practical accommodation is one thing, but a nonjudgmental, nondiscriminating acceptance is another. How tolerant can a society be and yet maintain itself in existence? Of course, where nothing is prized, everything can be tolerated.

Acceptance of the principle of tolerance necessarily leads even its defenders to the question of limits and leaves open the question of what should and should not be tolerated. It would be foolish, in the name of toleration, to ignore differences due to greater or lesser natural abilities, habitual patterns of good and evil, prudence and imprudence, and law-abiding and criminal actions. Toleration often turns out to be what those of a liberal perspective think ought to be and ought not to be tolerated. Since policy built upon a liberal concept of tolerance is often at variance with common sense and the desires of the great majority, it can only be implemented through some form of coercion.

Eventually the question has to be faced by our secularized, intellectual elites: Can Western institutions survive the repudiation or neglect of the sources that gave them birth? Friedrich Nietzsche, no friend of Christianity, recognized the issue. "It is an English inconsistency," he wrote, to be "rid of the Christian God" and yet "believe all the more firmly that they must cling to Christian morality. They have forgotten that the origin of their morality stands and falls with faith in God. The English do not recognize that what follows from the abandonment of their morality's guarantee is an expression of the strength and depth of the dominion of Christian judgment."[17]

Without the moral framework of Christian civilization that has made freedom possible, a framework that has defined the moral boundaries in which liberty could blossom, European society has but two ways to go: either toward the secular totalitarianism it has experienced in the past or toward the replacement of Christianity with a self-confident Islam. The multiculturalist liberals have regarded the Muslims as allies in their attempt to destroy Christian civilization but in the process may have signed their own death warrant. In its war with secular Europe, Islam is likely to emerge the victor.

Bertrand de Jouvenel, writing in occupied France in early 1940s, recognized another threat to the democratic franchise. Reflecting on the Roosevelt administration, barely ten years old at the time, he saw that the creation of commissions and agencies with legislative, executive, and judicial authority within the same organization could only lead to a disenfranchisement of the electorate. We see this happening in Europe as more and more power gravitates to Brussels and its numerous agencies. Policy decisions made far removed from a willing constituency can destroy inherited modes of production and social custom with little or no accountability to the populace affected.[18] To the extent that the European Constitution allows Brussels to become the organizer-in-chief of European society, it will become the enemy of democracy, shifting effective power from the people to a bureaucratic imperium that tolerates little authority outside itself.[19]

The Declaration of Laeken of December 2001 grapples with this issue. Yet to be resolved at that time was the question of federation or confederation, whether the European Union was to be governed by an intellectual elite from the top down or by regional constituencies from the bottom up, The Declaration of Laeken acknowledged that European institutions must be brought closer to the citizens while affirming at the same time that the European constitution should opt for "a clear, open, effective, democratically controlled community approach, developing a Europe which points the way for the world. An approach that provides concrete results in terms of more jobs, better quality of life, less crime, decent education, and better health care. There can be no doubt that this will require Europe to undergo renewal and reform." But of what kind? A cosmopolitan and homogenized Western Europe, severed from its traditions and controlled by a centralized bureaucracy?

The situation is not new. Subsequent to the American Civil War, the defeated Robert E. Lee in a letter to Lord Acton, dated December 15, 1866, fearful of the usurpation of power by the newly empowered federal government wrote: "I yet believe that the maintenance of the rights and authority reserved to the states and to the people, are not only essential to the adjustment and balance of the general system, but the safeguard of the continuance of free government. I consider it to be a chief source of stability to our political system, whereas the consolidation of the states in to one vast republic, sure to be aggressive abroad and despotic at home, will be the precursor of that ruin which has overwhelmed all that preceded it."[20] Lee may be considered, not only prescient with respect to the United States, but prophetic with respect to the European Union. The danger is perennial. Lee's judgment is echoed by James M. Buchanan who, writing in 2004, concluded: "The separate nation states of Europe are not likely to shed off their histories of national autonomy and jump in, as it were, into a new unitary monolith that remains in the process of being created . . . (yet) over a long period the European Leviathan may well become a dominant and dangerous force."[21]

In the United States it is beginning to be recognized that the most serious threat to democracy comes from a politicized judiciary. Appointments to the highest courts are made with a political objective in mind. The left recognizes that a liberal political agenda could never be implemented purely and simply through the legislative process. Given the nature of the legal system, those appointed to the judicial bench are more likely to be attuned to the liberal Zeitgeist of the academy than to the temper of the people. The chasm between the academy and Main Street is notorious. It is not so much that judges are often instruments of special-interest parties or sectional financial interests as it is the pragmatic and naturalistic conscience they have developed in their university years. The reigning philosophy of education disposes one to challenge an inherited moral and cultural order. Carried into the practical realm this often leads to a negative evaluation of an imperfect past in favor of an idealized future. Because both philosophy and theology are organically connected to political policy, we find federal courts in the United States ruling against the public display of the Ten Commandments and Christmas crèches, disregarding even from a secular perspective their symbolic value in calling attention to the principles undergirding the rule of law. At the time of the American founding the fathers of the new republic appended to the Constitution a Bill of Rights to guarantee explicitly that certain principles would prevail over the course of time. The First Amendment reads in part: "Congress shall make no law respecting an establishment of religion, or prohibiting the free exercise thereof." As understood at the time, the clause prohibited the establishment of a national religion but did not prohibit or abolish the state churches then existing in the majority of the colonies. The Supreme Court through a series of rulings since 1947 has all but prohibited the expression of religion in the public sector while at the same time it has attempted to impose secular norms on religious bodies. In responding to the Zeitgeist of the academy and by ignoring the beliefs of the overwhelming majority the Court provides another example of the fragility of democracy.

Another challenge to democracy arises when a nation perceives itself to be under attack either from within or without. George Washington in his Farewell Address, after serving two terms as the nation's first president, admonished his fellow countrymen to avoid foreign entanglements, advice rarely heeded in the following centuries.[22] The foreign policy of the United States has led to treaties and alliances that have involved nearly every generation in warfare since its founding. With every conflict new curtailments and abridgments to normal patterns of commercial and personal life come into being. Bureaucracies expand to meet the supposed threat. Although the United States has not been called upon to defend its borders since the War of 1812, it now has a Department of Homeland Security, with a director of cabinet rank.[23] This department now commands upward of 140,000 employees. Officials in its sister agency, the Transportation Security Administration, can issue directives that affect the lives of the entire populace.[24] Threats, real and imagined, curtail the ease of air travel, lead to previously unimagined security checks even to gain entrance to an art museum. These measures are instituted without the give and take of significant public discussion and offer no real recourse to the affected person. In the interest of security, the citizen not only loses considerable freedom but is often humiliated in the process. This takes place without an examination and public discussion of the foreign policy that brought on the threat that is ostensibly being met.

Apart from the surrender of popular or local control to a centralized bureaucracy, the most serious threat to democracy is the implicit repudiation of the charter that produced "government of the people, by the people."[25] In the fifth century B.C. Heraclitus of Ephesus wrote: "The people must fight for their laws as for their walls." After two-and-a-half millennia, the dictum must be taken seriously. Since the last half of the twentieth century, the people of the United States have seen their laws eroded as the federal judiciary, notably the Supreme Court, has struck down many legislatively enacted laws normally associated with the protection of life, property, and civility. The reasons for the invalidation of legislation by the courts are complex and often defy analysis, but this much can be said: judicial activism has become a feature of American life. The courts, notably at the federal level, seem peculiarly vulnerable to the ideology of the academy, often taking their lead from university discourse rather than legislative intent. Whereas legislation is necessarily hammered out in the give-and-take process of an assembly, where it is often a tissue of compromise and citizens at least have some representation, judge-made law is issued by decree. Courts are particularly vulnerable to persuasion by intellectual and media elites, who themselves are at war with the moral and cultural traditions of the nation. Given the monolithic posture of the media and the lockstep of the professorate, the people are left without adequate defense at the intellectual level of the beliefs they hold to be true. If the Supreme Court can contradict the clear intent of the First Amendment and all but abolish the public expression of religion, the fragility of democracy is all too apparent.

The United States is not alone in facing a threat to a democratic way of life. Christie Davies has entitled a recent book *The Strange Death of Moral Britain*.[26] Decades ago the British Lord Patrick Devlin reminded his fellow jurists that if the morality of a people deteriorates, the laws based on that morality will crumble.[27] The future of Europe under a European Constitution written in a moral vacuum is by no means secure.[28] The future does not bode well for Europe when a candidate for the European Commission can be rejected on the basis of his Catholic faith. Europe desperately needs leaders who are resolutely willing to defend its Hellenic and religious traditions against alien modes of thought. As Jacques Maritain has argued, sooner or later nations will have to declare for or against the Gospel, for without it, democracy cannot be maintained. The European Union's refusal to recognize its Christian origins is a visible sign that democracy is in crisis. To paraphrase Christopher Dawson, "Only a dying civilization ignores its dead." The European Constitution seems to be founded on the aberrant post-modern democratic values of tolerance, multiculturalism, and internationalism. Like Europe, the United States may be in danger of losing its way, but it is better positioned by reason of its founding documents, perennial standards to which appeals can be made in the interest of corrective action.

NOTES

1. From the notes of James McHenry, one of the delegates to the Federal Convention of 1787 and a signer of the draft of the U.S. Constitution (*Documents Illustrative of the Formation of the Union of the American States,* Government Printing Office).

2. "Democracy" as a term literally means rule of the people, from the Greek *demos* (people) and *kratos* (rule).

3. We are reminded of Paul Valéry's insistence that Europe cannot be understood apart from Roman Catholicism and Roman humanism. Heidegger, by contrast, put all the emphasis on the Hellenic patrimony of the West.

4. Hooker's *On the Laws of Ecclesiastical Polity* was first published as *Survey of the Summe of Church Discipline* in 1648. In 1972 the Arno Press, New York, reprinted the 1648 edition. John H. Hallowell is one of a number of scholars who recognizes the influence of Hooker and Williams in the drafting of the nation's founding documents. Speaking of Hooker, Hallowell writes: "The first stirrings of liberalism in America might be said to have found specific expression in [his] *Survey of the Summer of Church Discipline" (Main Currents in Modern Political Thought* [New York: Henry Holt & Co., 1950], 150).

5. Cf. D. Alan Heslop, "Richard Hooker's adapted Thomism," *Political Philosophy,* The New Encyclopedia Britannica (Chicago, 1943–1973), vol. 14, 689 ff.

6. John Locke, *The Second Treatise on Government,* ed. Thomas P. Peardon (New York: Macmillan/Library of Liberal Arts, 1952).

7. Cf. *Encyclopaedia Britannica, Micropedia,* vol. V, 121.

8. Brian Tierney, *The Idea of Natural Rights: Studies on Natural Rights, Natural Law and Church Law, 1150–1625* (Grand Rapids, Mich.: Eerdmans, 1997).

9. Harry V. Jaffa, *American Conservatism and the American Founding* (Durham, N.C.: Academic Press, 1984).

10. Without judging the merits of the claim, something like this may have happened when the United States invaded Iraq at the behest of a small group of like-minded officials and advisors who had gained control of the levers of power to advance an agenda contrary to the interest of the country and one that had been repudiated internationally. So weak was the case for the military invasion of Iraq that the U.S. Department of State sent five prominent Catholics to Rome to convince the Holy See of the righteousness of the war, a mission notably unsuccessful. Democracy, as Mill feared, may indeed be that fragile.

11. Jacques Maritain, *Christianity and Democracy* (London: Geoffrey Bles, 1945), 28. Maritain will also say, "Not only does the democratic state of mind proceed from the Gospel, but it cannot exist without it," Maritain, *Christianity*, 39.

12. Maria Mitchell, "Antimaterialism in Early German Christian Democracy," in *European Christian Democracy: Historical Legacies and Comparative Perspectives*, ed. Thomas Kselman and Joseph A. Buttigieg (Notre Dame, Ind.: University of Notre Dame Press, 2003), 174.

13. As quoted by Mitchell, "Antimaterialism," 174.

14. Mitchell, "Antimaterialism," 175.

15. John Rawls, *A Theory of Justice* (Cambridge, Mass.: Harvard University Press, 1971), 98.

16. Recognizing the importance of unity and its root in a common allegiance, George Washington in his Farewell Address to the nation (1796) explicitly called attention to the bond that unites them when he called upon his fellow countrymen to renounce their sectional differences and to look upon themselves as American and not as citizen of some section of the country. "With slight shades of difference," he said, "you have the same religion, manners, habits, and political principles . . . ; [you have] in a common cause fought and triumphed together; the independence and liberty you possess are the work of joint counsels, and joint efforts of common dangers, sufferings and successes."

17. Friedrich Nietzsche, "Twilight of the Idols," in *The Portable Nietzsche*, trans. Walter Kaufmann (New York: Penguin, 1976), 515–516.

18. Bertrand de Jouvenel, *On Power* (New York: Viking Press, 1949).

19. Writing in the later 1950s, the French Dominican R. L. Bruckberger, in a tribute to America reminiscent of de Tocqueville, wrote, "I feel certain that if the day comes when European nations, instead of moving toward more and more centralization, move toward more and more individual autonomy and give private initiative the greatest possible scope, Europe will once again astound the world" (*La Républiqu̧e Amèricaine* [*Image of America*], trans. C. G. Pauling and Vergilis Peterson [New York: Viking Press, 1959], 106).

20. Special Collections, Leyburn Library, Washington and Lee University.

21. "Competitive Federalism by Default," in *A Constitution for the European Union*, ed. Charles B. Blankart and Dennis C. Mueller (Cambridge, Mass.: MIT Press, 2004), 35.

22. Washington's exact words are: "It is our true policy to steer clear of permanent alliances with any portion of the foreign world; so far, I mean, as we are at liberty to do it."

23. In the Mexican war of 1846–1847, the United States was clearly the aggressor. Although the United States fought the Mexican forces in what is now Texas, California, and New Mexico, those territories became part of the nation only with the defeat of Mexico.

24. Amendment IV to the U. S. Constitution reads: "The right of the people to be secure in their persons, houses, papers and effects against unreasonable searches and seizures shall not be violated, and no warrants shall issue, but upon probable cause, supported by oath or affirmation, and particularly describing the place to be searched, and the persons or things to be seized." Heretofore it was accepted that under existing law a person cannot be arrested or detained without a charge being brought against him. Authorities were obligated at least to suspect one of a crime before detention, interrogation, or search. Yet at airports nationwide the law is clearly ignored, where the arriving passenger is automatically a suspect by virtue of his presence, no evidence of any kind required. It may be argued that even respecting the Fourth Amendment, the practice is justified given the threat of international terrorism. Yet the short-term benefits may not outweigh long-term dangers when Constitutional rights are readily surrendered because of an imagined threat.

25. I use the word "charter" loosely to stand for the Declaration of Independence, the Constitution, the records of the Federal Convention of 1787, and the *Federalist Papers*. These documents hold the key to the national identity of the American republic.

26. Christie Davies, *The Strange Death of Moral Britain* (London: Transaction Publishers, 2004). Toward the end of this work Davies writes, "The adoption of an ever-tightening European constitution will mean the end of Britain as a nation. Britain will fall, and it will have fallen because of the prior death of moral Britain, which reduced the national will to resist." Davies adds that "The willingness of successive British governments to relinquish British sovereignty over moral issues to the European Court of Human Rights has been matched by their far more dangerous willingness to hand over political and economic decision making to the European Union" (239).

27. Lord Patrick Devlin, *The Enforcement of Morals* (London: Oxford University Press, 1968).

28. In 1929, facing a disintegrating Europe, Werner Jaeger felt it necessary to call attention to a basic truth: "Our morality goes back to the Christian religion and our politics to the Greco-Roman conception of the state" (*Paideia: The Ideals of Greek Culture*, trans. Gilbert Highet [New York: Oxford University Press, 1929], xviii).

Chapter Eighteen

The Socialist Mind

Socialism is a coherent philosophical doctrine, but more than that it is a political program to be achieved. Its philosophical roots, identifiable in their own right, must be distinguished from its social and cultural aspirations and further from its political programs. It cannot be viewed as merely an alternative to a capitalist free market economy. Its revolt goes much deeper, challenging not only the economic but the moral and cultural traditions of peoples wherever it has gained ascendancy. Initially a Western movement (the term itself appears to have come into use in the early part of the nineteenth century), it has penetrated every part of the globe.[1] Given the socialists' ascendancy in Europe and American propensities to imitate Europe, it behooves us to look carefully at the origins of socialism for the ideas which the socialist mind takes for granted, commonplace ideas we find among our intellectual elite.

Not all socialist programs are as radical as those of Stalin or Mao Tse-tung, yet socialism is universally marked by certain features. Its creed, like other belief systems, may be imperfectly understood by its political adherents, but its power to motivate to determinate ends cannot be doubted. Those who subscribe to it do not have to communicate to know which cause to advance, which to oppose. They act in unison out of a shared conviction.

Like much of Enlightenment thought socialism may be characterized by what it repudiates as well as by its utopian goals. To focus on the West alone, the socialist creed is based on a denial of the existence of God and the transcendent end of human existence, features that until the eighteenth century characterized the Western mind since antiquity. Implicitly socialism denies a natural moral order to which man is accountable. Denying that man is self-directing, it affirms that individual choice is determined by psychological and social forces over which man has little or no control. Denying the reality of a universal and timeless human nature, it places no value on the lessons to be gained from the study of history, repudiating in effect the value of the Western literary canon. From its codification in eighteenth-century France it has sanctioned sexual license. This seems to be if not an essential feature, one that is nevertheless always a part of its social agenda. Socialist governments wherever they come to power sanction pornography, divorce, abortion, and in recent decades assisted suicide and euthanasia.

The socialist has long recognized that the success of his revolutionary agenda depends on control of information, primarily education; hence, his efforts to suppress parental rights in education. Control of the media is likewise a desirable objective. The socialist recognizes that in free and open debate, socialist ideas are not likely to prevail since many of its tenets fly in the face of the common perception of the good. In both Europe and North America and wherever the socialist mind prevails, obstacles are thrown up to prevent religious education. Throughout the West major media outlets in the hands of the left are grossly biased in a socialist direction, preventing a fair treatment or a hearing for alternative views. That socialism in its purest form can only be maintained through coercion is evident from events of the past century. We have notorious examples in the police states created by the Soviet Union, Nazi Germany, the Eastern bloc nations under Soviet control, Cuba, China, and North Korea, to name only the most obvious. In the democracies of the West coercion is subtle where socialist objectives are advanced through state control of education and through a sympathetic media. Media bias itself needs to be explained. The history of how the socialist mind-set captured the quasi-educated class which determines the outlook of the media has yet to be written. That history may be identical with the history of the secularization of modern culture, as Christopher Dawson has suggested. The mind of the secular majority, writes Dawson, has been so deeply affected by the process of secularization that it cannot view that process in an objective historical manner.[2] Without doubt the roots of socialism are deep in Enlightenment soil, nourished by Rousseau, Feuerbach, and Marx.

Rousseau, in his *Origin of Inequality* (1753), attributes all the ills of man not to man's own sin or to ignorance but to social injustice and the corruptions of an artificial civilization. In this and subsequent works Rousseau pleads the cause of the individual against society, the poor against the rich, the common man against the privileged classes, the cause of love against convention, and the intuition of the religious mind against the orthodox philosopher and ecclesiastical authority.

Rousseau fired the minds of his generation with the ideal of democracy not merely as a system of government but as a new way of life, a vision of social justice and fraternity. With boundless optimism he preached a social idealism, a religion of humanity, with a defined though simple body of dogma, designed to take the place of Christianity as the creed of a new age. His call for the complete reorganization of the social order became the creed of the French intelligentsia, a rationalized, humanitarian version of Christianity. Marx picked up the theme.

But more important for the development of Marx's thought was his reading of Ludwig Feuerbach's *Das Wesen des Christentum* (1841),[3] which denied the supernatural and everything in religion not of a naturalistic and human origin. In that influential work, Feuerbach systematically translated all statements about God into statements about man. Man is the measure: God conceived as a morally perfect being is the realized idea, the personified law of morality, the moral nature of man taken for absolute being. In the person of God, man celebrates his own personality in its limitless strivings. The word "God," Feuerbach explains, is but a designation for man's highest aspirations, a changing "ideal" that men establish for themselves. Put crudely, since the political and economic life of man is incapable of fulfilling his true self, he creates the illusory world of religion and its promise of eternal fulfillment.

In the eyes of the young Hegelians of whom Marx was one, Feuerbach appeared to have demolished Christianity and with it the social and political institutions grounded upon it, and in doing so prepared the way for a humanism freed from traditional moral and social constraints. This teaching was to leave its mark on a company of men who played an important role in the shaping of the modern mind, including Nietzsche, Scheler, Freud, Sartre, Fromm, and Dewey. Feuerbach aimed to change the friends of God into friends of man, worshipers into workers, believers into thinkers. Anthropology would replace theology, politics, and religion.

It is in this context that Marx will say of religion that it is man's self-administered opiate. Inasmuch as religion prevents man from seeking happiness when it can be found in this life, it must be attacked, and not merely at the theoretical level but in action. We cannot change society for the good simply by philosophizing about it; we must act. Philosophy must leave the plane of theory and with the help of the intellectual class tutor the masses. It must culminate in social revolution, a revolution of the proletariat against the established order. It is significant that in the *Communist Manifesto* Marx and Engels never use the word "capitalism." The terms employed are "bourgeois society" and "oppressing class," among others.

When Marx as a member of the Communist League was commissioned with Engels in 1847 to draw up a summary statement of socialist principles, elements of the socialist movement were well underway. Although socialism was a widely discussed theoretical topic, it was to that time merely a collection of insights and perceptions, still shapeless and inchoate. The resulting systematization became the *Communist Manifesto*.[4] The *Manifesto* itself refers to the writings of P. J. Proudhom, Claude Henri St. Simon, Charles Fourier, and Robert Owen. A half-century later Lenin was to write, "The theory of socialism grew out of the philosophic, historical, and economic theories that were elaborated by the educated representatives of the propertied classes and intellectuals."[5] The working class, Lenin was convinced, is unable to develop a social consciousness on its own. It must be "impregnated" with this consciousness from without. For Lenin this requires not only the unwitting cooperation of an intellectual class but the effort of persons engaged in revolutionary activities as a profession.

Marx and Engels in the *Communist Manifesto* were willing to sanction violence to attain socialist goals. Later, Marxists found legislation to be a surer path. Violence, they found, may be quicker, but legislative reforms are more lasting. In recent decades judicial decree has proved to be an even surer means. The legislative process is one of give and take, often leading to unwanted compromise. The judiciary by contrast can create law to reflect ideas pure and simple. Thus the battle in the United States is for the ideological control of the Supreme Court, a court all too willing to ignore constitutional limit in pursuit of idealistic goals.

The propensity to use the law to achieve socialist goals is not a new phenomenon. Marx was aware that many of his objectives could not be achieved without a complete restructuring of the then current legal system. His critique of bourgeois law was intended to show that the law of his day was the product of the capitalist ruling class, a class that created the law to sustain its mode of economic organization. Marx's critique focused on nineteenth-century tort law, which he thought tempered entrepreneurial risk with a doctrine that places accidents and product defects not on the maker but on the user.

Tort law is, of course, but one facet of a vast legal system, a system built upon an ancient philosophy of law and notions concerning the function of law in society. Marx's larger blueprint for the establishment of a socialist order called for the overthrow of the inherited in favor of laws that would promote his egalitarian conception of society. He recognized that before the socialist revolution could occur, the theoretical groundwork for it had to be laid. First, the belief structures that prevail have to be shown to be historically contingent. This he found easy, for they can be shown not always to have existed in their present form. Once contingency is recognized, the door is open to change: legal structures, just and unjust, are thus seen to be alterable. It may take courage and cunning to organize with others the struggle against the received, but once the new ideological structure is in place, the practical may be advanced.

An influential contemporary expression of Marxist legal theory is one which has come to be known as "critical legal studies."[6] Such studies emerged in the curriculum of some of the nation's most prestigious law schools in the 1960s and 1970s as thinly disguised socialist programs. Their intent, like that of Marx, is to challenge received notions of the nature of law and its function in society. Their proponents, known as "Crits, "recognize that law reflects, constitutes, and legitimizes commonly perceived notions of right and wrong. In pursuit of their own ends, the Crits seek command posts in the courts and in the law schools, and when it becomes possible, they do not hesitate, against precedent and constitutional restriction, to instantiate law that reflects their social objectives. In their hands law becomes a political instrument, allowing the courts to invade the democratic process. We have become accustomed to hearing judges described as "conservative" or "liberal," designations usually ascribed to politicians.

While judicial intrusion is destructive of the rule of law itself, equally serious is the fact that the political objectives in question are not likely to be those chosen in any democratic referendum. The objectives sought are most likely to have been framed by an intellectual elite and are often contrary to the judgment of the common man. Witness the many policies governing the use of land and policies determining university admissions, employment, and the awarding of contracts for public service, policies that have been introduced by judicial fiat rather than through the legislative process. Activist judges can easily find confirming legal rationalizations for their choices by drawing upon purely academic intelligence. It is clear that undergirding such judicial activism there is a conflict between belief systems, that is, between alternative views of human nature, human perfectability and responsibility.

A theoretical aim of law shared by socialists in Europe and North America is the correction of social imbalance and the leveling of natural inequality. Thus understood, the law may be used to remove inequalities, to redistribute income, and to remove as far as possible the ill effects of natural handicaps. The question that can only be settled in the light of a philosophy of human nature is: Should this be an aim of law, particularly of judge-made law?

As Marx clearly saw, tort law is an important part of legal theory because it affects not only the litigants but the economic activity of a region or nation. The traditional notion of tort law held it to be an instrument of corrective justice. Its intent was the restoration of the status quo that existed before any infringement of a person's right. Aristotle called this "rectificatory justice." The plaintiff in a tort action, it was thought, should recover because of an unlawful interference with his individual right not because of any general public goal of the state. By contrast, tort law from the socialist perspective is called upon not only to respond to the victim's injury as a result of negligence but to send a "moral" message to the perpetrator and beyond, perhaps to an industry.

Already in the nineteenth century Francis Wharton (1820–1889) objected to the use of tort law to achieve social objectives,[7] which he saw rashly placed upon capital the burden of not merely its own want of caution but of the want of caution of everybody else. Wharton distinguished between two views with respect to the nature of tort law: 1) the first holds a person liable for all the consequences that flow in an ordinary sequence from his negligence; this is the normal view of accountability; and 2) the second holds a person liable for all the consequences that could be foreseen as likely to occur, the "foreseeable test doctrine," as it came to be known.

The second view, Wharton argues, opens a Pandora's Box of philosophical as well as legal issues. If we can't predict the actions of others viewed as individuals, we may be able to predict the actions of others taken as a class. As insurers well know, behavior is so governed by natural laws that certain actions, including negligence, can be accurately predicted for the class provided the class is large enough. Yet predictions relevant to the aggregate tell us nothing about the likely outcome of an individual act. A manufacturer may be certain that a given number will abuse his product, but that does not make him responsible for the abuse. "To require us to act," writes Wharton, "in such a way that no action on our part may be the conditions of negligence on the part of strangers, would require us to cease to be."[8] If we do nothing, we are apt to omit something we ought to do.

> If we do something, owing to the imperfection of all things human, there will be some taint, no matter how slight, of imperfection in the thing we do. Yet whether in doing or omitting, we touch more or less closely multitudes of persons each with a free will of his own, each with idiosyncrasies with which we have no acquaintance, each of whom may by some negligence cross our path and make action on our part which is innocuous in itself injurious.[9]

The consequences of making one man liable for another's fault would lead to mischief. "Where would such vicarious liability end?" Wharton asks. "The consequences of this would be that capital would be obliged to bear the burden, not merely of its own want of caution but of the want of caution of everybody else."[10] Afraid that tort law interpreted through the socialist's prism could be used to destroy the economic underpinnings of society, Wharton wrote: "Here is a capitalist among these antecedents; he shall be forced to pay. The capitalist, therefore, becomes liable for all the disasters of which he is in any sense the condition, and the fact that he is held liable, multiplies these disasters."[11]

The natural affinity between the pragmatic naturalistic temperament, found in the disciples of David Hume and John Stuart Mill, and the socialist outlook is seen in Wharton's engagement with Nicholas St. John Green. Green was then a young instructor at the Harvard Law School and a member of the Metaphysical Club of Cambridge when it included William James, Chauncey Wright, and Oliver Wendell Holmes, well-known American pragmatists. Green, following John Stuart Mill, directly challenged the allied notions of "objective causation" and "causal chain." The legal implications are obvious. If no distinction is to be made, as Green argued, among occasion, condition, and cause, the true mechanism responsible for the effect is impossible to determine. In a court of law, without these distinctions, it becomes easy to argue for assessment of damages by the defendant with the "deepest pockets."[12] If Green's view were to prevail, Wharton argues, no factory would be built. "Making the capitalist liable for everything, therefore, would end in making the capitalist, as well as the non-capitalist, liable for nothing; for there would soon be no capitalist to be found to be sued."[13] Wharton saw that in divorcing responsibility from liability, capital is likely to be either destroyed or compelled to shrink from entering into those large operations by which the trade of a nation is built up.

Convinced that no corporation could be ruined without grave communal effects, he argued for a limit to entrepreneurial liability. He rejected the "foreseeable test" doctrine because it could only be made on a statistical basis. From a statistical point of view, he argued, all risks are predictable in the aggregate. In a world of randomness where there is no necessary connection between particular causes and particular effects, all that can be done is to statistically correlate acts in the aggregate with consequences in the aggregate. Moral causation and free agency are replaced by probabilities and statistical correlations.

Wharton adamantly challenged the tendency to look upon misfortune, whether inflicted by nature, by lack of self-discipline, or by accident, as somehow a social problem that ought to be rectified. If one begins with the principle that all loss should be compensated, the temptation is to search for a corporate or other affluent defendant at the expense of blurring the causal chain or placing all antecedents on an equal footing where there is no recognition of the distinction among occasion, condition, or cause.

Wharton, and the legal tradition he represented, assumed certain general principles, namely 1) that causes can be discerned; 2) that to the extent that they can be identified, responsibility can be assigned; and 3) that accidents do occur in which no one is at fault in any sense. An accident, by definition, is an unintended event, the intersection of independent causal chains. Wharton recognized that lack of intention may or may not mitigate liability; he would not abandon the "prudent-man test." Still, in any transaction there are at least two parties; intelligence must be assumed on all sides. Put another way, both buyers and sellers have reason to beware, lest hidden and unknown dangers become a reality.

Much has happened both in law and in the marketplace since Wharton's day, but clearly he was prescient. Whereas lack of caution or misuse of product in the nineteenth century would not have been allowed to serve as a basis for a claim, given shifts in legal theory, corporate leaders recognize that both judges and juries are likely to be swayed differently today and act accordingly.

Another front on which the socialist outlook is particularly pronounced is in the area of "civil rights," where in the formulation of welfare policy, we have the state being called upon to remedy self-inflicted wounds. In the delivery of health care we find numerous claims to benefits, for example, to publicly supported care where lifelong negligence in the care of one's health or reckless sexual behavior has contributed to illness or disability. The burden of an individual's want of prevention or proper care of health is thus placed upon the public, penalizing in effect through taxation those who exercised proper care. It makes a difference whether one speaks of "inalienable rights" or considers "rights" to be but a shorthand symbol for social practices that are espoused for political objectives. In the United States inalienable rights are protected by the Constitution, but they are limited in scope and do not entail the numerous rights claimed by the disaffected.

Similarly, the propensity of the socialist to legislate equality flies in the face of acknowledged differences between men and women in native intelligence, health, physical ability, and acquired skill, including moral and intellectual virtue. Other than equality before the law, equality is not necessarily a social value. It would be a strange world if all were equally athletic, equal in musical or artistic ability, or equally adept at manual labor. A well-ordered society can incorporate a wide variety of native talent and disposition. It is naive to assume that all are capable of high level management skills or of the professional skills of a surgeon or theoretical physicist. To artificially categorize on the basis of color, gender, or physique and then expect to find among the successful a proportionate number from each group would be merely nonsense if it were not for the socialist's propensity to legislate to achieve favored outcomes.[14]

The failure of socialism to promote prosperity wherever it has been tried does not seem to dissuade new adherents. Neither do its statist and totalitarian tendencies disturb those who in the pursuit of idealistic goals are willing to sacrifice personal and communal freedom.

In the godless world of socialism, achievement is necessarily measured in materialistic terms. Goals not achievable in the present generation are thought to be realizable in some future generation and hence worthy of continuous pursuit even though the present belies their attainability. Absent faith in divine providence, financial security and personal health assume exaggerated importance. Things of the spirit are neglected in favor of sensual pursuits. The self-identity provided by singular heritage is lost in the drive for homogeneity in the proletariat. No more egregious example is to be found than that of Mao Tse-Tung. Under Mao's regime art collections were considered bourgeois and were to be confiscated. Ancient artifacts representative of past achievement and insight were considered useless and at first Mao established "useless object stations," and connoisseurs were encouraged to dump precious artifacts and furniture lest they invoke a distinctive heritage at odds with the regime. Later in the 1960s art works were forcibly taken from the people.[15]

Although socialism may be intellectually profiled, socialism as a mindset exists in varying degrees among its adherents. Like any creed it may be imperfectly understood in theory and in its practical dimensions. That said, its characteristic dogmas are nevertheless definable and its objectives identifiable. In every generation it behooves those who find their identity in inherited classical Western and Christian culture to examine and understand the surreptitious threat which socialism presents to their accustomed view of life.

NOTES

1. In Great Britain the term was used to describe the teachings of Robert Owen (1771–1858) and in France the teachings of Charles Fourier (1771–1837) and Henri Saint Simon (1760–1852). Lorenz Von Stein wrote in 1844 a book entitled *Socialism and Communism in Present Day France.*
2. *The Gods of the Revolution* (New York: New York University Press, 1972).
3. Trans. George Eliot as *The Essence of Christianity* (New York: Harper & Row, 1957).
4. K. Marx, F. Engels, *The Communist Manifesto and Principles of Communism*, ed. Paul M. Sweezy and Leo Huberman (New York: Monthly Review Press, 1964).
5. V. I. Lenin, *What is to Be Done?,* in *Essential Works of Lenin and Other Writings*, ed. Henry M. Christman (New York: Dover Publications, 1966). Orig. pub. in 1902; included as an appendix in Sweezy.
6. Robert W. Gordon, "New Developments in Legal Theory," in *The Politics of Law: A Progressive Critique*, rev. ed., edited by David Kairys (New York: Pantheon Books, 1990).
7. Francis Wharton, *A Treatise on the Law of Negligence* (Philadelphia: Kay and Brother, 1878).
8. Wharton, *Negligence*, 134.
9. Wharton, *Negligence*, 134–135.
10. Wharton, *Negligence*, 136.
11. Francis Wharton, *A Suggestion as to Causation* (Cambridge, Mass.: Riverside Press, 1874), 11.

12. Numerous recent cases come to mind, i.e., the tobacco settlement; the Tylenol tampering case, wherein Johnson & Johnson Co. was held accountable because of the criminal activity of a deranged person who altered its product on a given shelf in a pharmacy; the federal appeals court sitting in Atlanta ruling that financial institutions can be held responsible for the toxic cleanup of tainted properties that they have taken over as a result of the default on a loan; and the case known as *Hymowitz v. Lilly*, wherein the highest New York State court applied the "market-share concept," holding a manufacturer responsible for a share of the awarded damages even when it could prove that the plaintiff did not use its product.

13. Wharton, *A Suggestion*, 11.

14. In a brilliant essay, "The Eclipse of Excellence," George Panichas asks, "How can standards of excellence survive, one may ask, when in fact the cabinet of the United States in its very composition must accommodate the idea of diversity and quota systems?" (George Panichas, *Growing Wings to Overcome Gravity* [Macon, Ga.: Mercer University Press, 1999], 32).

15. At first the Red Guards indiscriminately destroyed the confiscated artifacts. The intervention of museum curators managed to rescue from "collection dumps" a fraction of the confiscated pieces. Not surprisingly some items found their way into the homes of communist party leaders. The hard-line leaders of the Cultural Revolution, the notorious Gang of Four, were among the most ardent collectors of confiscated works. Mao's wife, one of the Gang of Four, allegedly purchased 536 works of art as well as 2,461 volumes for less than the equivalent of five U.S. dollars.

Chapter Nineteen

The Natural Basis of the Theological Virtue of Hope

Theognis of Megara, a sixth-century B.C. philosopher and poet, reflecting on the social deterioration of his day, lamented the lack of piety in the people. In a poetic work cited through the ages, notably by Plato, Xenophon, Aristotle, and Clement of Alexandria and known to us as a poem entitled "Hope," he claims that all the gods have left the earth and returned to Olympus. Faith and Temperance and the Graces have abandoned earth. Humans, having lost a sense of piety, no longer venerate those immortal gods. As a consequence, oaths are no longer reliable. The only divinity still remaining on earth is Hope. If this divinity were to leave, he warns, civilization would surely collapse.[1]

The poet stimulates reflection. What if a people, a community, a society, were to lose hope? Indeed, we may ask an even more fundamental question: Can there be "collective hope" or its contrary, "collective despair?" Each day we are informed by an omnipresent global media of a calamity in some part of the world where the victims are presented as having little more than hope. We need not look beyond this continent to find a culture under siege where thoughtful men offer little hope for the perpetuation of a once great civilization.

Following the lead of Theognis, I wish to discuss the role that hope plays within a community. Cultural historians tell us that discussions of hope usually emerge at a time of crisis. Indeed, theological discussions of hope gained a following in the middle decades of the twentieth century when, in the context of a Europe ravaged by two major wars, the topic was addressed by a number of German scholars. Jurgen Moltmann's *Theology of Hope* (1964)[2] is perhaps the most influential, although his work was preceded by that of Josef Pieper (1945) and Ernst Bloch (3 volumes, 1952–1959).[3] Hope is often presented as one of the three theological virtues, and indeed it has the status of a virtue but only within a religious context. In this presentation, I intend first to examine hope as a movement of the irascible appetite, treating it from a purely philosophical viewpoint. Only then will I ask: Is there a connection between the passion of hope and the theological virtue? As a passion, hope is not a virtue.

Hope has been discussed from a philosophical point of view since antiquity, through the course of Stoicism, to be sure. Like courage, the Stoics discussed hope as a movement of the irascible appetite, an emotive power. From that vantage point, human choice is a free initiative, but the outcome of choice is ruled by fate. Unable to change the course of sensible events, humans are able to control only their internal attitude toward the unfortunate events of life. Fate is inexorable, but hope is still possible.

St. Thomas similarly locates hope in the appetitive power, not in the cognitive faculty.[4] "Hope regards the good," Thomas writes, describing it as a "stretching out of the appetite to the good," that is, toward a possible good, attainable by one's own power or through another's activity. Hope presupposes the desire of some future good. When a person desires a thing, Thomas continues, it is because he has reason to believe that he can get it. But hope is more than that and rather different, too. We do not hope for what we are sure to obtain. What characterizes hope is the awareness that difficulties stand between our desire and its fulfillment. We only hope for what is more-or-less difficult to obtain. Thus, hope as an interior disposition is maintained in the face of some obstacle. If the obstacle becomes insurmountable, desire is succeeded by hate. Then not only is the pursuit abandoned but we no longer wish to have the impossible good so much as mentioned. You can imagine a disappointed teenager saying, "I did not want to go to the dance with him anyway, and besides I hate him." The retreat of the appetite from itself and the accompanying rancor against its former object is called despair.[5]

Hope is bound up, Thomas reminds us, with man's constant effort to live, act, and fulfill himself; it beats in the hearts of all. As a sensory passion, it may be predicated of dumb animals as well as of man. To illustrate this point, Thomas uses the homey example of a dog that sees a hare far off but makes no movement toward it because he has no hope of reaching it, whereas if the hare is near, the dog would likely make a movement toward it.

Given that the object of hope is an arduous good, one difficult to obtain, doubt with respect to its attainment may lead to despair. Experience may play a role in fostering hope, but it may just as easily lead to despair. Men of age and wisdom may be of great hope because their experience enables them to undertake tasks which seem to others impossible. In the course of a long life, how often have men seen the unhoped for come to pass? The young are full of hope but for the opposite reason.[6] The young have little past and a vast future, little memory and great expectations. The ardor of youth, which has never encountered a check, makes the young believe that nothing is impossible. The young will try almost anything and sometimes, to the surprise of all, succeed. Without doubt, hope is a driving force, but we must not make a virtue out of it. It remains an impulse of the sensitive appetite.[7] As an impulse of the sensitive appetite, it is not based on prudent calculation and chance of success. A daring man instinctively hurls himself into danger. Once he is at grips with it, he often finds more difficulties than he expected. Courage may then come into play. The merely daring man gives up, while the courageous man, once he has taken on the danger after reasoned deliberation, often finds the task less arduous than he feared and carries it through successfully.[8]

Following Aquinas, Pieper treats hope within the context of his discourse on human fulfillment, that is, within a teleological conception of human nature. It is an Aristotelian concept, to be sure, but one developed by Thomas within a theological context. Thus Pieper talks of man's *status viatoris*, man on the way, and means more by that than Aristotle could have meant since Pieper, even when writing as a philosopher, cannot forget man's eternal destiny as disclosed by revelation. "The positive side of the concept of being on the way, the creature's natural orientation toward fulfillment, is revealed, above all, in man's ability to establish, by his own effort, a kind of justifiable 'claim' to the happy outcome of his pilgrimage."[9] I am not sure that Robert Browning had hope in mind when he wrote: "Ah, but a man's reach should exceed his grasp—or what's a heaven for,"[10] but Pieper would find the notion congenial. The "way of man" leads to death as it does for all members of the animal kingdom. If man is merely a "being in time," as some philosophers would have it, man's ultimate fulfillment would be, as it is for dumb animals, merely the perpetuation of the species. Fulfillment beyond time escapes the purview of philosophers such as Heidegger and Sartre but not Aristotle, insofar as he saw that by nature man has a natural desire for immortality.

From a philosophical standpoint, it may be said that hope is something that can be empirically encountered, phenomenologically described, and understood as a function of the human psyche. The philosopher who reflects on existence as a whole cannot avoid attention to hope as a human disposition. What people hope for, almost by definition, is something that is welcome, desirable, loved, something good that can be attained. Josef Pieper, commenting on Johannes Hoffmeister's definition of hope as "joyful expectation" agrees that hope, given its implicit element of confidence, implies also the anticipation of fulfillment, namely, joy. Pieper adds this distinction: "Hope is aimed at being granted something good, and thus something loved, while joy is by nature nothing other than the response to being granted what we love."[11]

Turning to Jurgern Moltmann's *Theology of Hope* we find a suggestive passage in a section entitled, "The Tradition of Eschatological Hope," where he focuses on the social aspect of hope—that is, hope within a community—and speaks of the role that history plays by engendering hope or by dashing hope within a community. He speaks of "the messianic light of hopeful reason." "There is solidarity," he writes, "between the present and ages past, a certain contemporaneousness both in historical disappointment and eschatological hope."[12] The horrors revisited by history can undermine hope for the future, but on the other hand, recognition of positive elements in the present can engender hope. It is in this context that Moltmann explores the role that tradition plays in preserving equilibrium within a people, grounding hope and mitigating fear. "Traditions are alive and binding, current and familiar, where, and as long as, they are taken as a matter of course and as such link fathers to sons in the course of the generations and provide continuity in time. When this unquestioned familiarity and trustworthiness becomes problematical, an essential element in tradition is already lost. Where reflection sets in and subjects the tradition to critical questioning, with the result that the accepting or rejecting of them becomes a conscious act, the traditions lose their propitious force."[13] We are horrified, he says, by the error of those who in theology put the arguments of reason in place of the tradition of scripture and the fathers. Theology can teach only on the ground of the "word" given in tradition.

In approaching this topic I set out to determine the relation between the passion of hope and the theological virtue of hope. Two brief passages in Benedict XVI's encyclical, *Spe Salve*, illustrate the difference.[14] Benedict writes: "Young people can have the hope of a great and fully satisfying love; the hope of a certain position in their profession, or some success that will prove decisive for the rest of their lives. When these hopes are fulfilled, however, it becomes clear that they were not in reality the whole."[15] Aristotle would concur and add that human fulfillment is achieved only in and through the contemplative life. Benedict then moves to the theological level when he writes: "We need the greater and lesser hopes that keep us going day by day. But these are not enough without the great hope, which must surpass everything else. This great hope can only be God . . . who can bestow upon us what we, by ourselves, cannot attain. The fact that it comes to us as a gift is actually part of hope."[16] These passages make clear that natural reason can carry us only so far. The ultimate fruit of the contemplative life can be achieved only in union with God Himself. Yet we cannot fail to recognize that grace both makes possible and perfects a natural disposition. Revelation gives us a new perspective on human fulfillment and a hope that is beyond the grasp of unaided reason. Clearly the theological virtue of hope is consequent upon faith in the Risen Christ and the Revealed word of God. Still the irascible passion of hope fulfills its temporal function even in the larger context man's ultimate fulfillment in the Beatific Vision.

This paper was not conceived in a cultural vacuum. The present resembles the middle decades of the last century when, the Catholic Pieper, the Marxist Bloch, and the Protestant Moltmann were writing. This presentation has not focused solely on abstract or theoretical considerations of hope. It is the present that has generated discussions of hope on both sides of the Atlantic. Those of a certain age and experience recognize that within what was once called Christendom something has been lost. A sense of loss naturally leads to expectations for the future. The decline of the West is not a fiction.

Seventy-five years ago, the Spanish-born, American philosopher, George Santayana, lamented: "Our society has lost its soul. The landscape of Christendom is covered with lava: a great eruption of brute humanity threatens to overwhelm all the treasures that artful humanity has created."[17] Writing today, Pierre Manent reinforces Santayana's judgment, fearing that Europe is on the verge of self destruction. The democratic nation, he believes, has been lost in Europe, the very place where it first appeared. "Europe's political contrivances," he writes, "have become more and more artificial. With each day they recede further from the natural desires and movements of their citizen's souls."[18]

European countries, the political philosopher Pierre Manent is convinced, are no longer sovereign, nor do they aspire to retain their identity. European nations are caught between their old identity and that of a new European Union. After Maastricht, the EU's bureaucratic contrivance detached itself from the national political bodies that formed the Union.[19] The artifice, Manent thinks, took on a life of its own. "Europe" crystallized an idea endowed with legitimacy, suppressing all others, and that idea became equipped and fortified with institutional mechanisms capable of reconstructing all aspects of European life. Instead of increasing self-governance, Europe's new instruments of governance shackle it more with each passing day, promising an infinite extension that no one wills and no one knows how to stop. Enlightened despotism has returned in the form of agencies, administrations, courts of justice, and commissions that lay down the law or create rules, ever more meticulously contrived. In creating an uncontrollable bureaucracy, Europe, in effect, has institutionalized the political paralysis of democracy. So much so that its nations cannot control their borders let alone their economies and distinctive cultures.

We may ask, what does the future hold? With Santayana we recognize that the civilization characteristic of Christendom has given way. In his words, "The shell of Christendom is broken, The unconquerable mind of the East, the pagan past, the industrial socialistic future confront it with their equal authority."[20] What does this portent for the West? Should those who value their cultural heritage merely acquiesce and hope for the best? Of course not. Just as hope can play an important function in the life of an individual, it may stimulate a society as a whole. We have the example of Churchill and de Gaulle in the darkest hours of World War II and the more recent example of John Paul II, who through his leadership in the Solidarity movement inspired hope not only in his own people but in others of the Soviet bloc at the time. Hope is not a guide to be sure, but it can engender confidence and call men to action. Both the passion of hope and the theological virtue of hope can each play a positive role in the life of an individual. Hope as a passion is an integral part of human nature. The theological virtue is a gift but, I submit, it need not concern only "last things." To paraphrase the poet, God is in his Heaven and all may yet be right with the world.[21]

NOTES

1. *Theognis,* 1, v. 1135–1150, ed. D. Young (Teubner), 69. Cf. Gerard Verbeke, *Moral Education in Aristotle* (Washington, D.C.: The Catholic University of America Press, 1990), 32.

2. Jurgen Moltmann, *Theologie die Hoffnung*, 5th ed., trans. James W. Leitek as *Theology of Hope* (New York: Harper and Row, 1967).

3. Cf. Josef Pieper, *Über die Hoffnung* (trans. from the 7th ed. as *On Hope*) (Munich: Uber die Hoffnunf Munich: Kösel-Verlag, 1977); trans. Mary Frances McCarthy, in *Faith, Hope and Love* (San Francisco: Ignatius Press, 1986); and Ernst Bloch *Das Prinzip Hoffnung*, trans. as *The Principle of Hope* (Cambridge, Mass.: MIT Press, 1986).

4. St. Thomas recognizes six passions of the concupiscible appetite: love and hate, desire and aversion, joy and sadness; five for the irascible appetite: hope, despair, courage, fear, and anger (*Summa Theologiae*, I–II, Q.23, a.4).

5. Thomas Aquinas, *Summa Theologiae*, I–II 40, 4.

6. Aquinas, *Summa*, I–II 40, 6.

7. Aquinas, *Summa*, I–II 40, 8, ad 3.

8. Aquinas, *Summa,* I–II 45, 4.

9. Josef Pieper, *Faith, Hope, and Love*, trans. Mary Frances McCarthy et al. from the German *Liben, Hoffen, Glauben* (San Francisco: Ignatius Press, 1997), 93.

10. Robert Browning, *Andrea del Sarto*, 1855.

11. Josef Pieper, *Hope and History*, trans. David Kipp from the German *Hoffnung und Geschichte* (San Francisco: Ignatius Press, 1994), 21.

12. Jurgen Moltmann, *Theology of Hope: On the Ground and the Implications of a Christian Eschatology,* trans. James W. Leitch from the German (New York: Harper and Row, 1967), 291.

13. Moltmann, *Theology of Hope*, 291.

14. Pope Benedict XVI, *Spe Salve*, promulgated in English by Liberia Editrice Vaticana as *Saved by Hope* (San Francisco: Ignatius Press, 2008).

15. Benedict XVI, *Spe*, 64.

16. Benedict XVI, *Spe*, 66.

17. George Santayana, "Winds of Doctrine," in *The Works of George Santayana* (New York: Charles Scribner's Sons, 1937), 3.

18. Pierre Manent, *Democracy without Nations: The Fate of Self-Government in Europe*, trans. Paul Seaton from the French (Wilmington, Del.: ISI Books, 2007). 33.

19. Manent, *Democracy*, cf. 34 ff.

20. Manent, *Democracy*, 3.

21. Robert Browning, *Pippa Passes*, 1841.

Bibliography

Alfarabi. *The Political Writings, Selected Aphorisms and Other Texts*. Trans. and annotated Charles E. Butterworth. Ithaca, N.Y.: Cornell University Press, 2001.

Anscombe, Elizabeth. "Modern Moral Philosophy." *Philosophy* XXXIII (1958), 6.

Arberry, Arthur J. *The Koran Interpreted*. London: George Allen and Unwin, 1955.

Austin, J. *The Province of Jurisprudence Determined*. 2d ed. London: J. Murray, 1861 (Reprinted by Burt Franklin, New York, 1971).

Aquinas, Thomas. *Summa Contra Gentiles*. Trans. Anton C. Pegis as *On the Truth of the Catholic Faith*. Garden City, N.Y.: Hanover House, 1995.

———. *Summa Theologiae*. 3 vols. Trans. Fathers of the English Dominican Province. New York: Benzinger Brothers, 1947.

Aristotle. *Nicomachean Ethics,* in *Basic Works of Aristotle*. Ed. Richard McKeon. New York: Random House, 1961.

Ayer, A. *Language, Truth and Logic*. London: Victor Gollancz, 1936.

Bark, W. C. *Origins of the Medieval World*. New York: Doubleday, Anchor, 1960.

Barnes, Jonathan. *Aristotle*. Oxford, England: Oxford University Press, 1989.

Belloc, Hilaire. *The Great Heresies*. London: Sheed & Ward, 1938. Reprint Tan Books, 1991.

Benedict XVI. *Spe Salve*. Promulgated in English by Liberia Editrice Vaticana as *Saved by Hope*. San Francisco: Ignatius Press, 2008.

Bethell, Tom. *The Noblest Triumph*. New York: St. Martin's Press, 1998.

Block, Ernest. *Das Prinzip Hoffnung*. Trans. as *The Principle of Hope*. Cambridge, Mass.: MIT Press, 1986.

Boethius, Anicius Severinus. *The Theological Tractates*. Trans. H. F. Stewart, and E. K. Rand. London: William Heineman, 1918.

Boileau, David A. *Cardinal Mercier, A Memoir*. Leuven, Belgium: Peeters, 1996.

Brown-Fleming, Susan. *The Holocaust and the Catholic Conscience*. South Bend, Ind.: University of Notre Dame Press, 2006.

Bruckberger, R. L. *Image of America*. New York: Viking Press, 1959.

Cardoza, Benjamin. *The Nature of the Judicial Process.* New Haven, Conn.: Yale University Press, 1921.

Chadwick, Owen. *The Making of the Benedictine Ideal.* Washington, D.C.: St. Anselm's Abbey, 1981.

Cicero, Marcus Tullius. *De Officiis.* Trans. Walter Miller. Cambridge, Mass.: Harvard University Press, 1913.

———. "Discussions at Tusculum," in *Cicero: On the Good Life.* Trans. Michael Grant. London: Penguin Books, 1971.

———. *On Duties.* Trans. Walter Miller. Cambridge, Mass.: Harvard University Press, 1997.

Clark, M. L. *Higher Education in the Ancient World.* London: Routledge & Kegan Paul, 1971.

Clark, Stephen R. L. *Aristotle's Man: Speculations upon Aristotelian Anthropology.* Oxford, England: Clarendon Press, 1975.

Crombie, A. C. *Medieval and Early Modern Science.* Garden City, N.Y.: Doubleday, 1959.

Complete Correspondence of Sigmund Freud and Ernest Jones, 1908–1939. Ed. R. Andrew Paskaukas. Cambridge, Mass.: Harvard University Press, 1993.

Constitution for the European Union. Ed. Charles B. Blankart and Dennis C. Miller. Cambridge, Mass.: MIT Press, 2004.

Coulson, Noel James. "Islamic Law." Pp. 938–943, in *Encyclopaedia Britannica,* 15th ed. Chicago: Encyclopedia Britannica, Inc., 1974.

Crespi, Gabriele. *The Arabs in Europe.* New York: Rizzoli, 1979.

Crombie, Alistair. *Medieval and Early Modern Science.* Garden City, N.Y.: Doubleday, 1959.

Cua, Antonio S. "Confucian Ethics," in *Encyclopedia of Chinese Philosophy.* Ed. A. S. Cua. New York: Routledge, 2003.

———. *Ethical Argumentation.* Honolulu: University of Hawaii Press, 1985.

Dampier, Sir William Cecil. *A History of Science and Its Relation to Philosophy and Religion.* Cambridge, Mass.: Cambridge University Press, 1966.

Davies, Christie. *The Strange Death of Moral Britain.* London: Transaction Publishers, 2004.

Dawson, Christopher. *Dynamics of World History.* Ed. John J. Mulloy. Wilmington, Del.: ISI Books, 2002.

———. *The Gods of Revolution.* New York: New York University Press, 1972.

———. *Medieval Essays.* London: Sheed & Ward, 1953.

———. *Religion and the Rise of Western Culture (Gifford Lectures, 1948–1949).* London: Sheed & Ward, 1950.

De Jouvenal, Bertrand. *On Power.* New York: Viking Press, 1949.

Devlin, Lord. *The Enforcement of Morals.* London: Oxford University Press, 1965.

Dewey, John. *Experience and Nature.* New York: W. W. Norton & Co. 1928.

———. *The Quest for Certainty.* New York: Minton, Balch, 1929.

Durkheim, Emile. *Leçons de Sociologie: Physique des moeurs et du droit.* Trans. as *Professional Ethics and Civic Morals.* Glencoe, Ill.: The Free Press, 1958.

———. *Rules of Sociological Method.* Trans. S. Soloway and J. Mueller. New York: Free Press, 1964.

Dworkin, R. *Taking Rights Seriously.* Cambridge, Mass.: Harvard University Press, 1977.

Eco, Umberto. *Art and Beauty in the Middle Ages.* New Haven, Conn.: Yale University Press, 1986.

Edel, Abraham. *Method in Ethical Theory.* Indianapolis: Bobbs-Merrill, 1963.

Eldred v. *Ashcroft,* 537 U.S. 186, reh'g denied, —U.S.—, 123 S. Ct. 1505 (Mar. 10, 2003).

Ellul, Joseph. "God and Time: Islamic Philosophy and Mysticism," *Angelicum* 78, no. (2001): 651–668.

D'Entreves. *The Notion of the State: An Introduction to Political Theory.* Oxford, England: Oxford University Press, 1967.

Epictetus. *Discourses, Book I.* Trans., intro., and commentary Robert F. Dobbin. Oxford, England: The Clarendon Press, 1998.

———. *Moral Discourses.* Trans. and intro. Elizabeth Carter. London: Everyman's Classical Library, 1910.

Farrington, Benjamin. *The Faith of Epicurus.* London: Weidenfeld and Nicolson, 1967.

———. *Greek Science.* Baltimore: Penguin, 1961.

———. *Science in Antiquity.* London: Oxford University Press, 1967.

Feuerbach, Ludwig. *Das Wesen des Christentum.* Trans. George Eliot as *The Essence of Christianity.* New York: Harper & Row, 1957.

Freud, Sigmund. *The Future of an Illusion* in The Standard Edition of the *Complete Psychological Works of Sigmund Freud.* 24 vols. Ed. James Strackey. London: Hogarth Press and Institute of Psycho-Analysis, 1986.

Finnis, John. *Aquinas: Moral and Political Theory.* New York: Oxford University Press, 1998.

———. *Natural Law and Natural Rights.* Oxford, England: Clarendon Press, 1988.

Frankena, William. "Love and Principle in Christian Ethics," in *Faith and Philosophy.* Ed. A. Plantinga. Grand Rapids, Mich.: Eerdman's Publishing Co., 1964.

French, Peter A. *Collective and Corporate Responsibility.* New York: Columbia University Press, 1984.

Fried, Charles. *Saying What the Law Is.* Cambridge, Mass.: Harvard University Press, 2004.

Friedman, W. *Law in a Changing Society.* London: Pelican, 1964.

———. *Legal Theory.* London: Stevens & Son, 1944.

Fuller, Leon. *Anatomy of the Law.* London: Penguin, 1971.

Gaukroger, Stephen. *The Emergence of a Scientific Culture and the Shaping of Modernity, 1210–1685.* Oxford, England: The Clarendon Press, 2006.

Gerson, Lloyd. *Aristotle and Other Platonists.* Ithaca, N.Y.: Cornell University Press, 2005.

Gilson, Etienne. *Being and Some Philosophers.* 2nd ed. Toronto: Pontifical Institute of Medieval Studies, 1952.

——. *History of Christian Philosophy in the Middle Ages.* New York: Random House, 1954.

Goodman, Lenn. *On Justice: An Essay in Jewish Philosophy.* New Haven, Conn.: Yale University Press, 1991.

Gordon, Robert W. "New Developments in Legal Theory," in *The Politics of Law: A Progressive Critique.* Ed. David Kairys. New York: Pantheon Books, 1990.

Graglia, F. Carolyn. *Domestic Tranquility: A Brief Against Feminism.* Dallas: Spence Publishing Co., 1998.

Gratian, *The Treatise on Laws*: Decretum DD 1–20. Trans. Augustine Thompson, O. P. Washington, D.C., The Catholic University of America Press, 1993.

Hallowell, John H. *Main Currents in Modern Political Thought.* New York: Henry Holt and Co., 1950.

Hallyn, Fernand. *The Poetic Structure of the World.* New York: Zone Books, 1995.

Hare, R. M. *Essays on Religion and Education.* Oxford, England: The Clarendon Press, 1992.

Harré, Rom. *Principles of Scientific Explanation.* Chicago: University of Chicago Press, 1970.

——. *Varieties of Realism.* Oxford, England: Blackwell, 1986.

Hart, H. L. A. *The Concept of Law.* Oxford, England: Clarendon Press, 1961.

——. *Law, Liberty and Morality.* Stanford, Calif.: Stanford University Press, 1963.

Hatem, Sakr Muhammad. *Al-Sharq Al-Awsat,* 21 December, 2001.

Heidegger, Martin. *The Heidegger Controversy.* Ed. Gunther Neske and Emil Kettering. New York: Paragon House, 1990.

Hittinger, Russell. *A Critique of New Natural Law Theory.* Notre Dame, Ind.: University of Notre Dame Press, 1987.

——. *The First Grace: Rediscovering Natural Law in a Post-Christian World.* Wilmington, Del.: ISI Books, 2003.

Hooker, Richard. *On the Laws of Ecclesiastical Policy.* 1648 ed. reprinted. New York: Anno Press, 1972.

Hughes, Graham. "Rules, Policy and Decision Making," in *Law, Reason and Justice.* New York: New York University Press, 1969.

Hume, David. *Dialogues Concerning Natural Religion;* also *Treatise of Human Nature.* 18th printing. New York: Macmillan/Library of Liberal Arts, 1987.

Huntington, Samuel P. *Who Are We?: Challenges to America's National Identity.* New York: Simon and Schuster, 2004.

Husserl, Edmund. *The Crisis of European Sciences and the Transcendental Phenomenology.* Trans. David Carr. Evanston, Ill.: Northwestern University Press, 1970.

Jaeger, Werner. *Paideia: The Ideals of Greek Culture.* Trans. Gilbert Highet. New York: Oxford University Press, 1929.

Jaffa, Harry V. *American Conservativism and the American Founding.* Durham, N.C.: Academic Press, 1984.

Jaspers, Karl. *The Question of German Guilt.* Trans. E. B. Ashton. New York: Capricorn Books, 1961.

John Paul, II, *Fides et Ratio.* Washington, D.C.: United States Catholic Conference, 1998.

Kant, Immanuel. *Critique of Pure Reason*. New York: Macmillan, 1922.

Kass, Leon. *Life, Liberty and the Defense of Dignity*. San Francisco: Encounter Books, 2002.

Kaufmann, Eric P. *The Rise and Fall of Anglo-America*. Cambridge, Mass.: Harvard University Press, 2004.

Kibre, Pearl and Nancy Sirasi. "The Institutional Setting of the Universities," in *Science in the Middle Ages*. Ed. David C. Lindberg. Chicago: University of Chicago Press, 1978.

Kennedy, Robert. *Collected Speeches*. New York: Viking, 1993.

Kierkegaard, Søren. *Concluding an Unscientific Postscript* [*Afsluttende Uvidenskabelig efterskrift (1846)*], trans. D. F. Swenson. Princeton: Princeton University Press, 1941.

———. *Either/Or*, 2 vols. Vol. 1 trans. David F. Swenson, Lillain Marvin Swenson; Vol. 2 trans. Walter Lowrie. Princeton: Princeton University Press, 1944.

———. "The Self-Assertion of the German University," [Rector's Address, 1933/34], in *The Heidegger Controversy*. Ed. Gunther Neske, Emil Kettering. New York: Paragon House, 1990.

Koestler, Arthur. *The Lotus and the Robot*. New York: Macmillan Co., 1961.

Kristeller, Paul Oskar. *Medieval Aspects of Renaissance Learning*. Ed. and trans. Edward P. Mahoney. New York: Columbia University Press, 1992.

Lacey, W. K. *The Family in Classical Greece*. Ithaca, N.Y.: Cornell University Press, 1968.

Law and the Behavioral Sciences. Eds. Lawrence M. Friedman, Stewart Macaulay. Indianapolis: Bobbs Merrill, 1969.

Leclercq, Jacques. "Natural Law, the Unknown," *Natural Law Forum*, VII (1962), 15.

Lenin, Vladimir Ilyich. "What is to Be Done?" in *Essential Works of Lenin and Other Writings*. Ed. Henry M. Christman. New York: Dover Publications, 1966.

Lewis, Bernard. *What Went Wrong: Western Impact and Middle Eastern Response*. New York: Oxford University Press, 2002.

Lindberg, David C., ed. *Science in the Middle Ages*. Chicago: University of Chicago Press, 1978.

Livy, Titus. *History*. Cambridge, Mass.: Loeb Classical Library, 1924.

Locke, John. *The Second Treatise on Government*. Ed. Thomas P. Perdon. New York: Macmillan, 1952.

Lolordo, Antonio. *Pierre Gassendi and the Birth of Early Modern Philosophy*. Cambridge, Mass.: Cambridge University Press, 2006.

MacIntyre, Alasdair. *After Virtue*. Notre Dame: University of Notre Dame Press, 1981.

———. *Whose Justice, Which Rationality*. South Bend, Ind.: University of Notre Dame Press, 1988.

Manent, Pierre. *Democracy without Nations: The Fate of Self-Government in Europe*. Trans. Paul Seaton. Wilmington, Del.: ISI Books, 2007.

Maritain, Jacques. *Art and Scholasticism*. New York: Scribner's, 1960.

———. *Christianity and Democracy*. London: Geoffrey Bles, 1945.

——. *L'Église du Christ*, Trans. J. W. Evans, as *On the Church of Christ: The Person of the Church and Her Personnel*. Notre Dame, Ind.: University of Notre Dame Press, 1973.

——. *Man and the State*. Chicago: University of Chicago Press, 1951.

——. *The Person and the Common Good*. Trans. J. J. Fitzgerald. London: Geoffrey Bles, 1948.

——. *Three Reformers*. London: Sheed & Ward, 1950.

Mahdi, Muhsin S. "Islamic Theology and Philosophy," in *Encyclopedia Britannica*, 15th ed. Chicago: Encyclopaedia Britannica, Inc., 1974, pp. 1012–1025.

Marx, Karl, Engels, Friedrich. *The Communist Manifesto*. New York: International Publishers, 1935.

——. *The Communist Manifesto and Principles of Communism*. Ed. Paul M. Sweezy and Leo Huberman. New York: Monthly Review Press, 1964.

McInerny, Ralph. *Ethica Thomistica*. Washington, D.C.: The Catholic University of America Press, 1982.

Mill, John Stuart. *Principles of Political Economy*. Oxford, England: Oxford University Press, 1994.

Miller, Fred. *Nature, Justice and Rights in Aristotle's* Politics. Oxford, England: Clarendon Press, 1995.

Mitchell, Maria. "Antimaterialism in Early German Christian Democracy," in *European Christian Democracy: Historical Legacies and Comparative Perspectives*. Ed. T. Kselman and J. A. Buttiqieg. Notre Dame, Ind.: University of Notre Dame Press, 2003.

Moltmann, Jurgen. *Theologie die Hoffnung*. 5th ed. Trans. James W. Leitek as *Theology of Hope*. New York: Harper & Row, 1967.

Moore, Ruth. *Neils Bøhr: The Man, His Science and the World They Changed*. Cambridge, Mass.: MIT Press, 1985.

Munzer, Stephen. *A Theory of Property*. Cambridge, Mass.: Cambridge University Press, 1990.

Murray, Charles. "Measuring Achievement: The West and the Rest." American Enterprise Institute, *News & Commentary*, 6 August, 2003.

Murray, John Courtney. *We Hold These Truths*. New York: Sheed & Ward, 1960.

Newman, John H. *Historical Studies II*. London: Longmans, Green, and Co., 1872.

Niebyl, Karl. "Scientific Concepts and Social Structure in Ancient Greece," in *Philosophical Foundations of Science*. Ed. R. J. Seeger and R. S. Cohen. Dordrecht: D. Riedel, 1976.

Nietzsche, Friedrich. "Twilight of the Idols," in *Portable Nietzsche*. Trans. Walter Kaufmann. New York: Penguin, 1976.

North, Douglas. *Structure and Change in Economic History*. New York: Norton, 1981.

North, Douglas, and Thomas, R. P. *The Rise of the Western World*. Cambridge, Mass.: Cambridge University Press, 1973.

Panichas, George. *Growing Wings to Overcome Gravity*. Macon, Ga.: Mercer University Press, 1999.

Perspectives on Morality: Essays by William K. Frankena. Ed. K. E. Goodpaster. South Bend, Ind.: University of Notre Dame Press, 1976.

Panofsky, Erwin. *Abbot Suger on the Abbey Church of St. Denis and Its Art Treasures.* 2d ed. Princeton: Princeton University Press, 1979.

———. *Gothic Architecture and Scholasticism.* New York: Meridian Books, 1957.

Pieper, Josef. *Musse und Kult.* Trans. Alexander Dru, intro. by T. S. Eliot. New York: New American Library, 1963.

———. *Scholasticism: Personalities and Problems of Medieval Philosophy.* London: Farber and Farber, 1960.

———. *Scholastik.* Trans. Richard and Clara Winston as *Scholasticism: Personalities and Problems in Medieval Philosophy.* London: Faber and Faber, 1960.

———. Über die Hoffnung. Trans. Mary F. McCarthy as "On Hope," in *Faith, Hope and Love.* San Francisco: Ignatius Press, 1986.

Pipes, Richard. *Property and Freedom.* New York: Alfred A. Knopf, 1999.

Pound, Roscoe. *An Introduction of the Philosophy of Law.* New Haven, Conn.: Yale University Press, 1961.

Proudhon, Pierre Joseph. *Qu'est-ce que la Propriété*? Trans. Benjamin B. R. Tucker as *What Is Property?* New York: H. Fertig, 1966.

Putnam, Hilary. *Realism and Reason: Philosophical Papers.* Vol. 3. Cambridge, Mass.: Cambridge University Press, 1983.

The Qur_A_ Arabic Text with Corresponding English Meanings. English Revised and Edited by Saheeh International. Abul-Qasim Publishing House, Jeddah, Saudi Arabia, 1997.

Quine, W. *The Roots of Reference.* LaSalle, Ill.: Open Court, 1974.

———. *World & Object.* Cambridge, Mass.: MIT Press, 1960.

Ratzinger, Joseph. "Bishops, Theologians and Morality," *Origins* 13, (15 March, 1984).

Rawls, John. *The Law of Peoples: With the Idea of Public Reason Revisited.* Cambridge, Mass.: Harvard University Press, 1999.

———. *A Theory of Justice.* Cambridge, Mass.: Harvard University Press, 1971.

Robinson, Daniel. *Aristotle's Psychology.* New York: Columbia University Press, 1989.

Reformation Writings of Martin Luther, Vol. I: *The Basis of the Protestant Reformation.* Trans. Bertram Lee Wolf. London: Butterworth Press, 1952.

Rist, John M. *Real Ethics.* Cambridge, Mass.: Cambridge University Press, 2002.

Russell, B. *Religion and Science.* London: Allen and Unwin, 1935.

Saliba, George. *Islamic Science and the Making of the European Renaissance.* Cambridge, Mass.: MIT Press, 2007.

Sandel, Michael J. *Democracy's Discontent.* Cambridge, Mass.: Harvard University Press, 1996.

Santayana, George. *The Idea of Christ in the Gospels.* New York: Charles Scribner & Sons, 1946.

———. *Interpretations of Poetry and Religion.* New York: Charles Scribner's Sons, 1900.

——. *The Life of Reason.* New York: Charles Scribner & Sons, 1933.
——. "On the Unity of My Earlier and Later Philosophy," in *The Works of George Santayana.* New York: Charles Scribner & Sons, 1937.
——. *Persons and Places.* Cambridge, Mass.: MIT Press, 1986.
——. *Soliloquies in England and Later Soliloquies.* New York: Charles Scribner & Sons, 1937.
——. *The Winds of Doctrine.* New York: Charles Scribner's Sons, 1913.
Sayers, Dorothy. "The Lost Tools of Learning." 1947 lecture at Oxford University. www.bsccs.org/Sayers.
Schimmel, Annemarie. *Islam: An Introduction.* Albany: State University of New York Press, 1992.
Schnürer, Gustav. *Church and Culture in the Middle Ages.* Trans. George Undriener. Peterson, N.J.: St. Anthony Guild Press, 1956.
Schuhl, Pierre-Maxime. *La Formation de la Pensée Grècque.* Paris: Felix Alcon, 1934.
Scruton, Roger. "Freedom and Custom," in *Of Liberty.* Ed. A. P. Griffiths. Cambridge, Mass.: Cambridge University Press, 1983.
Selznick, Philip, Ed. "Natural Law and Sociology," in *Natural Law and Modern Society.* Cleveland: World Publishing Company, 1963.
Sertillanges, A. G. *The Intellectual Life: Its Spirit, Conditions, Methods.* Trans. Mary Ryan (reprint). Washington, D.C.: The Catholic University of America Press, 1987.
Sim, May. *Remastering Morals with Aristotle and Confucius.* Cambridge, Mass.: Cambridge University Press, 2007.
Smith, John. *The Spirit of American Philosophy.* Rev. ed. Albany: State University of New York Press, 1983.
Sokolowski, Robert. *Husserlian Meditations: How Words Present Things.* Evanston, Ill.: Northwestern University Press, 1974.
Spengler, Oswald. *The Decline of the West.* New York: Alfred A. Knopf, 1926–1928.
Stahl, William H. *Roman Science.* Madison: University of Wisconsin Press, 1962.
Stevenson, C. *Ethics and Language.* New Haven, Conn.: Yale University Press, 1944.
Strawson, P. F. *Individuals: An Essay in Descriptive Meta-physics.* London: Methuen, 1959.
Su, Zhixin. "A Critical Evaluation of John Dewey's Influence on Education," in *American Journal of Education* 103 (May 1995).
Thaumaturgus, Gregory. In *Origenem oratio*, quoted by M. L. Clarke, *Higher Education in the Ancient World.* London: Routledge & Kegan Paul, 1971.
Tierney, Brian. *Religion, Law and the Growth of Constitutional Thought, 1150–1650.* Cambridge, Mass.: Cambridge University Press, 1982.
Tolstoy, Leo N. *What is Art.* Trans. Almyer Maude. New York: Thomas Y. Crowell, 1998.
Truman, Margaret. *Harry S. Truman.* New York: William Morrow & Co., 1973.
Ueberweg, F., M. Heinze. *Grundriss der Geschichte der Philosophie.* Vol. III, 1914.
Valéry, Paul. *Collected Works.* Trans. Denise Folliot and Jackson Mathews. New York: Bollingen Foundation, 1962.

Van Steenberghen, Fernand. *Aristotle in the West*. Louvain, Belgium: E. Nauwelaerts, 1955.
———. *The Philosophical Movement in the Thirteenth Century*. London: Nelson, 1955.
Verbeke, Gerard. *Moral Education in Aristotle*. Washington, D.C.: The Catholic University of America Press, 1990.
Von Gierke, Otto. *Political Theory of the Middle Ages*. Trans. F. W. Maitland. Cambridge, Mass.: Cambridge University Press, 1900.
Wallace, William A. *The Modeling of Nature: Philosophy of Science and Philosophy of Nature in Synthesis*. Washington, D.C.: The Catholic University of America Press, 1996.
———. *From a Realist Point of View*. Washington, D.C.: The University Press of America, 1981.
Weisheipl, James A. "The Nature, Scope, and Classification of the Sciences," *Science in the Middle Ages*. Chicago: University of Chicago Press, 1978.
Wharton, Francis. *A Suggestion as to Causation*. Cambridge, Mass.: Riverside Press, 1874.
———. *A Treatise on the Law of Negligence*. Philadelphia: Kay and Brother, 1878.
White, Jr., Lynn. *Machino ex deo: Essays in the Dynamism of Western Culture*. Cambridge, Mass.: MIT Press, 1968.
———. "Dynamo and Virgin Reconsidered," *American Scholar* 27 (1958): 187.
Whitehead, Alfred North. *Science and the Modern World*. New York: The New American Library, 1948.
———. "Technology and Invention in the Middle Ages" *Speculum* 15 (1940).
Williams, John A. "History of Islam," Pp. 938–943 in *Encyclopedia Britannica*. 15th ed. Chicago: Encyclopaedia Britannica, Inc., 1974.
Witt, Charlotte. *Substance and Essence in Aristotle*. Ithaca, N.Y.: Cornell University Press, 1989.
Wolfe, Tom. *A Man in Full*. New York: Farrar, Straus, Giroux, 1998.
Wolf, Bertram Lee. *Reformation Writings of Martin Luther*, Vol. I: *The Basis of the Protestant Reformation*. London: Lutterworth Press, 1952.

Index